# Satire TV

# Satire TV

*Politics and Comedy in the
Post-Network Era*

EDITED BY

*Jonathan Gray, Jeffrey P. Jones,
and Ethan Thompson*

*NYU Press*

NEW YORK AND LONDON

NEW YORK UNIVERSITY PRESS
New York and London
www.nyupress.org

Library of Congress Cataloging-in-Publication Data

Satire TV : politics and comedy in the post-network era /
edited by Jonathan Gray, Jeffrey P. Jones, and Ethan Thompson.
p. cm.
Includes index.
ISBN-13: 978-0-8147-3198-7 (cl : alk. paper)
ISBN-10: 0-8147-3198-8 (cl : alk. paper)
ISBN-13: 978-0-8147-3199-4 (pb : alk. paper)
ISBN-10: 0-8147-3199-6 (pb : alk. paper)
1. Television in politics—United States. 2. Television and politics—
United States. 3. Television talk shows—United States. 4. Political satire,
American. I. Gray, Jonathan (Jonathan Alan) II. Jones, Jeffrey P., 1963–
III. Thompson, Ethan.
HE8700.76.U6S37    2009
791.45'6582831—dc22                2008045772

New York University Press books are printed on acid-free paper,
and their binding materials are chosen for strength and durability.
We strive to use environmentally responsible suppliers and materials
to the greatest extent possible in publishing our books.

Manufactured in the United States of America
c   10 9 8 7 6 5 4 3 2 1
p   10 9 8 7 6 5 4 3 2

# Contents

‖‖‖‖‖‖‖‖‖‖‖‖‖‖‖‖‖‖‖‖‖‖‖‖‖‖‖‖‖‖‖‖‖‖‖‖‖‖‖‖‖‖‖‖‖‖‖

*To W,*
*An inspiration to satirists (and satire scholars) everywhere*

||||||||||||||||||||||||||||||||||||||||||||||||||||||||

# Foreword

At a time when 24/7/365 fails to adequately quantify the world's informa-tion-gathering capacity, people cannot be blamed for finding themselves in need of a good laugh more than knowledge of the events that spawned it. Nevertheless, a small but growing segment of the American television audience is discovering that keeping up with The News is more necessary than ever. Why are people young enough to know better putting them-selves through the horror show of disappointments, brutality, dysfunction, stupidity, and greed that plays out daily on video screens and, if rumors are true, newspapers? There simply is no other way to follow a monologue by Jon Stewart or Bill Maher or to separate the absurd from the ridiculous on *King of the Hill* or *South Park*. Preparation for topical entertainment has joined celebrity trials, natural disasters, and product recalls among the attractions that have thus far saved The News from going the way of the variety show on English-language channels.

As may be the case with life itself, the definition of "satire" is becom-ing more obscure as its fan base expands. In its long development from ancient Greek theater to the inky page, satire was a term reserved for a particular kind of humor that makes fun of human folly and vice by holding people accountable for their public actions. Darwinists and other nonbelievers might be tempted to ask, "Accountable to whom?" But they usually don't. Laughter—a visceral, involuntary reaction that feels good— is a more rewarding experience than pointing out yet another proof of humanity's pathetic, aimless existence. Samuel Beckett knew this when he consented to the casting of Steve Martin and Robin Williams as the leads in Mike Nichols's 1988 New York production of *Waiting for Godot.*[1]

To find oneself laughing at an outtake of George W. Bush playing pres-ident on *The Late Show with David Letterman* is evidence of a personal moral context for viewing events—and no Camus novel can refute it. If you laughed, you have discovered what you might have already known if you hadn't skipped Walt Whitman in college lit: the president of the

United States is personally accountable to you for his actions, whether he's waging war on terror, health care, education, the national debt, national solvency, or the English language.

Many Americans born before Al Gore failed to invent the Internet find it surprising to see satire carving out a place for itself on television. TV became diffuse at a particularly unpropitious moment for satire—what history profs and buffs sometimes refer to as the McCarthy era (the quantitatively inclined count it as the early 1950s). But there was more to it than that. Madison Avenue had made a stunning success of commercial radio broadcasting during the unlikely economic climate of the Great Depression. Flush with the profits after World War II, the ad agency chiefs began to believe that their *real* job—the big job, the job for guys too real and big to even have jobs—was not so much to sell people one of these or a half dozen of those, as it was to sell people a life organized around buying things.[2] Work on that project, they told the junior account execs, and the details—hamburger-buying, car-buying, cigarette-buying, and so on—will, by and by, take care of themselves.

The sitcom, which ran a poor second to comedy-variety shows in the lost world of radio comedy, became the dominant format for humor on television during the 1950s. Far from satirical, sitcoms then, as now, tend to flatter their viewers by ridiculing personal behavior rather than the people who run things. In the sitcom world, nonconformity—whether it is found in Cliff the postal worker in *Cheers,* Endora the mother-in-law witch in *Bewitched,* or Newman the postal worker in *Seinfeld*—is often indistinguishable from antisocial behavior. That puts a writer in a position about as far away from the satirist's barbed word processor as virtual space will allow. Norman Lear's attempt at sitcom satire during the 1970s, *All in the Family,* is an exceptional proof of this rule. While Lear was no doubt pleased to have produced one of the biggest hits in TV history, he was dismayed to find that a fair share of the show's audience did not see anything satirical about the principal character, Archie Bunker, or his outspoken racist and sexist views. Quite to the contrary, these viewers appreciated the TV exposure for their otherwise suppressed political positions, and many of them articulated that sentiment by slapping "Archie Bunker for President" bumper stickers on their cars. Lear had adapted the show for U.S. commercial television from a British sitcom, *Til Death Do Us Part* (BBC, 1966–75), where the show had been successful for the politically correct reasons. There may have been more of a context for satire in the kingdom of *Monty Python, Punch* magazine, and Jonathan Swift.

But there didn't seem to be a context for satire in a broadcasting system whose bread was buttered by making unkeepable promises about the satisfactions of keeping up with one's Joneses.

What changed?

For one thing, the means of transmission. Cable improved the atmosphere for TV satire in too many ways to list in a limited memory format. It suffices to say that by expanding the channel spectrum to a bandwidth that mocks the dreams of old-time believers in ultrahigh frequency, cable made more room on television for virtually everything. Cable actually began in the 1950s as a technologically modest way of selling people out in the sticks a couple of extra stations that could be picked up off an industrial-size antenna. But once the Earth was encircled by more satellite transponders with stable footprint than anyone knew what to do with, cable morphed into a big tent, inclusive and diverse.

Before cable remade life as we view it, television was more reliable as an object of satirists than a medium for the presentation of their work. Nonetheless, primitive television was not without satirical avatars. Ernie Kovacs, for example, is said to be among the first to surmise the essential nature of television, and he was certainly the first of the early surmisers to actually appear on it, beginning as a local station morning guy in Philadelphia in 1950. "You can tell that TV is a medium," Kovacs said. "It's neither rare nor well-done." Kovacs moved through a succession of TV genres that could neither contain nor package him, and constrained by a Federal Communications Commission (FCC) that could actually yank a station's license at renewal time, he did very little material that would be considered political by current standards. But in making fun of TV's conventions when it was hardly old enough to have any, he invoked a kind of bohemian *artiste*'s angle of vision that implicitly mocked the medium's painfully overscrubbed face. He didn't need to criticize John Foster Dulles; he *was* criticism of John Foster Dulles. Besides, as a creative taxpayer (he owed millions to the Internal Revenue Service), Kovacs was more comfortable flying below government radar.

During a period when live television seemed to hold most of the best possibilities, Kovacs was already advancing into the realities of the prerecorded future. He hosted his monthly ABC prime-time comedy specials in 1961–62 from a TV director's booth, presenting sketches in a style and with an attitude that would be adopted over the next decades by avant-garde performance artists. As might be expected, critical notices were higher than ratings. In perhaps his greatest work of genius, he managed to stay on the air by always appearing on camera with a lit cigar, which was all his sponsor, the Dutch Masters Cigar Company, required of him. There are, however, some systems you cannot beat; he died in a car accident in 1962.

Jack Paar, who hosted the *Tonight Show* (1957–62) and later did a prime-time talk-variety hour for NBC (1962–65), ran a somewhat unorthodox green room. It included Fidel Castro, who came on to promo revolutionary Cuba in 1959; Jack Douglas and Reiko, TV's first Amerasian husband-and-wife comedy team and frequent guests; and John F. Kennedy and Richard Nixon, who appeared on separate episodes during the 1960 presidential campaign (in the run-up to the first-ever televised presidential "debate"). Asked why he chose to tape a show at the Berlin Wall while it was under construction, Paar said, "The public always enjoys going behind the scenes in show business to see how sets are built. Besides, having Fidel on made people call me a leftist. Having on the East Germans building this wall will make people say I'm on the right, though I can assure you that William F. Buckley will not be one of them. I'll let them argue it out until I'm restored at the center." Paar got out while the getting was good, buying a TV station in Poland Springs, Maine, where he lived for the next 40 years.

*That Was the Week That Was* (NBC, 1964–65), like *All in the Family*, was an American adaptation of a BBC series. The American *TW3*, created and sometimes hosted by its British producer, David Frost, debuted in January 1964. It was the first no-doubt-about-it political satire show on U.S. prime-time network television, offering a "news-of-the-week-in-comic-review" format for its entire half hour each week, more than a dozen years before *Saturday Night Live*'s "Weekend Update" segment hit the air. Regulars whose careers survived included Buck Henry, Alan Alda, and Tom Bosley. Appearing during the TV programming nadir of the mid-1960s (the heart of "least objectionable" programming darkness), *TW3* attracted attention, and sometimes audiences, with sketches that included a news send-up featuring United Nations paratroopers sent to rescue civil rights activists in Mississippi and some unflattering ditties about the pope, nuclear weapons, and suburbia by satirical song stylist and Harvard professor Tom Lehrer. Barry Goldwater, today the iconic granddaddy of contemporary political conservatism but then just a right-wing senator from Arizona, was a frequent target of jokes on the show. After Goldwater's nomination as the 1964 Republican presidential candidate that summer, viewers tuning in for *TW3* were disappointed most weeks to find the talking heads of politicians, unmocked by satirical comment. "Perhaps by chance, perhaps by design, *TW3* was repeatedly pre-empted during the fall and replaced with low-rated political speeches and documentaries paid for by the Republicans," wrote former NBC executives Tim Brooks and Earle Marsh.[3] Given all existing data about the degree of care that network television programmers take in placing shows in prime-time slots, the "perhaps by chance" scenario is a call for a documentary best handled by the Sci-Fi Channel. By the time *TW3* was back on the air with any regularity, *Petticoat Junction* (CBS) and *Peyton Place* (ABC) had cannibalized its audience.

A few years later, *The Smothers Brothers Comedy Hour* (CBS, 1967–70) introduced jokes about recreational drug use and U.S. foreign policy in Southeast Asia to prime-time television. Guests included Pete Seeger, a blacklisted, unplugged-in folksinger who performed a tune he wrote about a powerful country that gets involved in an overseas war from which it can't extricate itself because of a president who seems more beholden to the military-industrial complex than the Constitution he has sworn to uphold. What crazy times those were. Pat Paulsen, a previously little-known comedian who was a regular on the show, began a recurring sketch as a double-talking presidential candidate, which became his life's work. *The Smothers Brothers Comedy Hour* did well in the ratings, but the CBS brass, still bringing home megabucks with *The Beverly Hillbillies* and *Green Acres,* thought it wasn't worth the trouble and cancelled the show on a contract technicality when the producers failed to get a tape of the next episode to the network censor on time.

Premiering a year after *The Smothers Brothers Comedy Hour, Rowan and Martin's Laugh-In* (NBC, 1968–73) was number one in the Nielsen ratings for two of its five seasons. It marked the first time that the highest-rated comedy show on television wasn't a sitcom since Milton Berle had turned the trick with his variety show in 1951. *Laugh-In* pulled off one of the greatest feats possible in the American mass media environment of its time: it was topical, irreverent, and funny but contained few written jokes that could be described (by a network censor or anybody else) as "political." George Schlatter was among the first prime-time television producers—and certainly the first comedy producer—to explore the emerging possibilities of videotape editing technology, and he created a kind of visual political slapstick, custom-made to chase the vanishing attention span. Richard Nixon, for example, performed on the show while running for president (that's a quarter of a century before Bill Clinton wailed sax on *Arsenio* or talked underwear on MTV). In an unintroduced three-second spot, Nixon stared at the camera and said, "Sock it to *me*?" 'Nuff said.

Curiously, the success of *Rowan and Martin's Laugh-In* did not spawn a recipe for making more dough with the prime-time cookie cutter. The series generated no spin-offs or imitators, but its socko ratings—a weekly audience averaging from 26 to 32 million—demonstrated conclusively that making jokes about The News was more popular on television than was The News itself. Moreover, *Laugh-In* proved that McCarthy-era fears of organized product boycotts and licenses lost over political content—the reasons that network executives had always trotted out to explain their timidity—were not just weightless but groundless.

Having overturned these long-held axioms of network thinking, *Laugh-In* helped smooth the way at NBC for late-night comedy shows that made topical humor part of viewer expectation. These included Lorne Michael's *Saturday Night,* which premiered in 1975 and added "Live" in its second season, and *SCTV Comedy Network,* a Lorne Michaels–related Canadian video troupe whose half-hour syndicated show was supersized by the network to 90 minutes for its 1981 Friday late-night schedule.

From its earliest days out of the laboratory to the end of three-network rule, American television had always been better at satirizing itself than politics. Since that time, cable, direct satellite, and the Internet have turned the political life of the nation into a form of video, and as the essays in this volume show, made The News fair and often entertaining game on the rising tide of satire upon whose waves we now surf.

DAVID MARC
Bradford Heights, New York

### NOTES

1. For a penetrating discussion of this subject, see Louis Menand, "Now What Do I Mean by That?" *Slate,* 26 August 1996, at http://www.slate.com/?id=3319.

2. To get in the mood for this kind of thinking, read Hans Enzensberger, *The Consciousness Industry* (New York: Seabury, 1974); for compelling dramatizations, see *A Face in the Crowd* directed by Elia Kazan (1957).

3. Tim Brooks and Earle Marsh, *The Complete Directory to Prime Time Network and Cable TV Shows* (New York: Ballantine, 1999), 1015.

# Part I

# Post 9/11, Post Modern,
# or Just Post Network?

||||||||||||||||||||||||||||||||||||||||||||||||||||||||

# The State of Satire, the Satire of State

*Jonathan Gray, Jeffrey P. Jones,
and Ethan Thompson*

Few would have guessed that one of the most talked about American television broadcasts of 2006, and what *New York Times* columnist Frank Rich would declare as the defining moment of the 2006 midterm elections, would be on C-SPAN, the congressional access channel.[1] Though congressional or parliamentary access channels have cropped up around the world, offering citizens the ability to watch the political process at work and hence to serve as more knowledgeable political deliberators, such channels have tended to attract more ridicule than ardent viewers. Ironically, though, it was ridicule on offer when millions downloaded C-SPAN's blockbuster hit of the year via YouTube and other streaming websites.

Stephen Colbert, host of Comedy Central's *The Colbert Report*, had been invited to speak at the White House Correspondents Association Dinner on April 29, where he used the opportunity to launch a satiric attack on President George W. Bush and on the Washington press corps. Though many mainstream media sites hardly covered the event at first, soon the buzz that surrounded its viral spread—via emails, blogs, and conversation—forced attention. With the president meters away, Colbert's signature satirical take on a right-wing pundit had likened the president's few remaining supporters to the backwash at the bottom of a glass of water and, tongue firmly in cheek, praised the president for trusting his gut over facts found in books. The president's initial laughs grew increasingly uncomfortable, as did those of Colbert's live audience, for the satirist laid in to them, too, for being a flabby press corps that refused to question the administration. Many in the press argued that the speech was simply unfunny. But the speed and relish with which the speech circulated on the Internet attests to its popularity and resonance with a wider home audience.

This single event tells us much about the state of television satire, politics, political reporting, and television culture in the first decade of the twenty-first century. First, it speaks of the immense popularity of satire TV: being funny and smart sells and has proven a powerful draw for audiences' attention. Second, the rapid spread of the clip highlights satire's viral quality and cult appeal, along with the technological apparatus that now allows such satire to travel far beyond the television set almost instantaneously. Consigned to basic or pay cable channels (as it often is in the United States), satire has nevertheless frequently commanded public attention and conversation more convincingly than shows with ten times the broadcast audience. Third, since multiple commentators criticized the speech for not being funny, the speech illustrates how the presence of "humor" in political humor can rely quite heavily on one's political worldview. It demonstrates that some satire may not even intend to be funny in a belly laugh kind of way. Fourth, Colbert's boldness as the comedian in a room full of politicians and journalists crystallized the sad irony that contemporary satire TV often says what the press is too timid to say, proving itself a more critical interrogator of politicians at times and a more effective mouthpiece of the people's displeasure with those in power, including the press itself. Good satire such as Colbert's has a remarkable power to encapsulate public sentiment. Finally, then, the incident tells us of how satire can energize civic culture, engaging citizen-audiences (as few of Colbert's press corps audience rarely can), inspiring public political discussion, and drawing citizens enthusiastically into the realm of the political with deft and dazzling ease.

Colbert may have garnered the headlines for a time, but he has many peers. In October 2004, Jon Stewart of Comedy Central's *The Daily Show with Jon Stewart* created a similar stir when he appeared as a guest on CNN's *Crossfire* and lambasted the hosts for a "dog and pony show" debate format that, he charged, hurt the state of U.S. politics more than it could possibly help it (figure 1.1). In that presidential election year, Stewart was the go-to public figure for political commentary, as *The Daily Show* regularly featured heavily in discussions of politics. Stewart also swept up an impressive array of accolades, ranging from *Entertainment Weekly*'s "Entertainer of the Year" to Peabody Awards for *The Daily Show*'s election coverage in 2000 and 2004, and from numerous Emmys to the

Fig. 1.1 With millions of views (over 1 million views of this upload alone), Jon Stewart's 2004 appearance on CNN's *Crossfire* soon went viral, becoming one of the most talked about media events of the year.

Television Critics Association Award for "Outstanding Achievement in News and Information." Four years later, as 2008 began with the Writers Guild of America strike still on, many worried about a presidential primary season without Stewart's sage and witty coverage. Some people somewhat jokingly posed that *The Daily Show* should be declared an essential service (and therefore immune to the writer's strike conditions for guild members).

*South Park*, another show on the same cable network, continued to grab headlines for its treatments of political affairs, such as the right-to-die debates surrounding the Terry Schiavo case, immortalized in the episode "Best Friends Forever." Less scathing in nature, *The Simpsons* and *Saturday Night Live* continue to launch occasional satiric missives from their beachhead on network television. Back on cable, Aaron McGruder brought his popular comic strip *The Boondocks* to television in late 2005, which, along with *Chappelle's Show* and *The Mind of Mencia*, have mixed edgy racial politics with edgy political satire. President Bush's career was bookended by caricatures on *That's My Bush!* and *Lil' Bush*. Earlier, Michael Moore's *TV Nation* and *The Awful Truth* had presented satire to audiences in the United States, the United Kingdom, and Canada. Indeed, satire has thrived in other nations, too. In Canada, *This Hour Has 22 Minutes* and *Rick Mercer Report*'s imprint on popular culture has been matched by few Canadian Broadcasting Corporation (CBC) shows other than *Hockey Night in Canada*. British television has also long featured cutting political satire, including *That Was the Week That Was* in the 1960s, *Spitting Image* in the 1980s, *The Day Today* and *Brass Eye* in the 1990s, and the more recent *Have I Got News for You* and Sacha Baron Cohen's meteoric rise to international fame in the guise of his characters Ali G and Borat.

Although the collection of essays in this volume focuses on television in the United States, United Kingdom, and Canada, the unique ability of satire TV to speak truth to power (and quality demos) is apparent throughout the world. Ever mindful of expanding markets, *Variety* reported that comedy shows with a "satirical spin" were all the rage in China, "especially with younger, savvier urban audiences."[2] When Saddam Hussein was toppled, a new age for Iraqi television began, and one of its most successful genres was satire. The Al-Sharqiya channel was launched with political comedy as its main theme, and though its Baghdad operation was shut down by the government in early 2007, it continued to satirize war-torn Iraq via satellite transmission. A government spokesman vowed that he would love to get his hands on the producers beyond his reach: "Iraq's anti-terrorism laws are applicable to Sharqiya because it is provoking people."[3]

Television satire is flourishing in the post-network era. Indeed, with the increase in satirical programming and with the increase in the sociocultural status and prominence of such programming, it is no longer enough to refer to "satirical television," for satire is no longer simply an occasional style (though at times it is that, too). It is its own genre, and a thriving one at that. Just as there is reality TV, self-improvement TV, teen TV, and court TV, so there is satire TV. Moreover, with many satirical shows involving politicians as guests or in caricature, with several airing on the same day and with all addressing current political issues, today's class of satire TV forms a key part of televised political culture. Similarly, discussion of such shows informs and finds its way into all manner of discussions of local, national, and international politics. The essays in this collection seek to make sense of these programs' role in nurturing civic culture, as well as their potential place as sources of political information acquisition, deliberation, evaluation, and popular engagement with politics.

Alongside the enthusiastic accolades for Colbert, Stewart, and company (and offsetting the shows' fans) have been detractors who have either questioned satire's ability to engage citizens in any meaningful way or alleged that satire may merely inspire a cynical superiority complex in viewers that removes them from politics. Writing of Stewart in the *Boston Globe*, for instance, Michael Kalin charged that

> Stewart's daily dose of political parody . . . leads to a "holier than art thou" attitude toward our national leaders. People who possess the wit, intelligence, and self-awareness of viewers of *The Daily Show* would never choose to enter the political fray full of "buffoons and idiots." Content to remain perched atop their Olympian ivory towers, these bright leaders head straight for the private sector.[4]

Fox News' irascible Bill O'Reilly infamously posed that Stewart's audiences were "stoned slackers," and even Stewart, albeit rhetorically, for years fondly clung to the mantra that his show followed a program in which puppets make prank phone calls and hence hardly positions itself as heavy politics. *The Simpsons*, for its part, has also been charged with being "cold," "based less on a shared sense of humanity than on a sense of world-weary cleverer-than-thou-ness" that as a result "does not promote anything, because its humor works by putting forward positions only in order to undercut them."[5] Sometimes even compliments of contemporary satire amount to criticisms, as *The Simpsons* and *South Park* in particular are frequently noted to be willing to attack "everything," thereby not amounting to any form of "meaningful" political discourse.

In response to such criticisms, some have pointed to the National Annenberg Election Survey or Pew Research Center figures that suggest *Daily Show* viewers, in particular, are a more politically knowledgeable bunch than nonwatchers.[6] But attempting to rate a show's political value by counting audiences, or even by testing their political knowledge, is both problematic (assuming, for example, that political knowledge correlates neatly to active political involvement) and insufficient. Let us as volume editors show our cards here at the outset by stating that we believe contemporary satire TV to have considerable political value, and we find many of the criticisms of satire to be weak and based on erroneous assumptions of audiences, the nature of politics, and the nature of humor, satire, parody, and entertainment more generally. As such, in this introductory chapter, we aim to define and theorize what humor, satire, and parody are, as well as their relationship to politics. We offer sections on humor, satire, and parody before turning to a cultural history of how they have evolved into their current televisual forms. We also believe that, in order to inquire into the broader questions of how contemporary television satire positions and addresses people as citizens, as well as how such shows interact with politics, close study of the programs is required. Television's glossy surface, never-ending delivery of shows, and ephemeral nature have long seduced many into thinking that it can be criticized at speed and at a distance, but in truth it is a complex medium. Thus the authors of the chapters within this collection offer deep analyses of satirical programs in order that, together, they might provide a rich appraisal of the state of satire TV.

## What Are You Laughing At? Humor as Social Critique

The initial obstacle blocking many critics of satire from seeing its political potential arises because satire is coded as a subgenre of comedy, and comedy and humor represent for many the opposite of seriousness and rational deliberation. Thus before we discuss and define satire, we find it necessary to clear a path between humor and the political. Admittedly, some simply do not *want* humor to have any substance, preferring to regard it as a zone of escape from real world problems that require pensive stroking of the chin, not laughter. But a closer look at humor reveals a form that is always quintessentially about that which it seems to be an escape from, and hence a form that is always already analytical, critical, and rational, albeit to varying degrees.

As Simon Critchley begins his treatise *On Humour,* "Jokes tear holes in our usual predictions about the empirical world. We might say that humour is produced by a disjunction between the way things are and the way they are represented in the joke, between expectation and actuality. Humour defeats our expectations by producing a novel actuality, by changing the situation in which we find ourselves."[7] This change of expectation may take various forms—from a reversal of fortunes (a rich and pompous man trips on a banana peel), to exaggeration (his trip sends him flying across four lanes of traffic), to the grotesque (in the trip, his leg falls off), to stark contrast (his trip cures his limp)—and the stakes involved will change from situation to situation and from one genre of humor to the next. But all humor challenges social or even scientific norms *at some level.* As Critchley notes, in listening to a joke, "I am presupposing a so-cial world that is shared, the forms of which the practice of joke-telling is going to play with." In turn, all laughter (in assuming social norms) also challenges or otherwise toys with these norms, producing "anti-rites," as Critchley dubs them, that "mock, parody or deride ritual practices of a given society."[8]

If all humor plays with social norms, all humor carries the potential for reflection on, or even criticism of, those norms. In Mary Douglas's formu-lation, "A joke is a play upon form that affords an opportunity for realis-ing that an accepted pattern has no necessity."[9] If we laugh at a rich and pompous man slipping on a banana peel, for example, it may be in part because his wealth almost suggests divine luck or provenance that is now unexpectedly and violently disturbed and in part because his walk is so rehearsed and deliberate that a fall challenges his seeming control of his body. In either situation, then, we are invited to reflect on our attitudes toward the wealthy or on the rigidity of certain pompous walks and the social sentiment that they appear to reflect. This process and "reflection" may be unconscious, but humor always, at least potentially, offers the pos-sibility of *defamiliarization,* allowing us to see the social and scientific or-der anew, inviting us "to become philosophical spectators upon our lives. It is practically enacted theory."[10] As much as humor might *seem* escapist, as Critchley states, alluding to Don Quixote's famous tilting at windmills to the bemusement of his traveling companion, "the comedian behaves like a visitor from another planet, vainly trying to disappear into practices that we take for granted. . . . But *we* watch the comic from a this-world perspective, like Sancho Panza, enjoying . . . from a distance, where we can suspend reality, and yet still engage in reality testing."[11] Humor may be off the wall, but it makes us laugh at and contemplate the wall, the here, and the now.

Certainly, it is for this reason that one of humor's greatest theorists, Mikhail Bakhtin, writes of laughter as unique in allowing social analysis, reflection, and criticism. Laughter, he argues, allows us to approach any object from a healthy distance, "drawing it into a zone of crude contact where one can finger it familiarly on all sides, turn it upside down, in-side out . . . doubt it, take it apart, dismember it, lay it bare and expose it, examine it freely and experiment with it."[12] In this respect, Bakhtin staunchly denies that humor and laughter are not serious—or, rather, that such a hard binary exists—as he sees the continual reflection, analysis, and ridicule of social norms as enacted by humor as a necessary device warding off the entrenchment of any norm into becoming wholly accept-able and beyond rebuke.[13] As should be evident, Bakhtin thus regards hu-mor and laughter in terms of the *power* they allow the laugher vis-à-vis the laughed-at object. Here, his enduring image for understanding hu-mor is as "carnival" (see chapter 10 in this volume)—that time of year in medieval society when serfs gave up work and partied with licentious, lascivious behavior, bawdy and rowdy humor, parodic plays that mocked those in power, and, in general, a "temporary liberation from the prevail-ing truth and from the established order."[14] Carnival was, on one level, an escape from social expectations, norms, and power structures. The hu-mor, comedy, and play that ensued, though, frequently challenged those same expectations and structures. Indeed, comedy is a realm in which indecorum is not only welcome but also expected, producing a situation whereby comedy is sometimes one of the only spaces in some societies in which social controls can be resisted and interrogated.[15]

Bakhtin's notion of humor as a realm outside of regular society that allows or even encourages critique of that society is echoed in Sigmund Freud's equally famous psychoanalytic framework for understanding hu-mor. Freud saw jokes and humor, especially "tendentious jokes" and hu-mor, as acting similarly to dreams, controlled by and giving voice to un-conscious desires and repressed feelings or anxieties. "The pleasure in the case of a tendentious joke," he explained, "arises from a purpose being satisfied whose satisfaction would otherwise not have taken place."[16] In particular, Freud saw humor as frequently harboring our aggression to-ward forces, institutions, and individuals that hold power over us. Laugh-ing at someone slipping on a banana peel, in other words, can often be an act of *release* of aggression when the individual is perceived as hav-ing some form of power over us, hence the slip being funnier the more powerful the slipper is. As Susan Purdie argues, "'laughing at' is always aggressive, it 'puts people down' in signaling that they are down-put, but that could not happen unless they were originally perceived as 'up'—as in some way holding power over."[17] Once again, then, humor is revealed to be something that encourages criticism and reflection about prevailing systems of power, and it can be a discursive tool used by both parties in a struggle between dominant and resistive forces.

In the wake of Bakhtin's theory of carnival especially, comedy theo-rists have long debated how transgressive and how politically meaningful laughter will be in any given situation. Umberto Eco, for instance, regards carnival as presenting a zone for critique, but a zone that is separated from social reality, thereby ensuring that the critique and reflection stay vacuum-sealed within the comic realm. Carnivals end, in other words, and while we might laugh when we hear the joke, that is it.[18] Purdie also notes that carnival's long-term effects may even be constraining, in that the comic "release" may deflect or dissipate energies that might otherwise be directed toward resolving power differentials or enacting social change outside of the comic realm.[19] A continuing question for any humor—satire, parody, or other—that would engage in critique, then, is, "What comes after the laugh?" Others have pointed out that whether it succeeds in moving out of the comic zone in any given instance, humor is always at least *potentially* transgressive.[20] Humor allows a relatively open space for critique and reflection, one that is rare in many societies. Far from being solely light, frivolous, and wholly apolitical, humor is able to deal powerfully with serious issues of power and politics. Its most overtly political genre is satire.

### *A Scathing and Scornful Smile: Political Satire*

From Horace and Juvenal to Swift and Twain, satire's long and rich history within literature is well established. As discussed in this volume, however, satire's role as an expression of social and political criticism within the medium of television has been much more tenuous. For reasons that have as much to do with the political economy of network television (especially in the American context) as with the particular demands that satire places on writers and audiences alike, satire has been one of the medium's most underused forms of political discourse (not to mention entertainment). Such underutilization has been to the detriment of a more-engaged citizenry, for to satirize is to scrutinize and therefore to encourage one's audience to scrutinize as well.

Thus, whereas news—television's privileged discourse on public life—most often posits politics as something to learn, satire not only offers meaningful political critiques but also encourages viewers to play with politics, to examine it, test it, and question it rather than simply consume it as information or "truth" from authoritative sources. As Bakhtin suggests, by comically playing with the political, one can gain a greater sense of ownership over it and, in turn, feel more empowered to engage it. Charles Schutz reminds us that the Roman satirist Horace favored satire because it deals with important issues in a simple, approachable manner, thereby bridging the divide between philosophy and the general public.[21] As the authors in this book point out, contemporary satire TV offers viewers a means for playful engagement with politics that has been sorely missing through much of the medium's history. But before examining that history, we should interrogate what satire is, what makes it a politically important form of critique, and how it is distinguished from other comedic forms.

One particularly useful definition posits satire as "verbal aggression in which some aspect of historical reality is exposed to ridicule. It is a mode of aesthetic expression that relates to historical reality, involves at least implied norms against which a target can be exposed as ridiculous, and demands the pre-existence or creation of shared comprehension and evaluation between satirist and audience."[22] As a form of political discourse, two of the most important components of this definition are the verbal *attack* that in some way passes *judgment* on the object of that attack, thereby enunciating a perceived breach in societal norms or values. Again, Freud noted that many jokes perform a momentary act of aggression directed toward that which has power over us (whether a person, an idea, or an institution), for in that moment we free ourselves from that power. Similarly, while satire enables broader social commentary, it is the ability to attack power and pass judgment on the powerful while doing so in playful and entertaining ways that makes satire a particularly potent form of political communication.

Satire takes natural human emotions—"anger, shame, indignation, disgust, contempt"—and channels or domesticates them, transforming "a potentially divisive and chaotic impulse . . . into a useful and artistic expression," and one with enormous political power.[23] The purpose of satire is not negativity but positive change. The satirist can channel that anger, contempt, etcetera, by enunciating a particular "truth" or "standard of rightness."[24] As George Test notes, the satirist's truth can be "not only moral but also ethical, political, aesthetic, common sense, or shared prejudices."[25] Satirists see their job as helping "to distinguish right from wrong in society and [are] willing to attack the wrong without reservation."[26] But it is in the act of focusing attention on the object of attack that the satirist demands communal evaluation and rebuke. As G. K. Chesterton writes, "The essence of satire is that it perceives some absurdity inherent in the logic of some position, and . . . draws the absurdity out and isolates it, so that all can see it."[27]

In so doing, the aesthetic or artistic dimension in exposing such folly or vice is manifest in satire's most notable feature: ridicule. Satire's calling card is the ability to produce social scorn or damning indictments through *playful* means and, in the process, transform the aggressive act of ridicule into the more socially acceptable act of rendering something ridiculous. Play typically makes the attack humorous, in turn enlisting the audience in a social rebuke through communal laughter. Though some critics of popular, entertainment-based political discourse suggest a link between laughter and cynical attitudes or even a trivialization of public life, they fail to recognize the empowering role of laughter as a means of public judgment and rebuke.[28] Similarly, critics tend to see irony, parody, and satire as diminishing meaning (by belittling the subject), but as Harold Bloom reminds us, the great ironists such as Shakespeare tended to expand meaning.[29] Satire is provocative, not dismissive—a crucial point that critics typically ignore when assessing its role in public discourse.

Test argues that these four features—aggression and judgment, play and laughter—constitute and define all satiric undertakings and distinguish it from other forms of aesthetic expression with which it is sometimes confused, namely "humor, comedy, social criticism, parody, burlesque, farce, and travesty."[30] While laughter is certainly an important outcome if satire is to have its full effect, we disagree that laughter is a necessary component or distinguishing feature of satire. Laughter is ultimately something satire may or may not produce within the audience; it is not something that resides in the artistic expression itself. As others have argued (and as we show in this book), satire need not be funny.[31] *Gulliver's Travels* is perhaps one of the better-known examples of this; *Lil' Bush*, perhaps the most recent. Any requirement that satire must produce something as mysterious, complex, and socially situated as laughter limits its definition unnecessarily.

But therein lies the first problem in the relationship between satire and television. While satire need not be funny, television networks and producers (and perhaps even audiences) generally expect it to be, seeing it as another form of "comedy" that should be comprised of the same textual features (e.g., jokes) and produce the same audience reactions (e.g., laughter) as, say, a sitcom or variety show. Peter Keighron argues that television is the "least confident" of media, "the most terrified of rejection, scared that if you stop being funny for a single moment its audience will have reached for the remote."[32] In his interviews with numerous British satirists, he quotes one who complains that

> we haven't moved away from the idea of jokes, that you have to have a gag every few seconds. . . . If humor could take its place in the arts as simply being part of the oral tradition, that comedy and poetry and political speaking

all exist alongside each other and are connected, then there wouldn't be this desperation for everything to be structured in the form of jokes.[33]

Instead, entertainment programming that deals with social or political issues has tended toward the safer and ultimately more conservative route provided by sitcoms. As Michael Mulkay argues in reference to television's dependence on the sitcom, "much television humour depends on the constant repetition of the same underlying joke and on the repeated representation of the same unchanging stereotypes."[34] Most situation comedies are safe and predictable, whereas most satire is typically neither.

This observation leads to a second important feature of satire that militates against its place as a favored form of television programming: satire is ultimately a negative form (albeit with positive intentions) and therefore runs the risk of alienating the audience through its negative properties. "In such attacks," Test argues, "we have on public display some of the least socially acceptable emotions: anger, indignation, frustration, righteousness, hatred, and malice. As in actual social relationships, the venting of such emotions . . . creates an adverse reaction in the audience."[35] In the network-era model of maximized audience share, we can easily see how such forms of television programming have been typically unwelcome in prime-time (though occasionally tolerated in fringe hours such as late-night). Test argues further that "the general attitude toward satire is comparable to that of members of a family toward a slightly disreputable relative, who though popular with the children makes some of the adults a bit uncomfortable."[36] Which is perhaps an amusing way of also understanding why cable television channels such as Comedy Central have embraced satire as a brand marker—"popular with the children" is economically sufficient when focusing on narrower demographics and being content with smaller audience share. Those features of satire that might suppress mass audience appeal (aggression and judgment) are the same features that can create popular appeal in post-network economic models (even for upstart networks, as was seen in FOX's decision to air *The Simpsons*). Satiric programming offers markers of distinction for both the channel and audiences alike—forms of smart (or puerile) television that provide distinctive appeal and a seemingly unique perspective on the world not found elsewhere on television.

But Test argues that *each* characteristic places difficult demands on audiences. By extending his observation to television, we see why satire can be such a dangerous programming choice:

Satire in effect asks—demands—that its audience engage in a dialogue of a special kind. In addition to making associations, the audience is expected to assimilate the special mixture of aggression, play, laughter, and judgment that is set before it. Each of these alone can create difficulties. Aggression may cause resentment or other unfavorable reactions. Differences of opinion concerning the judgments are potential sources of contention. The playfulness of satire, especially when yoked with serious questions, may disconcert some. The complicated nature of laughter provides another dimension of difficulty. Together the possibilities for problems are compounded moment by moment.[37]

Furthermore, satire is rarely a form of discourse with clear-cut or easily digestible meanings. Satire can be "work," and therefore it tends to require a level of sophistication that network television infrequently demands of audiences (again, largely because satire is so often tied to the production of "comedy").[38] As Schutz has argued about political humor in general, "the best humor is always something of a puzzle in its camouflaged criticism, implicit standards, and negativism. Its appreciation requires mental participation by the audience, and its lessons are not hortatory, but self-learned."[39]

Yet here are two final dimensions of satire that make it such an important form of political discourse. Satire demands a heightened state of awareness and mental participation in its audience (not to mention knowledge). It is a historically persistent form of cultural expression that is spawned by societal and individual *needs* for such forms of expression. When historical reality presents periods of social and political rupture (such as culture wars, hot wars, and unpopular leaders) or mind-numbing manufactured realities (such as celebrity culture, media spin, and news management), satire becomes a potent means for enunciating critiques and asserting unsettling truths that audiences may need or want to hear. As Test notes, "satire is mainly about a time and a place and people."[40] In such times and places, satire becomes a means to "shake us out of our sense of apathy or indifference," a means through which citizens can become more critically aware.[41]

British comedian Mark Steel emphasizes the power of satire to stir audiences who are hungry for meaning:

You're not going to make a Tory into a socialist by doing comedy . . . but you can make [audiences] feel more confident about their ideas, which is not to be sneezed at. In a sense you are *changing* their ideas because you're making somebody who says, "Well I don't agree with all the injustices in society but nobody else seems to give a shit but me." . . . If you can make them think, "No, I'm not on my own. There are other people who think it's appalling. . . . I thought it was just me who thought that." You can make people feel that. You can make people *feel enthused about ideas.* (emphasis added)[42]

As Steel's comments make clear, satire and political comedy do not just speak to individuals but help individuals see their connections to others (or to communities of others). Certainly that is the case when conservatives see an affinity with the satirical critiques of liberals in *South Park,* or when liberal and progressive fans of Michael Moore's work appreciate the comedic humiliation of the agents of corporate and governmental power in his films and television programs.[43] But Schutz argues that, while all comedians are partisan,

the very nature of political humor as a communicative art requires its transcending of special interest in an issue and embracing a general interest of its audience. In the very act of challenging his opponent, then, the comic partisan by his humor declares for peace with him, calls upon the community of feeling, and reminds the audience of their moral commonality.[44]

Even satirists such as Jon Stewart recognize their representational role as a voice of a community—even if that community is the mainstream of the American polity. As he notes, "I represent the distracted center. My comedy is not the comedy of the neurotic. It comes from the center. But it comes from feeling displaced from society because you're in the center. We're the group of fairness, common sense, and moderation. We're clearly the disenfranchised center . . . because we're not in charge."[45]

Democratic theorists have tended to emphasize news as the most important form of political discourse because, in their formulation, it is the primary means through which individuals can make rational democratic choices based on information.[46] But as Jones has argued, news is only one narrative of public life, and a limited one at that.[47] Instead, political comedy, satire, and parody all provide important narrative critiques that enable democratic discourse and deliberation. Satire's lessons often enable people—as an audience, a community, a polity—to recognize the naked emperor and, through their laughter, begin to see realities that have been obscured. In that regard, satire provides a valuable means through which citizens can analyze and interrogate power and the realm of politics rather than remain simple subjects of it.

## Satiric Strategery: Parody as Satire

Confusingly, everyday vernacular often treats parody as synonymous with satire, but not all parody is satiric. Stephen Neale and Frank Krutnik explain that while satire draws on social conventions, parody draws on aesthetic ones.[48] Parody attacks a particular text or genre, making fun of how that text or genre operates. Pastiche merely imitates or repeats for mildly ironic amusement, whereas parody is actively critical. For instance, when an episode of *The Simpsons* loosely follows the plot of *Citizen Kane* (rendering Mr. Burns as Kane), no real critique is offered of Orson Welles's masterpiece, making this pastiche. Yet on a weekly basis *The Simpsons* plays with generic conventions of the traditional family sitcom. It also mocks forms of advertising and, particularly relevant for the essays in this collection, it occasionally lambastes the form and format of news, all with critical intent, thereby making such instances bona fide parody.[49]

Parody is common in many of today's class of satire TV, often working alongside the satire. For example, *The Daily Show* mimics the form of a news program with its grand music, set design, top corner insert graphics, beat reporters, and anchorman. As each show begins, Jon Stewart parodies real news anchors' apparently thoughtful notation and perusal of their script, by playfully or madly scribbling on his notes, ironically recontextualizing the ritually common act to suggest not up-to-the-second-of-broadcast tinkering or acquisition of information but, instead, simple play and love of doodling. As with much of his parodic schtick, this act robs anchors of their aura, coding them as kids with crayons. Likewise, British satirist and parodist Chris Morris's *Day Today* took the form of a news program. Morris often parodied the generic requirement of news teams to act as happy families working in perfect synergy with one another by, for instance, muttering into his microphone after signing off to a colleague, "Take her off the monitor. I can't stand to see her face." Stephen Colbert's entire persona is a parodic rendering of Fox News's Bill O'Reilly and hence a nightly character study and critique of both the person and the form.

Bakhtin wrote of parody with great enthusiasm, for in it he saw the marriage of two of his key theoretical interests—carnival and dialogism. Bakhtin saw texts as perpetually embroiled in discussion with one another, and both he and Valentin Volosinov wrote of "the social character of meaning" and of language as "a continuous process of becoming."[50] Texts do not take on meaning for any reader in a vacuum. Rather, a reader will always make sense of texts relative to other texts, "socially" or intertextually.[51] Parody exemplifies this process most clearly, for parody aims to recontextualize how we make sense of another text or genre. Parody involves "the structural superimposition of texts" that places the parody on top of the parodied text, a ghosted or parasitic covering.[52] As such, it offers "new" ways to make sense of "old" texts or genres. Moreover, just as humor in general can provoke reflection on the social convention that is targeted, parody aims to provoke reflection *and re-evaluation* of how the targeted texts or genre works. Laurent Jenny writes that the parody's author "repeats in order to encircle, to enclose within another discourse . . . to obliterate, to cancel," making parody "a mechanism of perturbation" whose function is "to prevent meaning from becoming lethargic—to avert the triumph of the cliché by a process of transformation."[53] Or as Bakhtin notes, "the process of parodying forces us to experience those sides of the object that are not otherwise included in a given genre or a given style."[54] Especially since parody frequently attacks genres, though, its lessons hold considerable potential to be far from fleeting. When we next encounter the once-parodied genre, we will now have added tools for making sense of it. Parody, as such, is a media literacy educator.[55]

As said, not all parody is satiric. However, news parody, parody of political speeches or debates, and parody of other genres of political discourse is often satiric. Because the news and political debates are the preeminent genres by which many of us learn of national and international politics, when parody attacks the woodenness of debates or the news for poor performance and for being more of a glossy show, it is by nature launching a satiric missive on the nature of the political process and our tolerance of the status quo. Making fun of the news is deeply political as such, and thus while parody is at root a form that is never inherently political, parody can *become* an important contributor to political discourse, encouraging critical viewing and a healthy cynicism about the mediation of politics. It can also prove satiric when transposing political figures into other genres, as when figures from the Bush administration populated the family sitcom parody *That's My Bush!* as typical sitcom archetypal characters. Savvy parody is a handy tool in the satirist's collection, and in various ways, contemporary television satire often uses parody to considerable effect. As many historians of parody have noted, parody (especially in periods of heightened interest in parody) often contributes to and signals the evolution of a genre; when a genre finds its most interesting and popular form(s) in its parodies, said genre is often dying.[56] Thus today's increase in news parody, in particular, may be signaling the genre's dire need for innovation and maturation and may be contributing to the push to rejuvenate it and make it evolve. To note this, though, is to plot the current era of satire TV on a chronology of satire and parody and hence requires that we now address these genre's cultural history in television.

## A Brief History of Satire TV:
### Turning the Dial and Targeting the Demo(cracy)

Today satire and politically tinged parody may seem plentiful on television, but this certainly wasn't always the case. Though it can be tempting to credit public backlash against a historically unpopular president as creating unprecedented audiences for such shows, the truth is that the tremendous changes in how television does business—namely, the shift from network broadcasting to cable narrowcasting—is the fundamentally enabling mechanism for these popular critiques of politics. Still, that shift, however massive, can't alone account for the boom in satire TV as an industry programming strategy and certainly can't explain its resonance with audiences. What precedents, then, have opened this televisual space for satire and parody? Satire has *not* been around since the earliest years of television. It is not a genre or format that has shifted and adapted to the modes of production or industrial imperatives the way in which soap operas, quiz shows, and sitcoms have from network radio to early TV to the network era and beyond. Instead, it represents a convergence of audience tastes, shifting programming strategies, and the gradual evolution of satiric and parodic television in other formats that has led to the current state of satire TV.

The cultural resonance of parody and satire may indeed decline and fall over the years, but even in decades renowned for their supposed domestic tranquility—say, the American 1950s—satiric voices have spoken to and for the disaffected, voicing criticisms that "official" commentators have not. Indeed, when one looks at the history of the twentieth century, the late

1950s and early 1960s stand out as a highpoint for social criticism in the form of satire and parody. The key caveat is that very little of that criticism was finding its way to television. Through the 1950s, parody had become a reliable strategy for television comedians to produce content to fill the long hours. But those parodies had for the most part focused on poking fun at film and television. If this variety of comedy was ever considered danger-ous, it was because network executives sometimes feared they were too esoteric—mass audiences might not get the jokes. Sid Caesar, for example, was well known for making parodies part of his shows, but one network executive feared that he was prone to err by doing "takeoffs on Japanese movies nobody has even been to an art theatre in New York to see."[57]

Instead of on television, it was in print culture and on vinyl records where social and political satire found a popular audience. *MAD* maga-zine, which began in 1953 as a comic book parody, had by the end of the 1950s become required reading for hip high school and college students. While the magazine could be expected to routinely lambaste familiar advertisements, films, and television shows, it also occasionally dipped into social criticism, such as in a piece that argued why the suburbs were on the way out or in a scathing parody of the Army-McCarthy hearings which reimagined the political and television event as a quiz show.[58] An-other magazine success story of the 1950s was *Playboy,* which ran features on socially conscious comedians like Mort Sahl (who hosted the first few Playboy Jazz Festivals) and Lenny Bruce. Founder Hugh Hefner even hired most of the *MAD* staff away in order to start what would become his first of two failed satire magazines.[59]

Satire cultivated something of a subterranean or outlaw image in popu-lar culture, despite the fact that it was a favorite of the new cultural elites: those who turned up their noses at both lowbrow or "mass cult" and the highbrow pretensions of old-school legitimate culture. Satire and parody proved potent weapons for those negotiating their identities in relation-ship to postwar popular and political culture, those who—like Hefner's idealized playboy—didn't buy into the suburban ranch house dream but still wanted to enjoy the comforts and pleasures of postwar consumer cul-ture. Even if they couldn't see Lenny Bruce or Mort Sahl in person, they had access to them on LP records. The social satire of those comedians and others like Shelley Berman, Bob Newhart, Mike Nichols and Elaine May, Stan Friedberg, Dick Gregory, and Godfrey Cambridge made the long-playing comedy album a great culture industry success story. Although all of those comedians were socially abrasive in one way or another, they did not espouse an explicit partisan viewpoint or ideological dogma. Instead, they articulated alternative ways of making sense of postwar culture, resonating with fans while rankling the cultural and political establishment.

As a counterpoint to the boom in satire TV during George W. Bush's historically contentious presidency in the conservative 2000s, historian Stephen Kercher designates 1962 as the highpoint of what he calls "liberal satire"—a year in the midst of the storied American "Camelot." Even with the corporate liberals in power, satire crested after developing an audience first as dissident, underground humor during the Truman and Eisenhower years, then packaged as popular entertainment and made available for popular audiences through magazines, comedy albums, theater companies, and the occasional toned-down TV appearance. "With the young, witty, urbane John Kennedy in the White House," he notes, "satiric expression, long a resource for cultural dissent, became for many American liberals a source of affirmation and a sign of better days to come."[60]

Still, that warm regard for satire did not carry over to the television executives and advertisers. A rare exception (and one that ultimately proved the rule) was ABC's short-lived but much-loved *That Was the Week That Was* (*TW3*). Another in a rich history of transatlantic crossovers, the key creative force behind *TW3* (and its British Broadcasting Corporation [BBC] antecedent) was writer/producer/performer David Frost. Its staff and cast included a long list of notable American writers and performers, including Buck Henry, Alan Alda, Calvin Trillin, and Gloria Steinem. The program was produced by Broadway bigwig Leland Hayward, known more for middlebrow extravaganzas like *South Pacific* than for dissident humor. Ostensibly structured as a satiric take on the week's news, the program today looks like a cross between *The Daily Show* and a variety show. While *TW3* became a national sensation in the U.K., it struggled in the American context, mostly, as Kercher shows (and David Marc notes in his foreword to this book), because of the reluctance of Hayward and the network brass to ruffle the feathers of advertisers and the politically powerful.

With the exception of news coverage, television content in the 1960s was notorious for ignoring the massive social conflicts and changes taking place. Network television executives were in the business of appealing to as many people—and alienating as few advertisers—as possible. That meant pursuing the "least objectionable" types of programming, with the effect that comedies were overwhelmingly escapist sitcoms. Work in television studies, however, has usefully noted the social criticisms latent in some of those programs. Lynn Spigel, for instance, has argued that the fantasy sitcom cycle of the 1960s (programs such as *The Addams Family, Bewitched,* and *The Munsters*) articulated popular disaffection from those suburbs and gender roles idealized in domestic sitcoms.[61] Aniko Bodroghkozy has also shown how even the sanitized counterculture of *The Monkees* could serve as sites for the articulation of nascent countercultural identities.[62] Explicit social satire, though, did not qualify as mass entertainment, even when, with cultural clashes in the streets and an unpopular war in Vietnam, Americans might have desired it the most.

Two programs in the 1960s that did manage to incorporate satire into their formats were *The Smothers Brothers Comedy Hour* and *Rowan and Martin's Laugh-In.* In both cases, however, the potential sting of the satire's politics was ameliorated, or in the case of *The Smothers Brothers,* proved fatal when CBS decided that hassling performers over politics wasn't worth the network's time or effort.[63] Still, the program did launch the faux presidential run of Pat Paulsen in 1968, which Heather Osborne-Thompson examines (in chapter 3) as a televisual "bridge" between politics and alienated voters in that tumultuous year. At NBC, *Laugh-In* simulated a party atmosphere by structuring itself as a swinging cocktail joke and skit party. As hosts, Dan Rowan and Dick Martin reprised their straight man/ dumb man nightclub act. This, along with the mod party atmosphere, served to frame whatever subversive quips might be made by the cast or guests within the sensibility of risqué nightclub routines rather than politically inflammatory stand-up or commentary. The atmosphere was safe enough for Republican presidential candidate Richard Nixon to appear a couple of months before the 1968 election, repeating the program's catchphrase "Sock it to me" (though he was not subsequently bombarded with the water or pies that usually followed that pronouncement).

We might understand the unwillingness of the television networks to promote satire as a popular form of television comedy throughout the 1960s as an acknowledgment that humor with political content could be potent enough to offend audiences, alienate advertisers, and undermine network economics. Indeed, in their examination of the socially transgressive nature of carnival culture, Peter Stallybrass and Allon White respond to the criticism (such as Eco's) that carnival functions as an official, sanctioned resistance and is therefore neutralized as an agent for social change. They point out that one need only look at the number of fairs outlawed through England and the ways in which bourgeois society defined itself against the carnivalesque to see that the subversive pleasures of the fair posed a threat to authority.

Of course, the willingness of the networks to consider socially relevant material as desirable fodder for television narratives—particularly comedies—changed in 1970. That's the year CBS gutted its lineup of successful though down-market comedies (such as *The Beverly Hillbillies*) to make way for more "socially relevant" programming designed to draw upscale audiences desired by advertisers back to TV. Prototypical of this new approach was *All in the Family*, a sitcom not radically different from its predecessors. The narrative structure of the show stuck firmly to the traditional sitcom format, yet with some "socially relevant" event temporarily disrupting the relative narrative equilibrium and agitation growing within the tenuous atmosphere of the Bunker household. *All in the Family* didn't parody the sitcom or satirize American life as much as it represented the generational conflicts playing out in homes around the country. Despite writer/producer Norman Lear's creation of Archie Bunker as bigoted oaf and obnoxious sitcom lead (but one audiences could nevertheless identify with), Archie could be very funny. Meathead's criticisms of Archie's outdated, conservative ways of thinking didn't sting as trenchant social criticisms. Rather, they were framed as the liberal ramblings of a grad student who could be read, as Archie maintained, as out of touch with the real world (or, in the case of Archie's feminist daughter, Gloria, hysterical). *All in the Family* was, in the end, a family of characters in conflict who said funny things in response to socially relevant issues, but the "sitcom" moniker fit those funny things better than "satire."

The television industry in the 1970s and 1980s seemed to tolerate satire as long as it cloaked itself in traditional sitcom trappings or hovered on the fringes of late-night TV. Lear's socially relevant sitcoms such as *Good Times* and *Maude* are examples, but they languished in the Reagan 1980s as neotraditional domestic sitcoms like *Family Ties*, *Diff'rent Strokes*, and *Growing Pains* rehashed plots and taught lessons about growing up that would have been completely at home on *The Adventures of Ozzie and Harriet*, *Leave It to Beaver*, or *Father Knows Best*. On the fringes, however, TV was learning how to appeal to smaller audiences through more cutting-edge humor. *Saturday Night Live*, particularly in its earliest years, was television comedy produced by a new generation for those coming of age during the social changes of the 1960s. The show funneled that cultural savvy into political and social satire acceptable on the late-night fringe. But as *SNL*'s popularity grew, so did producer Lorne Michael's desire to appeal to more people. As Jeffrey Jones notes in his essay in this collection (chapter 2), *SNL* would also learn how to properly neuter political critique

so as not to cross too many boundaries in upsetting the tastes of mass audiences. Social satire on late-night television during the 1980s was most
often subsumed into silly characters with little to no rebuke. For example,
the best *SNL* could muster as a response to the emergence of the religious
right as a potent political force was Dana Carvey's beloved "Church Lady."
*SNL* did repopularize news parody with its "Weekend Update" segment
(an obvious medium for satire), though often with a propensity for cheap
laughs and sophomoric humor.

Even on the fringes of pay cable, where some of the most biting political satire can be found these days, things were pretty tame in the 1980s.
HBO's *Not Necessarily the News* was yet another transatlantic crossover
(modeled off the BBC's *Not the Nine O'Clock News*) that parodied newscasts and commercials but possessed little political bite. The show also
draws attention to the fact that satire on TV in the United Kingdom has
regularly outpaced U.S. television. Also in the United Kingdom during the
1980s, the puppets on *Spitting Image* satirized Reagan, Thatcher, and other
politicos. Numerous international copies followed from Chile to Greece,
Israel to India, with Canal +'s *Les Guignols de l'info* (originally *Les Arènes
de l'info*) in France proving particularly successful. However, their U.S.
copy, *D.C. Follies*, managed to garner two Emmy nominations but contained little to no actual political humor and failed to capture the public's
attention. *Spitting Image*'s most lasting impact in the United States might
be the music video for the rock group Genesis's "Land of Confusion"—a
tidy example of just how banal the intersection of political and popular
culture in the 1980s could be.

Thankfully, television of the late 1980s did give the world *The Simpsons*
to accompany George H. W. Bush's extension of the Reagan years. Given
the current state of television comedy and all-permeating irreverence, it is
hard to recapture the sense of just how different *The Simpsons* really felt
when it first came on the air. As many observers have noted, *The Simpsons*
was and remains a show *about* television. Almost every televisual genre
has been parodied in one episode or another, with the news, ads, and
most of all the traditional family sitcom coming under particularly heavy
parodic fire. *The Simpsons* toys with American social vices by *playing* with
American television, realizing that in a televised nation, social satire must
often be both on and about television. When FOX had the audacity to pit
the program against *The Cosby Show,* it fired a volley in the culture wars
with more lasting impact on television than any of the flippant cultural
criticisms of George H. W. Bush, the man who bemoaned that we needed

a nation "closer to the Waltons than the Simpsons," or even his vice president Dan Quayle's vilification of Murphy Brown's choice to be a single parent as an example of Hollywood's lack of "family values."

Perhaps no single program is as important in creating the televisual space for the satire TV boom as *The Simpsons*. Like *Laugh-In*, *The Simpsons* promised irreverence and the breaking of television norms but rarely provided explicit and cutting-edge political satire. The all-pervasive parodic sensibility of that show, however, as well as its role in shaping the FOX network, cannot be overstated. Just the sheer number of writers and producers who have worked on the show before moving on to other projects has influenced the tenor of television comedy at large. Now that it is the longest running sitcom ever, it seems appropriate to consider that *The Simpsons* has established the satirization of sitcom and social norms as the norm. The programs examined in the essays in this collection all fall under the descriptor "post-network TV." As comedy television, they could all also be acceptably described as "post-*Simpsons* TV." And yet the two terms are somewhat linked, as *The Simpsons* proved one of the marquee programs in FOX's attempt to niche program its way into the American network lineup. ABC, CBS, and NBC had all sought to be "big tents," welcoming in all viewers, but FOX went after a specific demo, stylizing itself as young, irreverent, and brash, with shows such as *The Simpsons, Married . . . With Children, In Living Color,* and its now trademark reality television fare serving as its public face. With the monumental success of *The Simpsons* and its branding role for the FOX network as a whole, FOX gradually became first the fourth network and then one of the big four. When upstart networks The WB and UPN began in 1995, both mimicked FOX's strategy of targeting a specific demo, and in due time ABC began to program particularly for young female interests and NBC pursued the 18–49 demo. A look at the prime-time lineup today suggests, then, that the networks themselves have recognized and responded to "post-network" models of doing business.[64]

The changes in television comedy forthcoming in the post-network era could be seen most clearly through the launch of the cable channel Comedy Central and its strategy of using political humor and satire as a means of branding itself.[65] Formed through the merger of two competing comedy channels, Comedy TV (later renamed Comedy Central) launched in January 1991 and quickly sought to establish an identity as a location for more than reruns and stand-up comedy through topical humor. In 1992, the network launched its own brand of presidential election coverage from the party nominating conventions with "Indecision 1992," a special that has subsequently been repeated each presidential election year. As one producer noted at the time, "news has an interest in proving that the event is newsworthy. We have an interest in proving that it's comic," a statement that presages what would later become the network's slogan, "Same World, Different Take."[66]

But it was the network's launch of the humorous political roundtable discussion show, *Politically Incorrect*, in 1993 that garnered the network critical acclaim, wider cable system carriage, and brand identity. The show, hosted by comedian Bill Maher and featuring an odd assortment of celebrities, authors, musicians, comedians, and politicos, quickly became the network's flagship program by blending serious and humorous discussions about politics into a hybrid entertainment-political talk show. *Politically Incorrect* proved more humorous than satirical, but it also highlighted the artificial separation of politics from entertainment programming that defined the network era (where politics and public affairs programming was actually "narrowcasted" in ways that made it unattractive for mass audience viewing). Through its airing of *Politically Incorrect*, Comedy Central actually broadened television's horizon by blending entertainment and serious talk and by allowing both political experts and nonexperts to discuss, argue, and laugh about politics all in the same conversation.

Since the introduction of *Politically Incorrect*, Comedy Central has recognized that satirical treatments of politics are central to its identity, and, as documented in this volume, the network has been the one television network that has most thoroughly developed satirical treatments of state and society. Its programs have included *The Daily Show, South Park, That's My Bush!, Chappelle's Show, The Colbert Report,* and *Lil' Bush.* Such provocative programming has allowed network executives to contend that they offer more than simply the comedic. "Comedy Central is not a lifestyle channel," one executive stated. "Dare to watch our programs and you might think in a different way."[67]

Political humor and satire's further emergence in television's post-network era is seen in programs appearing on other cable channels, namely HBO and Bravo. With the introduction of *Dennis Miller Live* in 1994 and *The Chris Rock Show* in 1997, HBO provided a satirical platform to two former *SNL* alums, allowing both comedians to develop distinctively opinionated talk shows that helped redefine the genre of late-night talk while providing uncensored forums for aggressive political and social commentary.[68] Later HBO introduced America to Sacha Baron Cohen and his take-no-prisoners approach to satiric social and political commentary through his characters Ali G, Borat, and Bruno. Finally, while Michael Moore's parodic investigative newsmagazine show *TV Nation* originally aired on NBC and FOX (in 1994 and 1995, respectively), the reformulated version of his satirical take on the newsmagazine genre in *The Awful Truth* became even more biting during its two-season run on Bravo and the BBC (which cofinanced the production) from 1999 to 2000.[69]

In sum, beginning with *The Simpsons,* the 1990s saw the emergence of political and social satire in full form. By the end of the decade, *Politically Incorrect* had migrated to late-night network TV and *South Park* had taken over as Comedy Central's new flagship program. Immediately notorious for its trash-talking kids, *South Park* achieved ratings unheard of on basic cable, and, perhaps as importantly, proved a merchandising juggernaut. In the wake of *South Park's* phenomenal success, Comedy Central's status soared and it produced more and more original programming, a trend that other cable channels would follow and that would increase exponentially in the 2000s. If kids began the 1990s bedecked in Bart Simpson "Don't Have a Cow, Man!" shirts, the 2000s began with Eric Cartman demanding "Respect my authority!" Another highly influential and critically acclaimed Comedy Central show that began in the 1990s was the news-parody *The Daily Show.* Though originally hosted by Craig Kilborn, *The Daily Show* ultimately found its footing (and its satiric voice) when Jon Stewart took over the reins in 1999. Through the 2000s, *The Daily Show* collected dedicated viewers, as well as critical acclaim through numerous Emmy, Peabody, and TV Critics awards, meanwhile becoming a coveted arena for politicians to reach the American public.

A time in which television comedy—and particularly the ironic sort—received great attention (and hence was seen to matter) was the immediate aftermath of the 9/11 attacks. Suddenly it was assumed to be in poor taste for television comedians to crack topical jokes, and the leading late-night comedians (David Letterman, Jay Leno, et al.) decided to get solemn for a couple of weeks. Bill Maher's program was eventually canceled due to comments he made that were deemed inappropriate by the patriotism police in the immediate aftermath of the attacks. Dennis Miller seemingly lost his satiric instincts and quit his HBO program, but not before turning into a right-wing ideologue as a result of the tragedy. Lorne Michaels even needed on-air permission from Mayor Rudy Giuliani to be funny again. Perhaps most notoriously, Graydon Carter, editor of *Vanity Fair* and former editor of the 1990s satirical phenom

*Spy*, proclaimed the death of irony.[70] Luckily, the news-parody paper and website *The Onion* triumphantly issued a special edition the week after the attacks, bearing the slogan "Attack on America: Holy Fucking Shit." *The Onion* despaired that American life had "turned into a bad Jerry Bruckheimer movie," detailed the shock of the terrorist hijackers to find themselves in Hell instead of Paradise, and reported on a press conference held by God himself in which he angrily reiterated "Thou Shall Not Kill": "I'm against it, across the board. How many times do I have to say it? Don't kill each other anymore—ever! I'm fucking serious!"[71] Though *MAD* magazine was technically still around, it was *The Onion* and an endless supply of comedy websites and mash-up videos that were becoming the satiric counternote to what was available on television. *MAD* had once said what couldn't be said on television, providing an alternative language for meaning-making through parody and satire. Now *The Onion* was the news parody of record, as well as a veritable satire TV farm club, producing, most notably, Ben Karlin as head writer of *The Daily Show* and *The Colbert Report*.

Like that moment in the early 1960s when Mort Sahl wrote jokes for JFK and satire veered from the side of the road into the mainstream, satire TV today enjoys a privileged space from which to jab and prod the establishment. In fact, some of the most influential programs are now considered by the political establishment to be necessary stops to stoop for votes, remake public images, or build a nationwide persona. Jon Stewart may have landed a punch against CNN's *Crossfire* when he told hosts Tucker Carlson and Paul Begala that their partisan rantings were part of the strategy of politicians, but his show has become known as a key stop on what media strategists are calling the "satire circuit." Since their ratings skew much younger than *The O'Reilly Factor* or *Larry King Live*, *The Daily Show* and *The Colbert Report* have become "key to courting 'the irony demo': the coastal, college-educated cadre of young viewers who get much of their political analysis in the form of satire."[72] Researchers may issue battling studies over who gets their news or news analysis from the comedy shows, but the programs have certainly proven successful at getting a desirable demo's eyeballs to advertisers and politicos alike. Still, network television has mostly left it to the relative margins of cable television to take up the satiric sword. While *The Daily Show* dispatched a team to Ohio for the week of the watershed 2006 midterm elections, for instance, *SNL* broadcast a career retrospective of Darrell Hammond—who never even caricatured W.[73]

## Chapter Summaries

Continuing on from this introduction, our first two chapters further situate the current moment of satire TV by examining former models charting the recent development of satire. As Jeffrey Jones shows in chapter 2 on presidential caricature, *SNL* has had a checkered past as a source of meaningful social satire. Jones traces shifts in television's strategies of and willingness to caricature presidents and politicians, especially noting the distinction between the critical mode of caricature and mere impersonation humor. In contrast, he shows how, by "bookending" the Bush presidency, Comedy Central's *That's My Bush!* and *Lil' Bush* have laid the groundwork for a much more cacophonous and unruly variety of narrative critiques and interpretations than existed in the network era. In chapter 3, Heather Osborne-Thompson looks back at television's past to those "faux candidates" (such as Pat Paulsen on *The Smothers Brothers* and Jack Tanner in *Tanner '88*) who not only mimicked the election process for laughs but also worked to reconnect alienated voters to politics. "These representations," she says, "arguably created an empowering platform for demystification of the political double-talk and media-savvy of modern campaigns, and for expression of overt critiques of partisanship and 'old boys' networks' that have traditionally excluded the concerns of women, minorities, the poor, and the generally disenfranchised." Osborne-Thompson also looks at how Stephen Colbert's flirtation with running in the 2008 presidential race demonstrates the unique power that satire TV currently enjoys within the American political landscape.

In part II, we offer three chapters on the "fake news" genre that has challenged traditional norms of what counts as news and of how today's citizens do or "should" relate to the news. In chapter 4, Amber Day immediately takes issue with the term "fake news," noting that although *The Daily Show with Jon Stewart* is commonly referred to as such (owing to its parodic tone and content), "that label obscures the show's more complicated relationship to 'real' news programming, as well as the attraction it holds for fans frustrated with the compromised authenticity and relevance of straight news programming." To consider *The Daily Show* "fake news" risks dismissing its careful examination of political reality, but Day rejects the simplifying separation of satire and reality. Similarly, in chapter 5, Joanne Morreale examines the rhetorical strategies of *The Daily Show,* which, she says, not only impress with comedic wit but also include "incisive social criticism that teaches the skills of critical thinking and judgment that are essential to a participatory democracy." In chapter 7, Geoffrey Baym shifts the focus from Stewart to Stephen Colbert and his further play with distinctions between the real and the fake. In *The Colbert Report* (which follows *The Daily Show* nightly), Colbert embodies satiric parody. He confounds not only presidents, who tend to see things in black or white, but also anyone seeking easy divisions between real and fake, comedy and criticism, politics and entertainment. Baym's chapter examines Colbert's simultaneous indulgence in and ironic interrogation of postmodern simulation, spectacle, and epistemological relativity.

If critics of satire TV frequently stumble in creating binaries of the real and the serious, or the fake and the comic, another common misunderstanding of satire TV regards it as wholly critical, and in no way productive. The chapters in part III take aim at this criticism. First, in chapter 7, Jonathan Gray looks at two provocative television comedians from the United Kingdom, Chris Morris and Sacha Baron Cohen, who also include "real" interviews in their satiric programs, even to the point of drawing accusations that they victimize public figures. Television has been widely criticized for ushering politics into the age of the image, and comedy programming (such as talk shows) has often been accused of fawningly contributing to image politics. But Cohen and Morris, Gray writes, use savvy and astute satire variously to challenge or to redefine carefully manicured political imagery and to demand a more careful accounting of public image by citizen viewers. In chapter 8, Serra Tinic then writes that in Canada, where the quest for cultural self-definition has translated into a broadcasting policy obsession, satirical comedies have proved to be among the most popular television programs that resonate with a "national" audience in a regionally fragmented country. The work of Rick Mercer, in particular, provides a televisual forum for oppositional or resistant politics while simultaneously contributing to a sense of regional intersubjectivity and of national identity. Next, in chapter 9, Henry Jenkins looks at how online parody tries to negotiate a space betwixt and between participatory culture and participatory democracy. Picking up where his recent book *Convergence Culture* left off, Jenkins looks to the CNN/YouTube presidential debate (and its star, the global-warming Snowman) as an example of the emerging relationships between new and old media that are reshaping not just television but also democratic debate, discourse, and civic engagement. All three chapters illustrate the productive capacities of satire TV's critical approach.

In part IV, we turn to the limits of satire TV—how satire TV regularly violates standards of taste and conceptions of how politics work, as well as satire TV's capacities to enable audiences to deal with the complexities of party and racial politics. First, in chapter 10, Ethan Thompson examines how *South Park* has not just remained a ratings success but shown that television comedy in the post-network era can deal with timely and contentious political content in a way that spans ideological sensibilities that are too often simplified as "conservative" or "liberal," yet remains both provocative and meaningful. *South Park* continues to do this, he says, through its over-the-top, carnivalesque approach to satire that incenses critics, delights fans, and would make Bakhtin proud. In chapters 11 and 12, respectively, Bambi Haggins and Avi Santo examine satire TV's limit points through studying *Chappelle's Show* and *The Boondocks*. A number of the essays in this volume can be read as celebrations of satire TV's ability to popularize or defamiliarize "Politics with a capital P" for the public. But Haggins explores disquieting questions about the price of success for the comic, for the industry, and for both political satire and American popular culture at large when those in the audience may or may not be reading the social critique imbedded in the comedy. Also pointing an eye toward such concerns about reception, Santo examines the online discussion of fans (and critics) of *The Boondocks* to investigate how politics and political controversy are invoked by producers and viewers alike, and the extent to which political meanings are produced in the discursive interactions of online communities.

## Conclusion

Ultimately, the authors of all the chapters in this book, individually and combined, attempt to capture the state of satire TV at our current point in history. In this introductory chapter, we demonstrate how political comedy, satire, and parody *can* contribute meaningfully to political discourse and hence to the practice of citizenship. But no singular instance of satire will garner, impress, or inspire an audience simply because it is satire. Thus, in the rest of this book, we turn to specific examples of how a variety of programs have proven remarkably successful, as well as damn funny. We write this introduction in early 2008, during a contested American presidential primary season. Yet we find that amid endless polling statistics, stump speeches, *Groundhog Day*–style news coverage, and countless political ads in every medium, it is often in the realm of satire TV that we find some of the more intelligent, complex, and provocative analyses of the political landscape, as well as some of the more refreshing and unique voices and opinions on politics. Nor are we alone in this regard, as the mantra "Did you watch Stewart/Colbert last night?" initiates many a thoughtful discussion about politics. Even *Saturday Night Live* has found its way back into water-cooler conversations, though this may be due to its carefully manufactured candidate cameos rather than any cutting-edge satire. This collection represents an attempt to take these analyses, voices, and opinions seriously and to inquire into the processes behind the mantra and those conversations. When it works, satire TV is that rare delicacy: something that entertains, yet also makes us think critically, something that hails us as audiences looking for a laugh, yet also as citizens desiring meaningful engagement with public life. Gradually, satire TV has crept up on the news as one of the preeminent genres used to understand varied political realities, rendering it an ideal entry point for a study of politics, audiences, television, comedy, entertainment, and citizenship in the early twenty-first century.

NOTES

1. Frank Rich, "Throw the Truthiness Bums Out," *New York Times,* 5 November 2006.

2. Arthur Jones, "Among Urban Auds, Satire Takes Hold as Laffers Challenge Dramas," *Variety,* 3 April 2006, A18.

3. "Political Satire Flourishes on Iraqi TV," *All Things Considered,* National Public Radio, 21 September 2007. Reported by Anne Garrels.

4. Michael Kalin, "Why Jon Stewart Isn't Funny," *Boston Globe,* 3 March 2006, at http://www.boston.com/ae/movies/oscars/articles/2006/03/03/why_jon_stewart_isnt_funny/ (accessed 31 August 2006).

5. Carl Matheson, "*The Simpsons,* Hyper-Irony, and the Meaning of Life," in *The Simpsons and Philosophy: The D'Oh! of Homer,* ed. William Irwin, Mark T. Conard, and Aeon J. Skoble (Chicago: Open Court, 2001), 109, 118.

6. National Annenberg Election Survey, "Daily Show Viewers Knowledgeable about Presidential Campaign, National Annenberg Election Survey Shows," press release (21 September 2004), at http://www.annenbergpublicpolicycenter.org/naes/2004_03_late-night-knowledge-2_9-21_pr.pdf (accessed 31 August 2006); Pew Research Center for the People and the Press, "Public Knowledge of Current

Affairs Little Changed by News and Information Revolutions: What Americans Know 1989–2007," 15 April 2007, at http://people-press.org/reports/display.php3?ReportID=319 (accessed 29 August 2007).

7. Simon Critchley, *On Humour* (New York: Routledge, 2002), 1.

8. Ibid., 4, 5.

9. Quoted in ibid., 10.

10. Ibid., 18.

11. Ibid., 88.

12. Mikhail M. Bakhtin, *The Dialogic Imagination,* trans. Caryl Emerson and Michael Holquist (Austin: University of Texas Press, 1981), 23.

13. Mikhail M. Bakhtin, *Rabelais and His World,* trans. Helene Iswolsky (Bloomington: Indiana University Press, 1984), 123.

14. Ibid., 10.

15. Stephen Neale and Frank Krutnik, *Popular Film and Television Comedy* (New York: Routledge, 1990), 91. See also Chris Powell, "A Phenomenological Analysis of Humour in Society," in *Humour in Society: Resistance and Control,* ed. Chris Powell and George E. C. Paton (New York: St. Martin's, 1988), 103.

16. Sigmund Freud, *Jokes and Their Relation to the Unconscious,* trans. James Strachey (London: Hogarth, 1960), 117.

17. Susan Purdie, *Comedy: The Mastery of Discourse* (London: Harvester Wheatsheaf, 1993), 60–61.

18. Umberto Eco, "The Frames of Comic 'Freedom,'" in *Carnival!,* ed. Thomas A. Sebeok (New York: Mouton, 1984), 3.

19. Purdie, *Comedy,* 126.

20. Critchley, *On Humour;* Jonathan Gray, *Watching with* The Simpsons: *Television, Parody, and Intertextuality* (New York: Routledge, 2006); and Peter Stallybrass and Allon White, *The Politics and Poetics of Transgression* (London: Methuen, 1986).

21. Charles E. Schutz, *Political Humor: From Aristophanes to Sam Ervin* (London: Associated University Presses, 1977), 50.

22. M. D. Fletcher, *Contemporary Political Satire: Narrative Strategies in the Post-Modern Context* (Lanham, Md.: University Press of America, 1987), ix.

23. George A. Test, *Satire: Spirit and Art* (Tampa: University of South Florida Press, 1991), 4.

24. Schutz, *Political Humor,* 78.

25. Test, *Satire,* 29.

26. Gilbert Highet, quoted in Chris Lamb, *Drawn to Extremes: The Use and Abuse of Editorial Cartoons* (New York: Columbia University Press, 2004), 41.

27. G. K. Chesterton, quoted in Test, *Satire,* 28.

28. See, for instance, the persistently misguided critiques of Roderick Hart in this regard, the latest of which can be found in Roderick P. Hart and Johanna

Hartelius, "The Political Sins of Jon Stewart," *Critical Studies in Media Communication* 24, no. 3 (2007): 263–72.

29. Harold Bloom, *The Best Poems of the English Language: From Chaucer through Frost* (New York: HarperCollins, 2004), 138.

30. Test, *Satire*, 14.

31. Peter Keighron, "The Politics of Ridicule: Satire and Television," in *Dissident Voices: The Politics of Television and Cultural Change*, ed. Mike Wayne (London: Pluto Press, 1998), 128.

32. Ibid., 131.

33. Ibid., 130.

34. Michael Mulkay, *On Humor: Its Nature and Its Place in Modern Society* (New York: Basil Blackwell, 1988), 185.

35. Test, *Satire*, 17.

36. Ibid., 5.

37. Ibid., 32.

38. Though one might question, for instance, the conception of *South Park*'s audience as "sophisticated," a recognition that "scatology and vulgarity have a long lineage in satiric literature" may help us understand (if not appreciate) the particular popular appeal such satire provides (Edward A. Bloom and Lillian D. Bloom, *Satire's Persuasive Voice* [Ithaca, N.Y.: Cornell University Press, 1979]).

39. Schutz, *Political Humor*, 332.

40. Test, *Satire*, 35.

41. Lamb, *Drawn to Extremes*, 41.

42. Quoted in Keighron, *Politics of Ridicule*, 140.

43. Brian C. Anderson, *South Park Conservatives: The Revolt against Liberal Media Bias* (Washington: Regnery, 2005); Jeffrey P. Jones, "Moore Muckracking: The Reinvention of the News Magazine in the Age of Spin and Entertainment," in *Michael Moore: Filmmaker, Newsmaker, Cultural Icon*, ed. Matthew Burnstein (Ann Arbor: University of Michigan Press, forthcoming).

44. Schutz, *Political Humor*, 330.

45. Quoted in Jeffrey P. Jones, *Entertaining Politics: New Political Television and Civic Culture* (Lanham, Md.: Rowman and Littlefield, 2005), 114–15.

46. Michael Schudson, *The Good Citizen: A History of American Civic Life* (New York: Free Press, 1998).

47. Jeffrey P. Jones, "A Cultural Approach to Mediated Citizenship," in *Mediated Citizenship*, ed. Karin Wahl-Jorgensen (London: Routledge, 2008), 161–79.

48. Neale and Krutnik, *Popular Film and Television Comedy*, 19.

49. Gray, *Watching with* The Simpsons.

50. Valentin N. Volosinov, *Marxism and the Philosophy of Language*, trans. Ladislav Matejka and I. R. Titunik (London: Seminar, 1973), 27, 81.

51. For example, Bakhtin, *Dialogic Imagination*; Gray, *Watching with* The Simpsons; Julia Kristeva, *Desire in Language: A Semiotic Approach to Literature*

*and Art,* trans. Thomas Gora, Alice Jardine, and Leon S. Roudiez (Oxford: Basil Blackwell, 1980).

52. Linda Hutcheon, *A Theory of Parody: The Teachings of Twentieth-Century Art Forms* (New York: Routledge, 1985), 33.

53. Laurent Jenny, "The Strategy of Form," in *French Literary Theory Today: A Reader,* ed. Tzvetan Todorov, trans. R. Carter (Cambridge: Cambridge University Press, 1982), 59.

54. Bakhtin, *Dialogic Imagination,* 55.

55. Jonathan Gray, "Television Teaching: Parody, *The Simpsons,* and Media Literacy Education," *Critical Studies in Media Communication* 22, no. 3 (2005): [223-38].

56. For example, Dan Harries, *Film Parody* (London: British Film Institute, 2000); Hutcheon, *Theory of Parody;* Margaret A. Rose, *Parody: Ancient, Modern, and Post-Modern* (Cambridge: Cambridge University Press, 1993).

57. Gilbert Millstein, "TV's Comics Went Thataway," *New York Times Magazine,* 2 February 1958.

58. Ethan Thompson, "What, Me Subversive? Parody and Sick Comedy in Postwar Television Culture," unpublished ms., 2008.

59. Ethan Thompson, "The Parodic Sensibility and the Sophisticated Gaze: Masculinity and Taste in Playboy's Penthouse," *Television and New Media* 9, no. 4 (2008): 284–304.

60. Stephen E. Kercher, *Revel with a Cause: Liberal Satire in Postwar America* (Chicago: University of Chicago Press, 2006), 194.

61. Lynn Spigel, "White Flight," in *The Revolution Wasn't Televised: Sixties Television and Social Conflict,* ed. Lynn Spigel and Michael Curtin (New York: Routledge, 1997), 58–59.

62. Aniko Bodroghkozy, *The Groove Tube: Sixties Television and the Youth Rebellion* (Durham, N.C.: Duke University Press, 2001).

63. Ibid.

64. On post-network television, see Amanda Lotz, *The Television Will Be Revolutionized* (New York: New York University Press, 2007).

65. Jones, *Entertaining Politics,* 63–88.

66. Scott Williams, "Not the News: Comedy Central Plans Convention Coverage," *Associated Press,* 27 April 1992.

67. James Endrst, "Comedy Central Sends 'That's My Bush!' to the Movies," *Hartford Courant,* 3 August 2001.

68. Jones, *Entertaining Politics;* Jeffrey P. Jones, "Comedy Talk Shows," in *The Essential HBO Reader,* ed. Gary R. Edgerton and Jeffrey P. Jones (Lexington: University Press of Kentucky, 2008), 172–82.

69. Jones, "Moore Muckraking."

70. David D. Kirkpatrick, "A Nation Challenged: The Commentators, Pronouncements on Irony Draw a Line in the Sand," *New York Times,* 24 September 2001, C9.

71. *The Onion,* 26 September 2001, issue 37: 34, at http://www.theonion.com/content/index/3734.

72. Michael Learmonth, "The Lure of Latenight," *Variety,* 4 September 2006, 17.

73. Alessandra Stanley, "When It Comes to Political Parody, Upstarts Outrun the Classics," *New York Times,* 3 November 2006, E1.

## 2

|||||||||||||||||||||||||||||||||||||||||||||||||||||||||||||||

# With All Due Respect
## Satirizing Presidents from
## Saturday Night Live *to* Lil' Bush

### *Jeffrey P. Jones*

Embodying his on-screen persona as a conservative talk show host, faux television pundit Stephen Colbert offered a mouth-dropping satirical performance as the featured speaker at the White House Correspondents Dinner in 2006. As is typical in his television parodies on Comedy Central, Colbert proceeded to lambaste both the press and the president, neither of whom seemed to appreciate the effort. Not to make the same mistake twice, the organizers of the 2007 event took a safer route by hiring the crowd-pleasing presidential impersonator Rich Little for the evening's entertainment. But in reviving the long-since flagged career of the former late-night talk show staple, the event organizers reminded us of just how far television has come in its caricatures of presidents. For also appearing that same week on Comedy Central was the animated series, *Lil' Bush,* a portrayal of George W. Bush as a dim-witted and dangerous fifth-grader running amok in the White House and wreaking havoc across the world with his diabolical pals Lil' Cheney, Lil' Condi, and Lil' Rummy. The airing of these two different sets of caricatures demonstrated that the acceptable norms of television's treatment of the president have certainly changed.

Yet this was not the first time that Comedy Central had produced an entire series dedicated to satirizing President Bush. Beginning in April 2001, the network aired a short-lived series called *That's My Bush!,* a show with the announced intention of spoofing the sitcom genre, but also satirizing the current president and his family and staff in the process. In the

series, George W. Bush and Laura Bush are portrayed as the typical suburban sitcom couple, yet George is also painted as a simple-minded, lazy,
privileged, and easily distracted man. The show's writers and producers,
Trey Parker and Matt Stone of *South Park* fame, had planned to produce
the program irrespective of which presidential candidate won the 2000
election (Bush or Al Gore). But with Bush emerging victorious in the
contested election, he became the focus of the show. In turn, the series
became the first bold move by the network in satirizing a sitting president
in a not-so-flattering manner.

Taken together, *That's My Bush!* and *Lil' Bush* bookend the two-term
presidency of George W. Bush. These portrayals are instructive because
they represent how one cable network altered the course of how presidents are treated on television. Both programs are also series, representing
the first time that entire shows were dedicated to satirizing the president.
And, as discussed later in this chapter, both display an approach to political satire that is decidedly not the product of the safe, mass market thinking that is endemic to network television programming. To understand
the force of these portrayals as political statements, it is helpful to contrast
them with what came before. In this chapter, I chart the history of presidential caricatures on television, beginning with stand-up impersonators
such as Rich Little and continuing through to the groundbreaking sketch
comedy approach developed on *Saturday Night Live*. Since the mid-1970s,
*Saturday Night Live* (SNL) has regularly processed presidential politics for
viewers, offering interpretations that structured how images of the president were filtered through popular culture. But such caricatures are typically missing any form of meaningful political critique, instead depending
largely on impersonation humor that is focused more on personal mannerisms and political style than on politics.

The shows that bookend the Bush presidency, however, offer a broader
and more critical narrative frame for making meaning of the president as
politician and office holder. As sitcom-styled series, they provide a specific satirical framework for scrutinizing the features that characterize the
presidency in its historical context. They have also contributed to an era,
in conjunction with other non-network television programming, where
satire as a brutal art form has been revived. Hence, these shows lead us to
rethink the necessary place, role, and function of satire in contemporary
political culture and how such an important role has generally been absent from television for much of the medium's existence.

## Saturday Night Live

What is somewhat remarkable about television in America until the 1970s is how little the networks directly engaged in humor about the presidency. Their earliest attempt at presidential satire was in the form of presidential impersonations. Vaughn Meader, who impersonated John F. Kennedy, gained popular success through his comedy album *The First Family*. He parlayed that fame into several appearances on *The Ed Sullivan Show*, but his career ended abruptly with the assassination of Kennedy in 1963. Subsequently, one of the most famous presidential impersonators on television was Rich Little, who possessed an uncanny talent for capturing the voices and likeness of presidents. As luck would have it, he also bore a striking resemblance to President Richard Nixon and thus made a number of appearances on variety shows and late-night talk shows impersonating Nixon and, later, Presidents Carter, Reagan, and others.

In evaluating such performances as political satire, the question is whether the performers are criticizing the president or are simply using the president—the most familiar public figure in America—as part of their stand-up comedy shtick. With impersonation, the gist of the political performance is to look or sound as much like the president as possible. It is a mimetic performance, one in which the humor originates from hearing the president's voice come out of someone else's mouth. The interest for audiences resides less in any expectation of political critique and more in the simple pleasure of resemblance. As such, the performances are typically impotent politically, perhaps even flattering to politicians, with almost nothing in the routine that could be considered "satirical." This also suggests why such performances are popular: they are the lowest common denominator of political humor, with little to offend or provoke and much to share.

Presidential humor on television began to change in 1975, when a group of young comedians known as the "Not Ready for Prime Time Players" began regularly ridiculing the president on a program that began as a counterculture classic, *Saturday Night Live*. Presidents had rarely been made fun of on television, but this new program boldly announced that television had a role in mocking the office of the president. On the fourth episode, comedian Chevy Chase opened the program with his impersonation of President Gerald Ford as a bumbling fool in what became

Chevy Chase was the first *Saturday Night Live* cast member to satirize a president, although he never attempted to look or talk much like the real Gerald Ford.

a trademark opening sketch comedy skit. After Ford had experienced several public spills that were recorded by cameras and broadcast repeatedly on the news, he quickly became fodder for jokes in the press and on television. Chase jumped on the chance to hone a routine and create a persona for himself by portraying Ford as a klutz, including his stumbling over desks and falling off ladders, only to rise up and shout out the program's introductory line, "Live from New York, it's Saturday Night!" As Chase noted at the time, "Ford is so inept that the quickest laugh is the cheapest laugh, and the cheapest laugh is the physical joke."[1] Indeed, when watching Chase's skits, the viewer sees the beginnings of a physical comedy presence that Chase would develop further in hit movies such as *Foul Play* and *Caddyshack*. Nonetheless, Chase has suggested more recently that there was political intentionality in his portrayal: "He had never been elected [to higher office], period, so I never felt that he deserved to be there to begin with. That was the way I felt then as a young man and as a writer and a liberal."[2] Elsewhere he noted, "I took his career and put it in the dumper, because I did not want him to be president of this country."[3]

What was groundbreaking with Chase's portrayal of Ford was how the comedian "made absolutely no attempt to look like Ford," says Lorne Michaels, the show's creator and executive producer. "I loved that because it was so much in the spirit of the show. He just said he was Ford, and he was. He was playing an attitude."[4] Similar presidential nonimpersonations (based more on attitude than resemblance) would occur in the early years of *SNL* when Dan Aykroyd portrayed Richard Nixon and Jimmy Carter. Although Aykroyd attempted to imitate Nixon's gravely voiced speech, hunchback posture, and furrowed brow, his tall and lanky frame did not lend itself well to impersonating two short presidents. The lack of physical resemblance, however, did not mean the portrayal was necessarily off mark or unfunny. Perhaps the inability to impersonate with accuracy gave the performances special power or leeway for political commentary. Aykroyd was able to channel Nixon's dark and brooding nature, as well as Carter's piety, sincerity, and intellect, yet never doing so on the basis of "becoming" either president through resemblance.[5] *SNL* veteran Darrell Hammond (who later offered spot-on physical impersonations of Bill Clinton and Al Gore) noted that his favorite presidential portrayal on *SNL* was Aykroyd's Nixon because it wasn't a "direct impression, it's more of an interpretation. And even more effective, I think, than an accurate impression [because] it has more leeway for being funny."[6]

In contrast to pure impersonation, sketch comedy allows for humor or critique that does not depend on the comedian's ability to look or sound like the president. Rather, the comedian creates humorous situations that the audience *reads onto* the politician. Like an editorial cartoon, certain features are exaggerated for comedic effect. The comedic pleasure is typically more diegetic than mimetic; we enjoy envisioning the president articulate these comedic narratives. Therefore, we see a distraught and almost hysterical Nixon dragging Henry Kissinger to his knees to pray with him in the Oval Office and Carter talking a telephone caller down from a bad acid trip. The scenes are creative and original, not depending on public foibles for laughs. Instead, the satire comes from taking central personal characteristics that shaped the presidency of both men—Nixon's paranoia and Carter's go-it-alone, smarter-than-thou persona, both of which led to their downfall—and playing with them for comedic effect. It is a caricature, but one that, when placed in sketch comedy, allows for numerous satirical narratives to be played out.

This is why *SNL*'s political "disappearance" through much of the 1980s is so puzzling. Although Phil Hartman constructed at least one memorable sketch of President Ronald Reagan (in which the president's public persona as a genial, absent-minded grandfather figure is actually a ruse that hides a quick-minded, scheming president hell-bent on world domination), the program did little to satirize the president during the Reagan years. Lorne Michaels confesses that "we didn't do Reagan very often because there wasn't much to do. He was an actor, and people liked him. There just wasn't much there."[7] With a president who was unpopular and controversial in his first years in office, notoriously disengaged with the details of politics, and then became embroiled in two serious scandals (the Iran-Contra affair and the savings and loan debacle) later in his administration, excuses based on a supposed lack of material are both lame and unimaginative. But such a defense also highlights Michaels's increasingly conservative (and mainstream) approach to political comedy (discussed below) and how that approach differs from when the program initially established itself as a countercultural voice of a generation.[8]

In the late 1980s, *Saturday Night Live* once again made its cultural mark as a source for presidential humor with the arrival of cast member Dana Carvey. Carvey mastered an impersonation of George H. W. Bush, mimicking his patrician attitude, nasally voice, overused hand movements, empty rhetoric ("thousand points of light" and "stay the course"), and strange speaking style ("wouldn't be prudent"). Yet the portrayal was politically toothless because it was based entirely on impersonation humor, focusing on little more than the president's awkward personal style and rhetorical ticks. Certainly, the impersonation was funny because it combined the mimetic with the diegetic, adding a humorous narrative to the impersonation. But simply creating material that can be laughed at does not amount to meaningful political satire. Hence, it was not surprising when Bush later appropriated Carvey for his own political needs. Bush embraced Carvey, even inviting him to spend a night in the White House during his last days as president (using Carvey as a celebrity entertainment send-off to his staff). Bush also regularly imitated Carvey's impersonation of him in various public venues as a laugh line (and perhaps to show he is a good sport).[9] What is interesting about this embrace is that Bush is not known for appreciating satirical treatments of himself. Chris Lamb reports several instances in which Bush lashed out angrily at *Doonesbury* cartoonist Garry Trudeau for his depictions. Bush reportedly said, "I had the personal feeling that I wanted to go up there and kick the hell out of him, frankly," as well as "This *Doonesbury*—good God! He speaks for a bunch of Brie-tasting, Chardonnay-sipping elitists."[10] What distinguishes

Carvey from Trudeau is the lack of any real *politics* in Carvey's comedy that might irritate a powerful person such as the president.

Carvey's impersonations, which proved enormously popular with audiences (effectively embedding that imagery in the public's mind), set the tone for what would become the standard *SNL* approach to political humor: an emphasis on physical or phonetic resemblance that focuses on the politician's presentation of self. Hence, Carvey imitates Ross Perot's rhetorical quirkiness and goofy looks. Phil Hartman imitates Bill Clinton as an affably voracious consumer of junk food. Norm MacDonald renders Bob Dole as the "mean" housemate on *The Real World*. Darrell Hammond portrays Bill Clinton as an oversexed schemer and slick liar. Sometimes the impersonations were good (Hammond), sometimes much less so (MacDonald). As impersonations, though, the routines rarely proved to be political in the sense of critiquing the politician's policies or responses to world events or even showing how such personal characteristics could prove dangerous. Instead, the skits are about them as *people* more than as leaders. Viewers are led to laugh but not disdain, to appreciate affectionately but not really criticize. These are portrayals of human foibles, not sketches that suggest some inherent weakness in the person as a leader, weaknesses that viewers should consider before selecting him as president.

But as Ronald Lee has argued, politicians themselves have constructed a relationship with voters where politicians are to be seen as "feeling conduits." "Candidates' most important qualifications for office are not matters of administrative experience, legislative proposals, or foreign policy initiatives, but their ability to mirror the feeling of the electorate," he argues.[11] A quirky Perot, a sexualized Clinton, a mean Dole—these are the terms on which politicians can be judged by the average disinterested voter/viewer. Hence, *SNL*'s decision to evaluate candidates and presidents on these terms is not surprising, yet nonetheless politically impotent. When the personal and the political collided during the Clinton-Lewinsky scandal and Clinton's subsequent impeachment, *SNL* was served up a political situation that played to its strengths. Between Hammond's portrayals, the liberal use of a black beret, and numerous skits interpreting the scandal as a talk-show dream come true, *SNL*'s brand of political humor was the perfect vehicle for interpreting the silly and ridiculous nature of partisan politics at that moment in time.

Similarly in the 2000 presidential election, where the personal and political combined to produce two amazingly horrible if not outright surreal candidates, here again political reality played to *SNL*'s strengths. Darrell

Hammond began portraying Al Gore, and Will Ferrell played George W. Bush. Both comedians represented the contrasting style of *SNL*'s caricatures over the years. Hammond created an accurate impersonation of Gore by capturing the vice president's dialect, hand gestures, head tilts, and slow rhythmic way of talking that often came across as patronizing (and somewhat plastic). It was an uncanny resemblance. Ferrell, in contrast, maintained little physical or phonetic similarity to Bush but captured his attitude by portraying him as an intellectually challenged yet arrogant guy who was making it all up as he went along. *SNL* made its mark on the election with its parody of the first presidential debate. After both real-life candidates turned in breathtakingly pathetic debate "performances," *SNL* jumped on the comedic openings they were handed.

Hammond embodied a robotic and overcoached Al Gore who kept referring to a "lockbox" like a stuck phonograph, while Ferrell captured Bush's recurring problems with the English language by inserting lexical blunders such as "strategery." Both "candidates" offered these terms as the one-word summary of their campaigns, and in doing so, *SNL* had pretty much encapsulated the failings of both candidates through this skit. It also highlighted the tactics as well as specific performances of both politicians—Bush wasting time, Gore trying to take two turns; Bush's inability to handle the names of world leaders, and Gore's repeated sighing. Satire works best when it works from or advances a thesis. And *SNL* did that here by helping citizens see fairly clearly that the serious choice they were being asked to make was, instead, fairly ridiculous.

Still, one might argue that *SNL*'s political humor here is affirming rather than critical. Even though the show seemingly ridiculed each candidate's personal ticks or questionable strategies, the portrayal might have actually helped the politicians in crafting a popular appeal (that is, providing a means through which the public could actually engage with them). Two days before the election, *SNL* ran a special political edition of the show called *Presidential Bash 2000* (celebrating 25 years of political humor). Both candidates Gore and Bush participated by taping segments to kick off the program. The candidates made fun of themselves by accepting and playing on the caricatures that *SNL* had made famous. Why both campaigns decided to "play along" is not known. Perhaps they thought it helpful to show the candidates' humanness or sense of humor. Or perhaps it was simply a move to get free prime-time airtime two days before the election. Or perhaps they realized that by embracing the comedic routines of *SNL*, they were in essence neutralizing the routines from their potential negative effect. Whatever the reasons, *SNL*'s political humor did not seem dangerous enough for either candidate to refuse to poke fun at himself so close to an election.

But again, the central point is that *SNL*'s skits are relatively harmless because the humor is not really political. The show's writers and producers generally admit as much. For instance, *Newsweek* summed up its interview with show writer Jim Downey by saying, "His biggest concerns are being evenhanded and being funny in a way that mocks the candidates' performances, not their politics." And the show's executive producer Lorne Michaels agrees: "Jim's pieces are gentle, not vicious. They are the silly take, which in my opinion is also the smart take."[12] Michaels has tended to draw a particular (perhaps false) dichotomy between being funny and making a political point in satire: "First and foremost, it has to be funny. And I think that no matter what it is *you're trying to say in terms of how important it is,* the audience won't connect with it and we won't put it on unless we feel that it's truly funny" (emphasis added).[13] Positioning comedy and satire as potential opposites is, of course, questionable.

Despite such statements, Michaels believes that *SNL* continues to play a role as a satirical watchdog of power. "Whoever's in charge, that's who we're going to go after. The country was founded on distrust of authority, and . . . that's what we do," he notes.[14] Yet at least one ex-writer for the show disagrees with what he sees as empty rhetoric, arguing that the show has surrendered its role as a place for cutting-edge political humor by focusing much of its comedic efforts on wayward celebrities such as Britney Spears and Lindsay Lohan. Adam McKay, a writer for the show from 1995 to 2001, and its head writer from 1996 to 1999, contends that those subjects are "such a safe, wishy-washy target, as opposed to going after the powers that be. We always knew that the number one reason the show exists is to do impersonations of the president, our leaders, the Donald Trumps of the world—the people who need to be made fun of. And the show works when you do that, and it doesn't work when you don't do that."[15] McKay even suggests that 9/11 and the wars in Afghanistan and Iraq had affected how Michaels conceives of his political role. "In the name of political fairness or some odd sense of patriotism, Lorne has laid off the president for the last couple of years, and I don't agree with that move," he said.[16]

After 9/11 and the war in Afghanistan, Will Ferrell continued to portray Bush, but his take on the president as dim-witted but self-assured (and lexically troubled) became less funny as the public realized the seriousness of having such a man as president in perilous times. Ferrell left the show in 2002, and by the time of the 2004 presidential election, comedian Will Forte had assumed the role of Bush. Trying to repeat its success of 2000, *SNL* again featured the presidential debates, this time with Forte as Bush and Seth Meyers playing John Kerry. Both comedians attempted impersonation humor, and both failed miserably. Furthermore, the show did little more than play up the hype of both campaigns and repeat the accusations they levied at each other—Kerry as flip-flopper, Bush as obfuscator; Kerry's Vietnam record, Bush's 9/11 fear-mongering. The show had become little more than a community theater troupe's interpretation of political advertisements on TV, and perhaps even played an unwitting role in reinforcing the political messages that both campaigns wanted embedded in voters' minds. Under these conditions, then, "satire" becomes an accomplice to power, not an adversary of it.

In the meantime, serious—and seriously funny—political satire had moved elsewhere on television. Rather than recoiling after 9/11, another show written and produced in New York, *The Daily Show with Jon Stewart*, found its legs with an aggressive critique of the Bush administration's wars and terror(izing) campaigns. While *SNL* turned to safe and inoffensive humor about celebrities, *The Daily Show* and *Real Time with Bill Maher* were reminding viewers that satire could and should be both funny and biting. When Lorne Michaels was asked in an interview if *SNL* had ceded ground to its cable rivals, his response displayed the type of thinking that highlights not only the difference between the network and post-network eras of television but also why *SNL* has become irrelevant in the realm of political satire and humor: "We're a big-tent show. We bring a coalition of tastes. A cable show can do a 1 rating and be enormously popular. We're not that show. People who are staying to watch 'Update' or the people who want to see the music, or the people hoping we do a political sketch, all those audiences have to coexist."[17]

During the 2008 presidential race, *SNL* came roaring back into public consciousness as a site for political humor, thanks largely to Hillary Clinton's referencing a *SNL* skit in a debate to complain about her perceived mistreatment by the press and supposed press favoritism of Democratic rival Barack Obama. By using the skit to define political reality as she saw it, what had originated as a spoof of the news media became a weapon through which Clinton sought to shape the actual engagement between candidates and the press. Satire's role, it seemed, was to enunciate the particular reality that Clinton wanted the electorate to see, not the other reality (presented simultaneously in the skit) of Clinton as a vicious and whining candidate. In turn, the ever-jittery campaign press seemingly bought into Clinton's reality by hammering Obama to the point where he noted in dismay, "I am a little surprised that all the complaining about the refs has actually worked as well as it has for [Clinton]. This whole spin of how the press has been so tough on them and not tough on us—I didn't expect that you guys would bite on that."[18]

As if to return the favor Clinton had done by enhancing the credibility (and ratings) of the moribund show, *SNL* offered another debate skit the following week based on the same theme (a press that favors Obama), but this time featuring an appearance by candidate Clinton herself alongside her satirical doppelganger, Amy Poehler. While the entertainment press portrayed this turn of events (satire directly affecting the political process) as the return of an important voice of political satire and critique to television, what these events more clearly highlight is how *SNL's* brand of satire has moved beyond its previous low as an *accomplice* of power into a willing and active *agent* of it. The satirical critique doesn't attack power but instead is comprised of material that politicians can use, something they can and will appear willingly alongside, and just another popular culture text to be exploited for political gain (little more than George W. Bush appearing on the prime-time game show *Deal or No Deal* in the same year). In that regard, *SNL*—as with other forms of mass culture offered through the network model of television—erodes the inherent potential of popular culture (and satire, in particular) to criticize. Instead, network television entertainment participates in the same choreographed dance between press and politicians that constituted much of the relationship between media and politics in the last half of the twentieth century.

As *SNL* clearly showed in 2008, its political skits will continue to be both its most popular and prominently featured segments of the show. Because the skits focus primarily on impersonating the personal characteristics of politicians (not their politics), they also serve as safe forms of infotainment that can be played across NBC's various content-starved news outlets (*Today,* MSNBC, CNBC, *Meet the Press,* and so on). Furthermore, the skits tend to be better than much of the other material the writers produce, primarily because of their referential basis. That is, the audience maintains a relationship with these characters (politicians) and doesn't have to strain to connect with the humor (as is more often the case in some of the bizarre and unfunny skits that dominate the program). Political skits are also central to the *SNL* brand, a commodity that can be endlessly packaged in video and DVD after-markets and as election year specials that run in prime time.[19] Finally, political skits will continue on *SNL* because of the historical place and tradition they have on the show. For better or worse, both audiences and political observers alike expect *SNL* to comment on politics.

With the death of President Gerald Ford in December 2006, many commentators reflected on Chevy Chase's memorable caricature of Ford some 30 years earlier. Since Ford had never waged a national campaign for higher office, his public image had not been shaped by his own hand (as is ultimately the role of much campaign communication). Hence, Ford was somewhat of a blank slate on which Chase could write his critique. But as one commentator put it, "compared with the round-the-clock, often-substantive ribbing of the current President Bush, Chase's needling of Ford seems sweet in hindsight."[20] And that, I argue, is an apt description of *SNL*'s approach to political humor for much of the show's run. As citizens today constantly engage with serious forms of political satire on the Internet through video mash-ups, photo montages, and animated spoofs such as Jib-Jab (see chapter 9, Henry Jenkins's contribution to this volume), and as new cable television programs (such as *The Colbert Report* and *Lil' Bush*) offer scathing critiques of contemporary partisan politics, we can see more clearly just how much *SNL*'s counterculture roots have withered. The program has matured over the years, but it also represents an older network model of thinking about programming, mass market appeal, and the proper role for satire. Arguably, this type of thinking is not what drives the cable channel Comedy Central and its approach to political commentary in the post-network era.

## *That's My Bush!*

Almost from its inception, Comedy Central has used satire and comical political talk as a means of branding its network as a location for cutting-edge political humor.[21] The network continued in that vein in 2000 when they decided to work with Trey Parker and Matt Stone (the creators of *South Park*) to produce a comedy series about the president. Parker and Stone moved forward with planning a show that would satirize the situation comedy genre first and foremost, but use the First Family and the White House as the narrative center of the sitcom. As the show made its way onto the air, Parker and Stone defended their choice of ridiculing Bush by arguing that critics were missing the point. Both repeatedly contended that the show was intended as a parody of situation comedies, not as a sat-ire of Bush.[22] In fact, they suggested the show was somewhat of a love let-ter to Bush because they were going to make him the typical loveable "fa-ther" figure in the vein of Homer Simpson.[23] "The whole point of a sitcom is taking a character and forcing you to love that character," said Parker. "So what we are going to do is make everyone love George Bush."[24]

The program did skewer the inane suburban home and office situation comedies. The show begins with a bouncy theme song typical of sitcoms: "He's the president in residence, he's kind of in charge / He's got the whole country saying, 'That's My Bush!'" Much of the show occurs within the residence quarters of the White House and includes the ubiquitous subur-ban sitcom characters of a wise-mouthed maid (à la *Hazel*) and the next-door neighbor who is always dropping by and making himself at home (à la *Three's Company*). The show also makes fun of the office brand of sitcom, giving the president a dumb but sexy secretary whose every en-trance is accompanied by hoots and whistles from the supposedly "live" (actually canned) studio audience (à la *Married . . . With Children*) and an assistant (appropriately named "Karl Rove") who actually runs the opera-tion. As per the genre's conventions, each episode resolves a dilemma that typically arises from miscommunication (after much madcap zaniness), concluding with the "lesson learned" in the closing bedroom scene. And à la Ralph Kramden (*The Honeymooners*), the dialog ends with George re-citing the audience-echoed tagline, "One of these days, Laura, I'm gonna punch–you–in–the–face!"

The portrayal of Bush as an affable good-ol'-boy, yet dim-witted and lazy president doesn't allow for Parker and Stone's defense that their show was apolitical. The show included occasional political bon mots, such as when George dismissively asks the maid if she doesn't have some laundry to do. She replies, "Yep, I gotta do like your father did and separate the whites from the coloreds."[25] Furthermore, most of the episodes included some sort of commentary on intractable political issues. In "A Poorly Executed Plan," the president personally executes a death row inmate by pouring drain cleaner down his throat after reading him his last rights: "You have the right to die like a little bitch, have your soul sent to hell" (even though Bush thinks he is faking an execution to impress his old frat brothers). At the end of the episode, a distraught Bush exclaims to Laura, "I can't believe I killed that man!" to which Laura consoles him with the not so subtle political note, "It's no different from those 152 men you put to death in Texas. You just did it yourself this time." And in "An

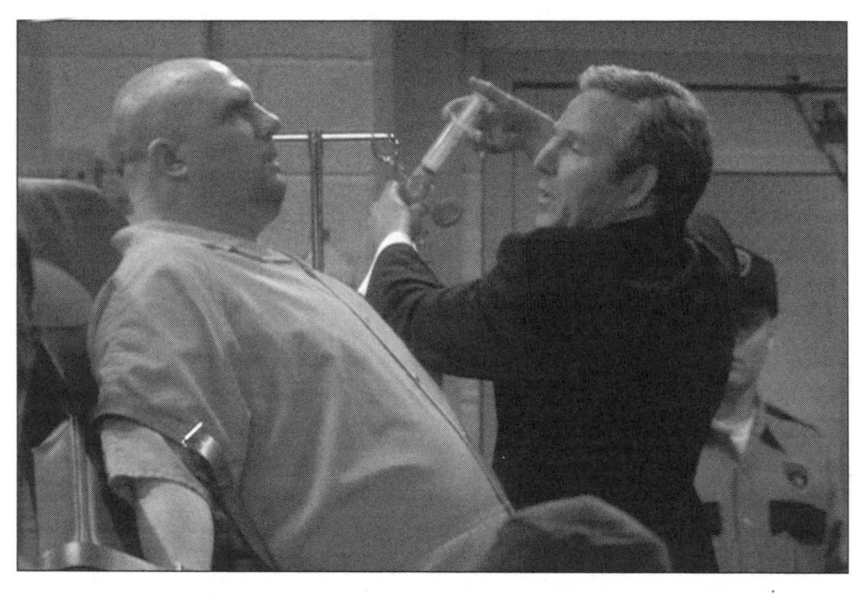

On *That's My Bush!*, President George W. Bush takes charge of a
prisoner execution, eagerly doing the job himself.

Aborted Dinner Date," George attempts to fulfill his campaign promise to
be a "uniter not divider" by bringing together the heads of the anti-abortion and pro-choice movements. The pro-choice character is portrayed as
a butch lesbian, while the anti-abortion leader is a fetus who survived a
botched abortion procedure 30 years earlier and is now really pissed.

Just as important as the overt satirizing of Bush's politics, the program also signals how far television has come in its satirical treatment
of a sitting president and his family. In one episode, after complaining
that nobody pays attention to her now that George is president, Laura
begs George to "spread me out on that massive table, right under that
big picture of Mr. Lincoln, and pound me." Perhaps the most telling
in this regard is the episode titled "The First Lady's Persqueeter." The
episode revolves around Laura trying to figure out why George no longer seems interested in performing oral sex on her. The communication problems ensue when she thinks that the "old and smelly" cat that
George is referring to isn't the 24-year-old family pet that George wants
put to sleep but her own feminine hygiene problems. Perhaps Parker
and Stone weren't satisfied with the raciness of the series title, so they

wrote this episode to make it abundantly clear. Either way, the program set a new standard for presidential satire in making jokes at the personal expense of the First Lady.

When the program appeared on Comedy Central, television critics were less enamored of it than audiences. Most found the program not very funny in either its parodic or satirical efforts.[26] A few believed the caricature served Bush well by painting him "dumb as a fox," a mask that therefore distinguished him from typical Washington elites.[27] But one critic from the *Buffalo News* expressed his shock and dismay at the turpitude of contemporary political satire when he wrote, "No president—not even George W. Bush—deserves the putrid adolescent japery of what I've seen on 'That's My Bush!' . . . If this isn't truly disgusting and reprehensible television, I don't know what is."[28]

Perhaps the most thought-provoking commentary, though, came from Doug Saunders, a writer for the Canadian newspaper the *Globe and Mail*. In his review, Saunders argued that while every president has "a comic alter ego, a satirical shadow that follows his every move" (such as those on *SNL*), Bush is perhaps the first president to "consist of nothing but a satirical shadow." A show like *That's My Bush!*, therefore, captures the nature or essence of "a profoundly average schmuck who has somehow wandered away from the backyard barbecue into the White House." Saunders extends the critique by arguing that the show also fits the larger myth that is the American dream cum American democracy. While the rest of the world is terrified by "this real-life, Washington version of *The Beverly Hillbillies*," he argues, the terror is also thrilling to Americans for it enunciates "the basic thrill of American life: While it is one thing to put a man on the moon, it is a truly democratic, patriotic thing to put a stupid man on the moon. Then he becomes a stand-in for all Americans." Saunders concludes his review of the show by arguing, "As Canadians, we may roll our eyes at the silliness of *That's My Bush!*, but we will never fully comprehend its earnestly patriotic motive: It is, at last, a level of television perfectly matched to the presidency."[29]

The criticism is apt in both content and form. Putting a dolt in the White House may make no sense in real life, but casting him in a sitcom does. The situation comedy may be the best way to come to terms with such a president, for as James Poniewozik also argues in *Time* magazine, the situation comedy is "our national storytelling form just as the epic poem was [to] the Greeks." Placing the president in this familiar genre then allows us to envision him in myriad ways beyond the sketch comedy of *SNL*. Here Bush is both lovable husband and a dumbass president; a guy who is "kind of in charge"; a guy whose wife is smarter than him; a guy who is lazy and defers to his advisors for the real work of the White House; and a guy who screws things up, despite his sincere desires otherwise. In hindsight, this reading seems quite prescient. Or perhaps the sitcom treatment allows viewers to make exactly the reading that Saunders proposes. The managing editor of the conservative magazine *National Review*, for instance, seemingly bought into Parker and Stone's encoding of Bush as a likeable guy, proclaiming that, despite his expectations otherwise, "Bush is shown not as a fool, but as a good-hearted American Everyman flummoxed by crazy situations that would, in reality, flummox the typical person of above-average intelligence."[30] Given either reading here, the portrayal of the president in a situation comedy certainly allows everyone to exclaim, "That's *Our* Bush!"

*That's My Bush!* was popular with audiences, averaging 1.7 million viewers, but the series was canceled after eight episodes because it was the most expensive program the network had ever produced (costing $900,000 an episode).[31] Surely the series would have been canceled after 9/11 anyway, but before such acts of self-censorship had to occur, the economics of cable programming showed that while satirical programming is popular, there are limitations to the types of satirical programs that make economic sense in the post-network era.

## Lil' Bush

In 2007, Comedy Central again returned to the Bush presidency, this time airing the animated situation comedy *Lil' Bush* (another show popular with audiences, garnering similar ratings as *That's My Bush!*, but costing much less).[32] Mocking the style of other animated children's programming where familiar older characters are cast as younger versions of themselves,[33] George W. Bush is portrayed as a moronic and hubristic First Child because his father, George H. W. Bush, is still in the White House. Each episode presents a new situation for Lil' George as he cavorts with his pals Lil' (Dick) Cheney, Lil' Condi (Condoleezza Rice), and Lil' Rummy (Donald Rumsfeld). Along the way, they engage various enemies such as Lil' Kim Jong Il, Lil' Al-Qaeda, and Lil' Al Gore. This portrayal is also an exaggeration of reality, but not necessarily in the form taken by editorial cartoonists or sketch-comedy writers (that is, exaggerating certain physical

Lil' Bush, with Lil' Cheney, Lil' Rummy, and Lil' Condi,
create another diabolical scheme of political mayhem.

or personal characteristics). The White House, for instance, is drawn with large nuclear weapons and oil rigs in the backyard. Donick Cary, a former comedy writer for *The Late Show with David Letterman* and *The Simpsons,* admits that he has created "this fantastical Bush World bridging the two Bush presidencies, where anything can happen."[34] But the fact that the show's chronology makes no sense matters not (Bush Sr. is still president, but the issues, characters, and world events tackled are all contemporary). Rather, it is the opportunity to portray George W. Bush as a petulant little child that merits the caricature ("He's got nuclear weapons *and* little-kid emotions!" exhorts Cary). But also, as Cary notes, "somehow, this president that we have lends himself to thinking in a simplistic, cartoony fashion. He's always been about sound bites, one-word answers, move ahead, act from the gut."[35] Such a portrayal works quite well if imagined as words and actions emanating from a fifth grader.

Such a portrayal, however, isn't just critical—it's downright brutal. The show's brief thrash-styled theme song is simply comprised of the lyrics, "Lil' Bush, He's the worst . . . Lil' Bush, Lil' Bush." George's brother Lil' Jeb is portrayed as an even more inarticulate imbecile (literally head-butting his way in and out of disasters, but enjoying the cartoon longevity of Kenny on *South Park*). Mother Barbara and Father George are seen as effete and calculating. One episode concludes with Father Bush saying, "The majority of voters think being gay is wrong, so we do too," to which Lil' George says, "That's because values matter, right Pop?" Father Bush replies, "That's right son. Every four years!" as the Bush family and Lil' Gang laugh diabolically. But if the writers of *That's My Bush!* took the gloves off in their sexualized portrayals of the First Family, *Lil' Bush* has shown a willingness to take it several steps further. In one episode, Barbara complains to her husband, "Oh George, you never visit the First Lady parts anymore." She then proceeds to have sex with Lil' Cheney who, over the course of 45 minutes of sex, gets absorbed by her vagina and enters her womb.

But the harshest personal portrayal of all occurs near the end of an episode in which Lil' George's parents think he might be gay because of his overly close friendship with Lil' Tony Blair. Father Bush finally confronts Lil' George after watching his cheerleading routine with Blair and says, "Your mother and I were afraid cheerleading might turn you gay," to which Lil' George replies, "Gee, Pops, you're the one who married a dude [referring to his mother]. Isn't that gay?" Father Bush answers by saying, "Your mother's not a man. She's a collection of reanimated ex-presidential body parts with female sex organs sewn on." Father Bush then proceeds to tell a story, seen in flashback, of how Barbara came into being. We learn that Mrs. Bush is a fabrication of George Washington's head and face (dug up from the grave), William Howard Taft's "tremendous ta-tas" and birthing hips, and Betsy Ross's "lady parts." When the story concludes, a dismayed Lil' Bush looks at his dad and says, "Wow, Pop, that's really fucked up," to which the elder Bush replies, "Yeah, I've done some weird shit in my life."

The portrayal of Bush's Lil' Gang isn't much better. Lil' Condi is seen as having romantic feelings for George. Lil' Rummy comes across as an evil schemer, as seen in one episode in which he draws a picture of a bunny rabbit with a knife in his belly and says, "That will teach you to hop in the woods without body armor." But hardly a scene of the gang goes by without Lil' Cheney being portrayed as evil incarnate. When he is lost in Barbara Bush's womb, the ultrasound picture of him shows "ID = Evil." Cheney's father is Darth Vader; their home, the Death Star. In several episodes, he is seen biting the heads off chickens and drinking their blood or eating bloody raw meat. When he speaks, it is primarily mumbled words (sounding like a penguin talking out the side of his mouth), with only the occasional decipherable word.

It is the Bush administration policies and means of conduct in office, however, that are usually at the center of the critique. Indeed, it is the connection between these personal caricatures and the political policies they beget that makes the satire so damning. In "Lil' George Goes Power Crazy," George is slated to make a class presentation on how a light bulb works. When called on, he says, "Sorry, Teachy, need more time. The science on this complicated issue is still out. But don't worry. I'm forming a panel that will deliver a report on this issue in the next five years." In the same episode, George continually makes fun of Lil' Al Gore for being fat. Lil' Condi finally says, "George, Lil' Al really isn't that fat," to which George replies, "I know that, but I'm saying it loudly and repeating it bunches of times so that everyone thinks it's true. It's called the 'No Spin Zone.'" Finally, in the episode "Camp," Bush's summer camp gang takes on Camp Al-Qaeda, and near the end, the gang must perform a song at a talent show. Lil' Condi is frustrated and announces, "I'm worried about the show tonight. We spent so much time pranking those hairy terrorists that we don't have a song for the talent show." Bush replies, "You're right, Con. There's only one thing left to do." Lil' Condi naively asks, "Spend the next few hours writing a really great song?" to which Lil' George replies, "No, no. Design such an awesome stage show that no one will notice how bad our song is. It's a policy I call 'Rock and Awe.'" After the band performs dressed as Kiss, the episode ends with words flashed on the screen: "Lil' George never stopped rockin' . . . until 1986, when, for political reasons, he was born again. His prank war against the terrorists continues to this day."

Cary defends the harshness of the critique by arguing it is an honest one. And sometimes the portrayal isn't too far from the truth. In the episode "Nuked," Lil' George complains, "I hate doing what I'm told. I want to be a decider!" whereas real-life President Bush proclaimed, "My job is to make decisions. I'm a decision—if the job description were, what do you do, it's Decision Maker. And I make a lot of big ones and I make a lot of little ones."[36] Each episode also features the Lil' Bush Band performing as a punk-rock group, singing tunes that illustrate the episode in some way. In "Nuked," the song "Decider" accompanies images of Bush launching nuclear strikes on Kim Jong Il, Hillary Clinton, Barack Obama, Nancy Pelosi, gay couples, antiwar activists, and blue states. The song's lyrics include "I'm the Decider making up my mind, blowin' up things, I'm feeling fine. Decide, decide, listen to my gut, going nu-cle-ar, I'm going all nuts. . . . Bringing death from above with no remorse, if you complain,

I'll just stay the course." The connection to punk rock, Cary notes, is an intentional commentary on the Bush administration's style of conduct: "Dive in headfirst. Break stuff up. Don't care what people think. It's *very* punk-rock" (original emphasis).[37] And indeed, punk rocker Iggy Pop provides the voice of Lil' Rummy just to keep it honest!

The press's reaction to the show was even more aggressive and negative than the reviews for *That's My Bush!* Most complained that the show was not funny and that the critique was not timely (appearing after the 2006 electoral setbacks for the Republican Party).[38] Others complained that nothing in the episodes amounted to real satire or contributed significant insights.[39] Such critiques, though, miss the (punk-rock) point of the show. Punk has never tried to provide cutting-edge musical innovations or offer cerebral dissertations on the need for political change. Punk is reductive and simplistic, aggressive and loud. It makes its point succinctly and moves on. It takes no prisoners and ultimately doesn't give a fuck if you like it or not. The punk point of *Lil' Bush* is not to mimic the conventions of television humor (that is, the expectation to be funny or satirically insightful). Instead, it is to mimic and mock the style, attitude, and conventions of the president and his administration, yet warped just enough to get our attention and offend in the process.[40]

This cartoon is rarely "ha-ha" funny. But perhaps that is because the show is more intent on pointing out the relationship between real-life absurdity and its cartoon variety to always go for laughs. By making Bush infantile, the program shows not only how ridiculous he is but also how ridiculous we are for letting this "child" get away with it. Bush exhibits behaviors we wouldn't tolerate in our own children (petulance, arrogance, material destruction, refusing to apologize), and, hence, we are all indicted in the process. That, too, on reflection, is not very funny.

## Bookending Bush

*That's My Bush!* and *Lil' Bush* bookend the Bush presidency. Both proved popular with audiences, but more important, both served as vehicles for processing the "meaning" of the president in real time (as does the news). If the president himself spends great effort in manufacturing and shaping his own imagery (again, as does the press), then it is rather significant that satirical television programming does the same, for the president is nothing if not symbolic.[41]

As bookend means of making sense of George W. Bush, the changed and different portrayals over the span of six years are instructive. Bush moves from being a father figure to a small child. His stupidity is no longer harmless but instead quite dangerous. He is no longer simply daft yet affable and loveable but now stupid, arrogant, and mean-spirited. The caricature changes from Bush as President of the United States ("He's the president in residence, he's kind of in charge," as the theme song puts it) to Bush as "Resident of the United States" (as the presidential seal that comprises the *Lil' Bush* logo states). The image thus moves from Bush being "kind of in charge" to simply being an occupant of the residence/office (as are the other "unelected" children of presidents). The portrayal of Bush's consorts has changed as well—from neighborly and sexy to vicious and wicked. And the political issues highlighted no longer transcend the Bush presidency (gun control, the death penalty, abortion). Instead, they are political issues and events that are specific to Bush's time in office—Al-Qaeda, the Iraq war, relations with North Korea, global warming—and, in particular, issues that his administration has handled poorly.

The different portrayals are the result, of course, of the specific historical context in which they were written and appeared. Yet it is too simplistic to argue that one represents a naive pre-9/11 America and the other a wiser but disillusioned post-9/11, post–Iraq war nation. The writing in *That's My Bush!* certainly reflects the political mood and culture of pre-9/11. There are seemingly no pressing political issues, only intractable ones that politics either exacerbates or can't resolve. The comedic interest in the president is not his conduct as a politician but his characteristics as a man. As noted earlier, Trey Parker and Matt Stone argued that they weren't out to make Bush "look like an idiot" because "he's going to do that fine on his own." Instead, they argued, by placing him in a situation comedy (even as a parody), they were going "to do something very, very subversive and actually make you really love this guy."[42] But perhaps Parker and Stone can be forgiven for their immature conception of politics and even political satire. The country had just spent eight years in a seemingly constant battle between Republicans and President Bill Clinton, waged largely at the personal level (what Clinton labeled the "politics of personal destruction"). Clinton proved so politically similar that Republican Party officials in the 1996 election complained that he had stolen their political ideas. But that didn't stop them or right-wing media commentators from waging war daily on Clinton and his wife for their supposed personal failings as human beings.

In that context, the *South Park* approach to placing characters in stupid situations, offering up double entendres, and relying on puerile sexual humor fits well with both the popular culture and political culture of the Clinton years.[43] Besides living in a thoroughly sexualized culture, Clinton himself sexualized the office of the presidency by engaging in actions that led to accusations against him for sexual indiscretion from numerous women. Therefore, the play on Bush's name as female anatomy in the show's title and in the episode "The First Lady's Persqueeter" is not only what passed for political humor and commentary by 2000–2001, but also the language offered up by politicians themselves (see, for instance, *The Starr Report*). With that said, perhaps *That's My Bush!* was exactly the type of political humor *needed* at that time. If these two candidates (Bush and Gore) were the best the two major political parties had to offer, then parodying the president as the central figure of a dysfunctional family in a parodic sitcom not only summarizes the moment but also created a scenario in which either candidate or president could be ridiculed on those terms.[44] With Bush as the eventual lead character, those terms became (as one critic put it) "President Dumbass."[45] Those terms, then, were the "language" of the moment.

By the time *Lil' Bush* aired in 2007, American political culture had changed drastically, largely related to events such as the shock of 9/11, two disastrous wars, the flouting of the Geneva Conventions abroad, threats to civil liberties at home, a lapdog Congress, Republican Party corruption and scandals, and an endless barrage of PR, smear campaigns, fake news, spin, and outright lies—and nary an admittance by the administration that mistakes had been made. The ignorance and arrogance of Bush and his team of advisors no longer seemed benign, but childish. The public mood had soured from its somewhat disinterested stance toward politics to one of extreme displeasure (as seen by Bush's historically low approval ratings).[46] But the changes in political culture did not lead citizens to be more mindful and watchful by intensifying their newspaper reading or network television news watching.[47] Rather, citizens seemingly sought some form of solace by either watching the patriotic cheerleading supplied by Fox News (resulting in Fox becoming the cable news ratings leader) or watching new satirical forms of political television that supplied quite meaningful critiques of politics for those disgusted with the state of affairs and journalism's seeming disinterest in helping to rectify it. From *The Daily Show with Jon Stewart* and *The Colbert Report* on Comedy Central to *Real Time with Bill Maher* on HBO, cable television now regularly supplied programming that was entertaining, yet highly critical of politicians and the news media that support them.[48]

*Lil' Bush* reflects the frustration of the times. Its caricature is not nuanced, and it is more amusing than belly-laugh funny. It is an exercise in contempt. It is satire largely because of its gross exaggerations of political figures and their policies. But satire is not *necessarily* funny. Dictionary definitions of satire often include the notion of holding something or someone in contempt. And British satirist Rory Bremner contends that satire includes a "comic resolution of anger."[49] Jonathan Gray has written of the need for audience researchers to recognize the viewing practices associated with anti-fandom, or the visceral enjoyment that comes from loathing certain programs or personalities.[50] The observation can be extended to include the representation of politics and political figures on television. Some forms of political satire may be enjoyable to watch for no other reason than they offer a venue through which citizens can revel in their disgust, loathing, and outright anger at certain aspects of political life.

*Lil' Bush* is not necessarily funny or profound but is dripping with contempt for the Bush administration. *Lil' Bush* reminds us that while television as an entertainment medium usually demands that all satire be funny, simply being able to participate in the public display and celebration of contempt, anger, and outrage is why *Lil' Bush* matters. It also matters because it becomes one of the several television programs that have helped write the "meaning" of the Bush presidency while he is still in office. If journalism is the first draft of history, as the saying goes, then the elevation of television satire as a popular and legitimate avenue for processing the meaning of politics in contemporary society means that programs like *That's My Bush!* and *Lil' Bush,* as bookends to the Bush presidency, provide a poignantly sour counterpoint to those early drafts. And the second draft that emerges from the caricatures in these shows is not the "fallible yet funny" human being qua *SNL.* This draft, instead, is about the person who inhabits the most powerful political office in the world—the President of the United States— whether it be written as "President Dumbass" or "Resident Evil."

## The Age of Brutal Satire

As brutal and powerful as these bookend shows might be, it is important to note that they exist in the same time and space as, and hence play off of, other satirical discourses occurring simultaneously. For instance, portrayals of Vice President Dick Cheney as Darth Vader and having a voice that sounds like a penguin probably originated through Jon Stewart's impersonations on *The Daily Show*. *Lil' Bush*, however, picked up and used the same imagery to greater effect. Yet when the vice president's wife visited *The Daily Show*, she attempted to make several "being-hip-with-pop-culture" references to her husband's satirical image (such as his biting the heads off of chickens), believing (incorrectly) that they derived from Jon Stewart (right network, wrong show). The point here is that it would be a mistake to see any one show described in this chapter (or this book) in isolation. Rather, they interact with other comedic material, including network programming, as well as viral and mash-up videos on the web. These satirical interpretations help shape a broader comedic framework through which citizens make interpretive sense of political life, and in turn, the programs and the language they provide help shape political culture.

Returning to where we began, we have seen that impersonations are too circumspect to be called satire and therefore lack much in the way of political punch. *SNL* will still rely on them to attract audiences, largely because they are one of the most popular segments of a show that is typically poorly written. And they continue to garner attention for the program in the press because, ultimately, *SNL* marks the realm of safe "critique." Stephen Colbert's performance in front of the president and press corps, on the other hand, shows exactly what political satire is or should be. It often mimics its object of ridicule where it matters most—in its essence, not surface. True political satire can be funny or prescient, but it always attacks power with cheekiness rather than tickling its cheeks powerlessly.

What comes after W? That is, will the next president be greeted by such brutal forms of ridicule or caricature as we have seen in the Bush years? It is impossible to know, but the groundwork has certainly been laid for a much more cacophonous and unruly variety of narrative critiques and interpretations than existed in the network era. Despite the *Buffalo News* critic's desire for a return to an era where presidents were treated respectfully by television, it is probably safe to say (especially after the almost surreal Clinton and Bush presidencies) that there is really no going back. But I would argue that satire is not some cheap formula that gets trotted out by network execs in need of a new hit. The writing emerges from the *need* for it to be said. As Jon Stewart said in 2002, "There are times when it's not about making a joke; it's about having to acknowledge what is going on so you can feel like you're still in the same world as everyone else."⁵¹ As I have argued with both *That's My Bush!* and *Lil' Bush,* the times seemed to call for each resulting satirical treatment. Hence, a new president will likely not be hammered right out of the gate just for ratings sake. But should the times call for it, and should the next president engage in the absurdities that have marked the last two-term presidents, American television has shown that it has matured to the point where it will take off the gloves and offer viewers something more than "funny" pratfalls and "hilarious" vocal inflections. Satire, then, will have done its job.

### NOTES

1. "The Ridicule Problem," *Time,* 5 January 1976.

2. "Chevy Chase Turned Star Athlete into a Klutz," *Toronto Sun,* 28 December 2006, 7.

3. "President Pratfall? Enough Already!" *Los Angeles Times,* 1 January 2007, E6.

4. Diane Holloway, "Presidents Become Boobs, Bumblers on 'SNL,'" *Washington Times,* 24 February 2001, D4.

5. Lorne Michaels later expressed his frustration with Aykroyd for refusing to shave his moustache when he began playing Carter (Holloway, "Presidents Become Boobs").

6. Transcript of program broadcast, *Today Show,* NBC, 3 November 2000.

7. Holloway, "Presidents Become Boobs." Elsewhere Michaels argues that the show never could find its "take" on Reagan (transcript, *Larry King Live,* 3 November 2000).

8. Or, as the 31-year-old Michaels said in 1976, "I wanted a show to and for and by the TV generation. Thirty-year-olds are left out of television. Our reference points, our humor, reflect a life-style never aired on TV" ("Flakiest Night of the Week, *Time,* 2 February 1976).

9. For instance, "George Bush Lampoons Dana Carvey," *Associated Press Online,* 6 December 1997.

10. Quoted in Chris Lamb, *Drawn to Extremes: The Use and Abuse of Editorial Cartoons* (New York: Columbia University Press, 2004), 30–31.

11. Ronald Lee, "Images of Civic Virtue in the New Political Rhetoric," in *Presidential Campaigns and American Self Images,* ed. Arthur H. Miller and Bruce E. Gronbeck (Boulder, Colo.: Westview, 1994), 52.

12. Marc Peyser, "Al and Dubya after Hours," *Newsweek,* 30 October 2000, 38.

13. Transcript of program broadcast, *Larry King Live,* 3 November 2000.

14. Ibid.

15. Dave Itzkoff, "The All Too Ready for Prime Time Players," *New York Times,* 2 January 2005.

16. Ibid.

17. Ibid.

18. Rory O'Connor, "Hillary Clinton Was 'Working the Refs,'" *Alternet,* 5 March 2008, at http://www.alternet.org/election08/78759/.

19. For instance, the skits on the Clinton scandal were packaged as part of the show's "Best of" video series, titled "The Best of the Clinton Scandal" (1999).

20. Paul Brownfield, "On TV, He Was Stumbler-in-Chief," *Los Angeles Times,* 28 December 2006, A35.

21. Jeffrey P. Jones, *Entertaining Politics: New Political Television and Civic Culture* (Lanham, Md.: Rowman and Littlefield, 2005), 64–74.

22. For instance, Walt Belcher, "Oval Office Gets It Square in the Funny Bone of New Sitcom," *Tampa Tribune,* 2 April 2001, sec. Baylife, p. 1.

23. James Poniewozik, "10 Questions for Matt Stone and Trey Parker," *Time,* 5 March 2006.

24. Quotes are attributed to an *Entertainment Tonight* interview with Parker and Stone on 12 April 2001, titled "First Family Frolics," at http://www.uti.com/~peterg/ThatsMyBush.html.

25. This refers to the infamous remark George H. W. Bush made to President Ronald Reagan in pointing out his son's children: "That's Jebby's kids from Florida, the little brown ones." For a recounting of the incident, see Russell Contreras, "Gorgeous George," *Austin Chronicle,* 14 August 2000, at http://weeklywire.com/ww/08-14-00/austin_pols_feature2.html.

26. David Bianculli, "'Bush' Ain't the Ticket," *New York Daily News,* 2 April 2001, 86; Matthew Gilbert, "'That's My Bush!' Isn't a Capital Idea," *Boston Globe,* 4 April 2001, C1.

27. Joshua Gamson, "The President Has No Pants," *American Prospect,* 21 May 2001, 36.

28. Jeff Simon, "Trashy 'That's My Bush' Cheapens Real Political Satire," *Buffalo* (New York) *News,* 10 June 2001.

29. Doug Saunders, "The Washington Hillbillies," *Globe and Mail* (Toronto), 18 July 2001, R1.

30. Michael Potemra, "That's Our Bush," *National Review,* 6 April 2001, at http://web.lexis-nexis.com.

31. John M. Higgins, "Comedy Central Impeaches Bush," *Broadcasting and Cable,* 6 August 2001, 12.

32. *Lil' Bush* averaged 1.7 million viewers, including being the number one show for men ages 18–24 in its time slot. The show was renewed for another season in 2008—a presidential election year. The show was originally developed as animated shorts for Amp'd Mobile, and as reported in the press, "Comedy Central claims it is the first show to transition from mobisode to TV series" (Lisa de Moraes, "Doubled Over in Laughter: 'Mencia' and 'Lil' Bush' Renewed," *Washington Post,* 2 October 2007, C07).

33. Such programming includes *The Muppet Babies, A Pup Named Scooby Doo, Flintstones Kids, The New Archies,* and *Baby Looney Tunes.*

34. Frazier Moore, "Heckuva Job: Comedy Central's New Satire, 'Lil' Bush' Takes a Cartoon Look at the President," *Associated Press,* 11 June 2007.

35. Ibid.

36. Ibid.

37. Ibid.

38. Mike Hale, "The President and His Friends, Younger and More Animated," *New York Times,* 13 June 2007, E10.

39. For instance, one critic argues that the show is "mostly just outrageous, designed to offend as much as to make any salient point. . . . Yet little of it adds up to much of anything but foul-mouthed mischief" (Diane Werts, "Not Bush League, But It's a 'Lil' Close," *New York Newsday,* 13 June 2007, B21).

40. This argument was first developed in an article for the online academic journal, *FLOW* (Jeffrey P. Jones, "Punk-Rock Presidency: The State of Presidential Satire on Television," *FLOW* 30 August 2007, at http://flowtv.org/?p=731).

41. Barbara Hinckley, *The Symbolic Presidency: How Presidents Portray Themselves* (New York: Routledge, 1990).

42. Interview with Parker and Stone, "First Family Frolics."

43. For example, in the *South Park* episode "Chinpokomon," the Japanese assure President Clinton that he has "a very large penis."

44. The theme of the Clinton sex scandal making the nation into a "dysfunctional family" was played out across various media forums. For examples on *Politically Incorrect with Bill Maher* and *This Week,* see Jones, *Entertaining Politics,* 152.

45. Joyce Millman, "President Dumbass," *Salon.com,* 5 April 2001, at http://web.lexis-nexis.com (accessed 2 September 2007).

46. Peter Baker, "Disfavor for Bush Hits Rare Heights," *Washington Post,* 25 July 2007, A3.

47. See Pew Research Center for the People and the Press, "Public's News Habits Little Changed Since September 11," at http://people-press.org/reports/display.php3?ReportID_/156(accessed 25 September 2005).

48. Jones, *Entertaining Politics.*

49. Quoted in Peter Keighron, "The Politics of Ridicule: Satire and Television," in *Dissident Voices: The Politics of Television and Cultural Change,* ed. Mike Wayne (London: Pluto, 1998), 133.

50. Jonathan Gray, "New Audiences, New Textualities: Anti-Fans and Non-Fans," *International Journal of Cultural Studies* 6, no. 1 (2003): 64–81.

51. Jane Ganahl, "Comic Release," *San Francisco Chronicle,* 23 April 2002, D1.

*3*

||||||||||||||||||||||||||||||||||||||||||||||||||||||||||

# Tracing the "Fake" Candidate in American Television Comedy

## Heather Osborne-Thompson

My family has a tradition of talking back to politicians on television. From my days as a Watergate-era preschooler, I had less an understanding of the power of television to craft political images than I did an inkling of the pleasure involved in taking those images apart. Indeed, before I knew of Richard Nixon's tearful TV declaration that he was *not* a crook, I observed my father telling the televisual Richard Nixon that he *was* (and why). Later, I learned that my father had observed his father saying the very same thing to a much younger televised version of Nixon during the then-Congressman's participation in the hearings before the House Un-American Activities Committee.

On one hand, such memories provide a convenient justification for my chosen career path, as I teach others how to talk back to television. On the other hand, they have also informed my weakness for political comedy on American television, which has always provided a forum for talking back to official images that don't quite ring true. Other chapters in this collection examine how contemporary programs like *The Daily Show* talk back to politicians through meticulously parsed sound bites and irreverent interviews. In this essay, however, I focus on a type of television comedy that historically has responded to the increasingly alienating process of televisual politics by instructing viewers on how to talk back: the fake campaign. Specifically, I consider three examples of this phenomenon: Pat Paulsen's bid for the presidency in 1968 on *The Smothers Brothers Comedy Hour* (CBS, 1967–69), fictional congressman Jack Tanner's presidential run in *Tanner '88* (HBO, 1988), and comedian Stephen Colbert's effort to get his name on the ballot in South Carolina's 2008 Democratic and Republican presidential primaries.

While the faux campaign is not unique to television, I argue that these particular examples chart formative attempts by TV comedy to respond to significant moments of crisis in American political history: the presidential campaign of 1968; the Reagan-era penchant for highly mediated, image-dominated campaigns; and the seemingly diminished prospect of "serious" political engagement in the post-network, brand-savvy, multi-platform media age in which we currently live. Informed by the rise of what Nancy Fraser calls "subaltern counterpublics," or "discursive arenas where members of subordinated social groups invent and circulate counterdiscourses to formulate oppositional interpretations of their identities, interests, and needs," these three moments stand out for the ways marginalized perspectives on such issues as race, class, and gender emerged as legitimate topics for political discussion in a wider arena.[1] And faux campaigns arguably helped foster this emergence by enacting or modeling the parameters for such conversations. Through their combination of comedic genres and "reality-based" modes of representation, such as cinema vérité, these campaigns not only parodied the high-concept, stylized, and exclusionary process of politics waged on television but also made explicit the perspectives of counterpublics in order to expose the limits of American democracy as it was currently being practiced.[2] As such, the campaigns of Pat Paulsen and Jack Tanner both play an important role as precursors to the more contemporary political television comedies on which the other essays in this volume focus, while Colbert's faux run demonstrates the unique power such comedies currently enjoy within the American political landscape.

## Pat Paulsen for President

Although Richard Nixon was not the only politician to exploit television for political purposes, scholars frequently portray his use of the medium as emblematic of TV's influence on the modern political campaign. In his article "Television's Nixon: The Politician and His Image," David Culbert argues that "the origins of political television are closely related to the early career of Richard M. Nixon."[3] Moreover, Culbert places Nixon's televisual "ascendance" in the context of conflicting discourses about the medium's ability to both "make possible greater individual participation in political decision making" and make "impossible" the prospect of getting away from the "all-seeing eye" of the camera.[4]

Indeed, by the late 1960s, Nixon's influential approach to waging campaigns televisually—exemplified by his 1952 Checkers speech—held a prominent place in critiques leveled at the mainstream political establishment by such youth-oriented television comedians as Tom and Dick Smothers. As Aniko Bodroghkozy points out in her study of 1960s television, the brothers, who were famous for their comedic takes on folk music and sibling rivalry, increasingly used their comedy-variety program as a platform for echoing the sentiments of wider movements disillusioned with the United States's involvement in Vietnam and its abysmal record on civil rights.[5]

As part of their project to reach disaffected youth audiences during the tumultuous election year of 1968, the Smothers Brothers enlisted program regular Pat Paulsen to mount a fake presidential campaign. The stone-faced Paulsen was best known for his satirical editorials that were done in the manner of network news programming. Seated behind a desk and addressing the camera directly, Paulsen would espouse earnest-sounding but inept positions on such questions as "Are Our Draft Laws Unfair?" and "Should TV Be Censored?" Paulsen's deadpan delivery, odd facial ticks, and seeming unease before the camera radiated a lack of both sophistication and sincerity that linked him to the many politicians his commentaries took aim at on the show, including Nixon, California Governor Ronald Reagan, and President Lyndon Johnson. Similarly, his approaches to what were considered very real problems for the country (the inequities of a draft system that provided people of privilege with deferment options) and for the Smothers Brothers (censorship of television content) indicated a profound inability to understand complex issues.

For example, he proposed a new draft lottery based entirely on hat size, explaining, "The tiny heads will go into the military and the fatheads will go into government."[6] In response to the question of whether television should be censored, Paulsen seemed particularly interested in limiting TV's "all-seeing" potential for exposing the inadequacies of politicians, arguing:

> Let's face it, there have to be some realistic taboos, especially with political comment. After all, the leaders of our country were not elected to be tittered at. Censors have to draw the line somewhere. For instance, we are allowed to say Ronald Reagan is a lousy actor, but we are not allowed to say he's a lousy governor. Which is ridiculous. We know he's a good actor.

And you can't say anything bad about President Johnston [*sic*] because you shouldn't insult the president. But if you compliment him, who will believe it?[7]

Such statements alluded to the quandary in which many people critical of the state of American politics found themselves in 1968. With a field of potential presidential candidates that included alleged "crook" Richard Nixon, "lousy" actor and no friend to student demonstrators Ronald Reagan, and a Democratic Party in near disarray, the time seemed right for Paulsen to focus on presidential politics exclusively. Initially, his campaign unfolded under the guise of a number of "statements" in which he denied rumors that he was running while detailing his platform and qualifications for the job. Each of these statements juxtaposed Paulsen's seeming ineptitude with a shrewd parody of the ways the current field of candidates used coy reluctance, emotionalism, and seemingly spontaneous slogans to create the televisual personae on which they built their campaigns. A typical example occurred during the February 11 episode:

Thank you, Dick, Tom, the entire *Smothers Brothers Comedy Hour,* and the vast affiliated stations of the Columbia Television Network . . . for allowing me this opportunity . . . in front of 40 million fellow Americans to deny once again that I am a candidate for the coming election. . . . To prove the honesty of my denial, in a recent presidential campaign survey, my name was not even mentioned. I feel that this is unfair—I want my name right up there alongside the other men—uncandidates like Governor Reagan, Governor Rockefeller, and Senator Kennedy. Why should they get all the publicity for not running? I will not deny that I have considered the possibility of running for President. I owe that much to my public. . . . However, in spite of my repeated denials, the groundswell of popular support grows every day. I do not understand why this is happening. The fact that I have a surefire plan of action to lower taxes, solve our Civil Rights problems, obliterate the national debt, and put an end to the war in Vietnam obviously disqualifies me as a presidential candidate. I say leave politics to the politicians and leave me out of it. I don't want to be any more than I am today—a common, ordinary, simple savior of America's destiny.[8]

Paulsen's statement, which alternates between denying his presidential aspirations and highlighting his "surefire" plan for solving pressing national problems, attempts to position him incongruously as a political

Faux candidate Pat Paulsen looked presidential during a February 1968 episode of *The Smothers Brothers Comedy Hour*. Image from the documentary *Smothered: The Censorship Struggles of* The Smothers Brothers Comedy Hour, dir. Maureen Muldaur (New Video, 2002).

novice with savvy. He betrays knowledge about television as a medium governed contradictorily by a combination of corporate interests (Columbia Television Network) and the "public interest" (40 million prime-time viewers). He employs political "code" words, such as "my fellow Americans," "groundswell," and "common, simple, ordinary." He is pouty about not being included in the list of more glamorous "uncandidates" considering presidential runs in 1968. All together, these qualities connote a hubris associated with men who would be president but try to camouflage that ambition with a televisually manufactured humility.

Such signals that Paulsen had every intention of becoming a fake candidate were, of course, borne out. After "coming out" as the Straight Talking American Government (STAG) party candidate, his performances became increasingly grandiose as the general election drew near. Typically appearing in front of a podium awash in red, white, and blue bunting, and surrounded by giant Pat Paulsen for President portraits, Paulsen gave speeches and performed inspirational songs such as "You'll Never Walk Alone." These displays culminated in two kinds of "media events" before the 1968 election: the *Pat Paulsen for President* special that aired in *The Smothers Brothers'* Sunday night time slot on October 20, 1968, and Paulsen's version of a fireside chat that aired on *The Smothers Brothers* the following Sunday. Each bore the imprint of a particular facet of mediated campaigns: the cinema vérité–style documentary that often officially introduces a candidate to a national audience by showing him campaigning, receiving voter support, and detailing his vision for the future and the more intimate glimpse into a candidate's home and private life that "personality journalism" affords.[9]

*Pat Paulsen for President* follows a structure common to many films whose aim is to energize voters in the "home stretch" of a political campaign. Although it uses "slice of life" techniques common to cinema vérité, such as a handheld camera and an emphasis on "capturing" moments rather than composing them, it employs voiceover narration by Henry Fonda that ties together seemingly random moments of Paulsen's campaign into a coherent narrative. Although regular viewers of *The Smothers Brothers* would already have seen advance footage of the film in earlier episodes, the special places these events in the "proper sequence" that one associates with a candidate in ascendance: it begins with Paulsen taking inspiration from iconic Washington, D.C., landmarks; traces the blossoming of his campaign as empty streets give way to "throngs" of supporters; connects his voter appeal to his humble beginnings on a chicken ranch; and ends with his triumphant postprimary party. Comparing Paulsen with Miguel Cervantes's famously optimistic, if crazy, character Don Quixote, Fonda's voiceover recalls how Paulsen—"a dreamer who went out to joust windmills and jest a political system . . . somehow persuaded millions of Americans to join that dream."[10]

In typical Paulsen style, the overblown prose of the voiceover does not match the images. For example, during the sequence in which Paulsen is captured wandering around such sacred sites as the reflecting pool opposite the Washington monument, Fonda's voice poses lofty rhetorical questions about Paulsen's "call" to service:

> Was there a hushed moment when George Washington heard the clarion call of destiny? And are we again at one of those fateful moments when a needy nation cries out for leadership? It is said of destiny that many are called but few respond. The omen is plain: like Washington, he must test the waters of leadership. And thus equipped with a grammar school concept and a sense of history our simple savior sets out on a course to fulfill his destiny.[11]

Throughout this section, we see images of Paulsen, who has stepped in what appears to be dog feces and seems less engaged with any clarion call than he is with wiping his feet on the grass. Likewise, he "tests the waters" by stumbling into the reflecting pool, soaking both shoes. The last shot in the sequence is of Paulsen walking away from the camera shaking his legs and muttering to himself. Such awkward juxtapositions are repeated throughout the film, as Paulsen continues his quest to convert "a third grade idea [of running for president] into a reality."[12]

Though *Pat Paulsen for President* provides ample evidence that the comedian's "campaign" is a humorous exercise, it concludes with more somber images of Paulsen touring Resurrection City, "the shantytown capitol and symbol of [Martin Luther King, Jr. and the Southern Christian Leadership Council's] Poor People's Campaign" with some of its inhabitants.[13] On top of these images, Paulsen says in a voiceover:

> You know I've always had this dream. I guess it must sound kinda silly. I've always wanted to be president. A lot of people say I'm not much of a candidate. I do have a tendency to play things a little bigger than they are. In fact I embarrass myself sometimes. But I've never tried to embarrass our country. If I ever got to be president, I'd walk right out to that front gate and shake hands with anybody. And if anybody ever needed a friend to talk to, they'd be welcome to drop by anytime.[14]

The film closes with a zoom-in on the Lincoln Memorial and is followed by credits, which appear in the form of an election ballot and depict a hand writing Paulsen in as a candidate.

No such poignancy appears in the fake candidate's appearance on *The Smothers Brothers* the following week, when Paulsen invites his audience to join him for a "typical evening at home."[15] Such an appearance evokes Franklin Delano Roosevelt's use of radio to address his public as president. However, Paulsen's chat has more in common with the uses to which Richard Nixon put television in his early days as a national politician. In the Checkers speech, for example, he asked for the opportunity to make his case to the nation directly without any interlocutor.[16] Although Paulsen's appearance does not work to defuse a scandal, it does claim to want to "circumvent" the mediation of campaign speeches or interviews by speaking to supporters from a more "authentic" personal space. Of course, the armchair-sitting, smoking jacket–wearing, pipe-holding, ordinary dog-owning Paulsen fails in this endeavor. He nearly sets himself on fire with the pipe, kicks the dog because it growls at him, and attempts to take a nip from his flask while he thinks the camera is trained on something else. Perhaps most tellingly for the Smothers' audience, Paulsen's African American servant puts out the pipe fire by pouring water in his employer's pocket and says in an aside to the camera, "Don't want nothin' to burn around here until we get ready." This statement, undoubtedly a reference to rioting occurring in the nation's inner cities in 1968, as well as the Black Power movement, would have been obvious to an audience who was aware of the problems of poverty and racial injustice that fueled such expressions of outrage. When Paulsen patronizingly refers to his African American servant as "a real good boy," however, he reinforces the idea that he is un-aware of these inequities and therefore lacks the authority to represent all Americans.

The final insult to the audience in Paulsen's attempt to craft a real per-sona occurs when Paulsen is interrupted by a stagehand:

PAULSEN: Well, I want to thank you Americans once again for stopping by for a visit while I spend a typical evening at home. Just remember that I don't need a high-powered public relations firm to give me a phony, glam-orous image. This is my simple home. It's a common ordinary home—

STAGE HAND: I'm sorry Mr. Paulsen, we've got Nixon coming in in about ten minutes and we need the set. If it's okay we'd like to have it now, put it on another stage. All right, let's get it out of here.

PAULSEN: Well, my time is just about up . . .

The set on which he is sitting is wheeled off the stage to reveal a conduc-tor and choir, who up until this moment have been providing a sound-track of angelic "ah-ah-ahs" one might associate with 1950s-era biblical epics and Disney films. Their looks of embarrassment at being "outed" as part of Paulsen's homey façade simply reinforce the feeling that the entire exercise has been one of manipulation that will continue as Nixon steps onto another stage.

Such "fake" manipulation repeatedly informed Paulsen's campaign, which was similarly punctuated with other moments in which he seemed to be speaking directly to viewers, not so much as a candidate but as someone who also felt hopeless about the possibilities for a president who could lead the nation more honorably. During the last episode of *The Smothers Brothers* before the 1968 election, Paulsen interrupted his pre–election day monologue with a bit of advice:

> I'm honored by the fact that many thousands of you have indicated in the public opinion polls that you really do plan to vote for me. But please don't waste your vote if there really is a candidate that you can support. I hope you will look for a candidate who offers the best hope for world peace and a man who is interested in equality and justice along with law and order.[17]

No sooner had he made this plea than he returned to his more familiar shtick, removing his coat to reveal a World War II–era military uniform, weeping, and singing "God Bless America" in an attempt to sway voters.

Other than a humorous concession speech in which he announced to the press in true Nixonian fashion that they "[wouldn't] have Paulsen to kick around any more," Paulsen's presidential ambitions on *The Smothers Brothers* seemed to die with the election of Richard Nixon in 1968.[18] However, they are echoed in the perennial efforts of performers, activists, and ordinary citizens to run candidates for office who are simply not electable, such as the Birthday Party's "Nobody" (for President); the numerous parliamentary candidates of Britain's Monster Raving Loony Party; and the array of gubernatorial candidates in California's 2003 recall election, which included former child star Gary Coleman, among others. The absurdity of such candidates *usually* precludes them from being taken seriously *as candidates,* but it also makes it possible for them to highlight and enact public conversations about what Bodroghkozy refers to as "[crises] of authority" within the American political mainstream at a given moment.[19] As evidenced by Paulsen's campaign, the crises of presidential authority in 1968 emerged primarily around the ability of candidates to substantively address issues of race and class. As discussed in the next section, the 1980s witnessed a shifting of that focus toward a preoccupation with presidential politics under the scrutiny of 24-hour cable news coverage.

## *The Making and Meaning of a Real Fake Candidate in Tanner '88*

Compared with Pat Paulsen's deliberately fake presidential ambitions on *The Smothers Brothers, Tanner '88,* the "mockumentary" that Garry Trudeau and Robert Altman produced for HBO during the presidential election year of 1988, is perhaps the closest thing to the actual campaigns with which we are familiar today. Avoiding the gags, one-liners, and live audiences of the more "stagebound" performance traditions that inform such genres as the variety show, the 12-episode exploration of fictional former Michigan congressman Jack Tanner's bid for the 1988 Democratic presidential nomination uses the formal trappings of televisual "reality" (vérité-style camerawork and layered soundtrack) to create an atmosphere of "pure" observation.[20] In this respect, *Tanner* represents a forerunner to the kinds of comedy for which HBO is now well known. Although the premium channel had always provided a venue for comedy that would not survive on network television due to censorship constraints, the Trudeau-Altman collaboration's curious blend of fiction and reality has more in common with such edgy, reality-based series as *Curb Your Enthusiasm* (2000–   ) in that it seems determined to let its humor emerge from situations that are not consciously all that funny.[21] In this case, the "situation" depicted happens to be the 1988 American presidential election, which now holds a special place in Democrats' collective memory for its candidates' many missteps in front of cameras, such as Gary Hart's fall from grace after an alleged affair and Michael Dukakis's unphotogenic tank ride, all of which were rehashed repeatedly by mainstream media outlets.

Like these men, whose names are now synonymous with those offending images, Tanner is doomed by the disjuncture between his message and his ability to convey that message. Unlike *Pat Paulsen for President,* which uses film to satirize the predilection for casting candidates as noble characters who rise from nothing to assume the mantle of president, *Tanner '88*'s chosen mode of representation is video, a medium synonymous with television and its sense of immediacy and "liveness." Through this mode, the program portrays Tanner's presidential campaign less as a narrative of triumph and more as a catastrophic event that is always-already waiting to happen. That is, despite the Tanner campaign crew's attempts to maintain control over a message that defines their candidate as palatable to mainstream America, the "all-seeing eye" of *Tanner '88*'s camera provides a real-time account of the missteps that will make this task impossible. As Mary Ann Doane suggests about television in general, Tanner's TV image is coded as pure *information* (as opposed to representation) over which he has little control.[22]

An example of this difference between information and representation occurs at the conclusion of the two-part first episode ("The Dark Horse") in which Jack Tanner attempts to introduce himself to the voters of New Hampshire.[23] For most of the episode, the program offers two different perspectives: those of his campaign team, led by chain-smoking, battle-hardened T. J. Cavanaugh, who in this episode is showing Tanner's newly produced campaign video to a focus group; and of Tanner, who is traveling around the state to press the flesh with farmers, quilting bee members, and potential campaign volunteers. Ultimately, the view from either perspective is not good. Tanner's campaign video—in which he shovels snow and discusses how his 1960s activism helped shape his vision for the future—is openly mocked by focus group members for its lack of pizzazz and relevance. Similarly, his attempts to practice "retail" politics in one of the states that made the phrase famous are disastrous. Neither Tanner, who is hounded by fictional political reporter Hayes Taggerty and steamrolled (or worse, ignored) by savvy New Hampshire voters, nor T. J. can say that the campaign is off to a good start. When Tanner returns to his headquarters (a frigid hotel room), the team gives him the bad news: "The [focus] group didn't get it. . . . Why you're running, the point of your candidacy . . . they didn't get it."

Tanner's response to the crisis provides the first inkling that his campaign will falter under the media scrutiny that will dog him until the Democratic National Convention in Atlanta. He perceives this discussion with his team as an opportunity to explain why he feels compelled to run (his feeling that the country needs to get back to the ideals espoused by John Kennedy and 1960s liberals); the team perceives it as an opportunity to mine what he says for a new campaign image (their opportunity for manipulation through spin). Tanner tries to distinguish himself from the sizeable field of candidates by telling a story in which none of his contemporaries could answer his daughter Alex's question, "Who was your favorite Beatle?"

As Tanner proceeds to describe how the answer to this question indicates a potential Democratic candidate's right to his party's nomination, Altman's camera appears to wander around the room, settling for a few moments on the blank faces of each team member. Eventually, the camera trains its eye on Deke Connors, the New York University film grad who is charged with producing the campaign's advertising spots and is surreptitiously attempting to videotape Tanner with a camcorder resting on his lap. Tanner's speech not only communicates his anxiety about the future of the Democratic Party but also alludes to what he feels is the sabotaging of American democracy by politicians who would quell dissent with slick political slogans and false messages of hope—a criticism that many had lobbed at Ronald Reagan's team for creating such manipulative ad spots as "Morning in America." However, because we are viewing Tanner's impassioned speech from the point of view of Deke's camcorder, what the candidate says is perhaps only equally as important as the fact that we are seeing it shot guerrilla-style from a low angle through a glass coffee table. Tanner, fortified by these passionate ideals, makes a renewed pledge to run for president, regardless of what focus groups might think. His team only thinks about how to capitalize on the aesthetics of what they've just recorded. Predictably, the episode ends with a slow pan over a new campaign poster that contains a grainy, journalistic photo of a pensive-looking Tanner in mid-sentence. In the lower right-hand corner, the poster appears to be torn away to reveal the phrase "For real" beneath it.

This phrase, along with Tanner's Beatle litmus test, structures the fundamental tension of *Tanner '88*. According to Tanner, any democrat who laid "claim to generational leadership" in the 1988 election would need to choose John Lennon as their favorite Beatle because "the singer mattered as much as the song, [and] ideas were only as valuable as the people who thought them." However, because the series presents his campaign in two divergent formats (Altman's slow-roaming "video vérité" style and the over-the-top, experimental antics of Deke's camcorder), it seems to be suggesting that this "singer versus song" dichotomy no longer matters in presidential politics. Altman's camera cannot claim to be truly objective; occasionally it focuses on what might be construed as partisan objects, such as a bumper sticker that says, "Vote Republican—it's easier than thinking." However, Deke's manic, gimmicky setups, which include a pool's eye view at a Hollywood fundraiser and a helicopter stunt, suggest *nothing* substantive about politics per se. Both camera techniques are concerned with artifice, but one (Altman's) seems interested in exposing the artifice of presidential campaigning in the late twentieth century as part of its information-gathering mission, while the other (Deke's) seems intent on deploying artifice in the service of creating a representation that meets the needs of the media and the "modern" voter in the late twentieth century.

Because *Tanner* was shot and aired as the "real" Democratic presidential campaigns of 1988 unfolded, the program was able to capture footage of the actual political process in tandem with Jack Tanner's "fake" campaign stops. Episodes featured candidates (Pat Robertson, Bob Dole, Gary Hart, and Bruce Babbitt); entertainers (Waylon Jennings, Rebecca DeMornay, heavy metal band Harlow, and several young Detroit rappers); journalists (Linda Ellerbee and Tom Brokaw); and assorted other media personalities (Capitol Hill staffer and future *Hardball* host Chris Matthews). Their presence in Jack Tanner's world signals a breakdown between the realms of the "culture industries" and of "real" political campaigns that is reminiscent of Jürgen Habermas's analysis of the "transformation of the public sphere" under late capitalism. From this perspective, with the rise of space-merging technologies like radio and television, the arena once reserved for unfettered discourse about issues relating to the common good has become "infiltrated" by commercial entities, such as the news media, pollsters, lobbying firms, and the like.[24] These entities exist ostensibly to provide information that voters need to make informed decisions about candidates. However, because they are also governed by commercial logic, "they serve less as organs of public information and debate than as technologies for managing consensus and promoting consumer culture."[25]

Such a perspective puts *Tanner's* ubiquitous theme song "Exercise Your Right to Vote" in sharp relief. Part pep rally and part campaign jingle, the song's style contradicts its lyrical celebration of the power given to people in a participatory democracy:

> Exercise your right to vote.
> Choose the one you like the most.
> It's your individual right
> to choose the one you want to fight for you.

Much like a Rock the Vote campaign in which celebrities are used to motivate voter turnout, the song appears to be designed to present a vote as a kind of choice or product. Its repetitive, rhyming exhortation to Americans to "exer-cise [their] right to vote" has the effect of likening the choice not to careful consideration of candidates' stances on the issues but, instead, "to choose the one you like the most" the way one might select a brand of soda or a pair of sneakers. "Choice" as we once knew it, the show seems to suggest, does not exist in a world where media control our access to the political process.

Or does it? Although the series chronicles the demise of Tanner's campaign in excruciating detail—including his arrest during an anti-Apartheid demonstration, his clandestine romantic relationship with Dukakis's deputy campaign manager, his suggestion that drugs be legalized, and his campaign's effort to wrest convention delegates away from Dukakis by teaming up with Jesse Jackson—the last shot of the series depicts its main character's fate as open-ended, as he stares off into space equivocating about whether to continue running as an Independent. Indeed, in an interview for the Criterion Collection DVD of *Tanner '88,* Garry Trudeau suggested to Robert Altman that the series was not meant to signal their hopelessness about the state of politics in an era of unprecedented media coverage:

> TRUDEAU: But you and I aren't cynics. We're hopeful. We keep moving forward.
>
> ALTMAN: I'm a hopeful cynic.
>
> TRUDEAU: Is there such a thing?
>
> ALTMAN: Yeah, sure. It's like a person who lives in the desert. And hopes for rain.[26]

## *Stephen Colbert: I'm a Fake Candidate (And So Can You!)*

Although Robert Altman's contradictory image of the hopeful cynic was an example of his trademark irony, the presidential campaign of 2008 seems to have operated from this space of contradiction in earnest in that it witnessed not only a continuation of the intensely mediated image wars between potential candidates and members of the news media that *Tanner '88* satirizes but also the opening up of alternative spaces for discussion and creation of such images. The contradiction lies in the fact that this shift is largely made possible by vertically integrated media industries in which commercial interests and a seeming greater freedom of self-expression often go hand in hand. Large conglomerates with multiple media platforms have arguably created a space for many of the comedies discussed in this volume, such as *The Daily Show* and *The Colbert Report,* not simply to exist but to thrive. This landscape also helped transform the fake campaign. While Paulsen and Tanner provided disaffected voters with a blueprint for "talking back" to false political images largely outside of the mainstream media, comedian and conservative pundit-parodist Stephen Colbert modeled new possibilities for participation in the political process with his fake and rather short-lived run for president in the fall of 2007.

Colbert's journey toward becoming an official presidential candidate echoed Pat Paulsen's in that it began on *The Colbert Report* (Comedy Central, 2005– ) as a series of hints at his fitness for the job combined with the suggestion that he required evidence of a movement to support him. In this respect, Colbert received "the sign" he was looking for on September 13, 2007, when actor Viggo Mortensen appeared on *The Colbert Report* as

Aragorn (his character from the *Lord of the Rings* trilogy) to "call" Colbert to service. This moment, which Mortensen played with great theatricality by beseeching Colbert to enter the race and pledging his allegiance to the would-be candidate by offering him (albeit with some prompting from Colbert) the coveted elven "sword" Anduril, demonstrated Colbert's connections to a very different audience than the network or cable audiences addressed by Paulsen's and Tanner's fake campaigns. By drawing on imagery outside of what documentary scholar Bill Nichols refers to as the "historical world"—specifically, by inserting director Peter Jackson's filmic version of one of J. R. R. Tolkien's much-beloved fictional characters into the "nonfictional" space of presidential politics—this sequence bespeaks both an affinity for and a solidarity with the fan cultures who comprise part of Colbert's niche audience, as well as a continuing preoccupation with the blurring of the lines between "real" and "fantasy" in a postmodern media landscape.[27]

On October 16, Colbert upped the ante by officially announcing his desire to run for president as both a Democratic and Republican candidate in the South Carolina primaries, which were to be held in January 2008. Like Paulsen, who revealed at the end of *Pat Paulsen for President* that he never actually put his name on any presidential primary ballots, and Tanner, who never actually campaigned anywhere except within the space of his show, Colbert signaled his candidacy's "fakeness" by limiting the scope of his run. In contrast to those two candidates, however, Colbert based his logic to run only in South Carolina on the fact that he was *actually* born in the state and might therefore appeal to real South Carolina voters as a "native son." It's difficult to imagine real voters taking the campaign seriously, given Colbert's commercial sponsorship by Doritos snack chips and his pro–South Carolina campaign slogan ("First to secede, first to succeed"), which mocks the state's role in the lead-up to the Civil War as well as the South's devastating defeat. However, thanks to the fluid boundaries between television and commercially sponsored Internet sites, discussion of the would-be campaign among Colbert fans quickly morphed into action. Websites were set up to provide interested parties with instructions on how to petition to get Colbert on each party's respective ballot in South Carolina, and a survey conducted by polling firm Public Opinion Strategies showed him ahead of "actual" (but long-shot) Republican and Democratic candidates alike.

Similarly, the lead-up to and actual announcement of Colbert's campaign prompted an array of responses from so-called legitimate news sources, who in recent years have made attempts to become increasingly web-savvy, not only because of their own interests in cross-platform promotion but also because of the make-or-break political moments (such as Virginia Senator George Allen's now-legendary "macaca" reference) that unfold daily in user-generated web videos and have unprecedented influence on the political process. In this respect, although they are no longer able to act as "gatekeepers" by controlling the flow of information in the way that they once were, such media outlets are required to pay attention to these developments.

Perhaps the most interesting examples for the purposes of my argument are Stephen Colbert's October 14, 2007, guest column for Maureen Dowd in the *New York Times*—"I Am an Op-ed Columnist (and So Can You!)"—and his October 21, 2007, appearance with Tim Russert on *Meet the Press* (NBC). Both appearances were designed in part to promote the October 9 release of his much-anticipated (and self-promoted) book, *I Am America (and So Can You!)*, but each appearance also demonstrates Colbert's infiltration of the "real" world of politics in a way that is qualitatively different from the fake campaigns of Paulsen and Tanner. In the latter cases, "real" news people were certainly present within the space of the programs. Pierre Salinger, journalist and White House press secretary for both Presidents John F. Kennedy and Lyndon B. Johnson, made appearances in the *Pat Paulsen for President* special and, as noted above, *Tanner '88* featured on-the-fly interviews with several well-known network reporters and anchors. What distinguished Colbert's efforts, however, was his seeming unwillingness to respect generic boundaries in his quest to "talk back" to the highly mediated realm of presidential politics.

In contrast to accommodating "real" people within the limited entertainment space of a variety program or a "vérité" sitcom, the "fake" candidate Colbert ventured outside of his program into such venerated spaces as the pages of the *New York Times* and the longest-running Sunday news-talk show *Meet the Press*, not only to promote himself as a "serious" candidate but also to mock the outlets providing him with such a platform. Perhaps most important, despite his lampooning of the *New York Times*'s famously urbane Op-Ed staff (of Dowd, he writes contemptuously of what he imagines is her extravagant, *Sex and the City*–esque lifestyle: "As I type this, she's watching from an overstuffed divan, petting her prize Abyssinian and sipping a Dirty Cosmotinijito"), as well as Russert's rapid-fire, probing style of questioning, both commentators were willing participants in Colbert's satire of their places within the mainstream of American political discourse.[28] Borne from a commercial imperative to recognize the

power of alternative modes of such discourse, their willingness to accommodate Colbert's "back-talking" demonstrated both their need to appear
relevant to younger audiences turned off by their "political insider" status and to show that they "got"—and are even in on—the joke, even as
it made them (and their mode of discourse) look foolish to Colbert fans,
political bloggers, and other people fed up with politics as usual. It also
signaled how far satire has come in the post-network media environment,
when what were once either entertainment oddities or satiric discourses
that sat safely outside the realm of politics are now engaged with on even
the most venerated platforms of political journalism. The walls that for-
merly separated political insiders and outsiders, cable and network, pundits and parodists is now quite permeable.[29]

Despite the exhilaration that Colbert's tactics inspired in his supporters, however, not all participants in the sphere of "legitimate" politics
were so ready to provide a venue for his antics. Ultimately, although he
decided not to pursue a place on the Republican ballot, citing a cost-
prohibitive $35,000 registration fee, Colbert was denied a place on the
Democratic ballot by an official South Carolina party ruling that said he
did not meet the party's standards of "national viability," while the Federal
Election Commission deemed his commercial sponsorship by Doritos a
violation of campaign financing rules. Moreover, although Senator John
Edwards's campaign released a statement indicating their willingness to
play along with Colbert's fake efforts to appeal to South Carolina voters
(distinguishing their candidate by his refusal to be influenced by "taco
chip lobbyists"), CNN reported that supporters of Senator Barack Obama,
the eventual winner of the South Carolina Democratic primary, actively
sought to keep Colbert's name off the ballot.[30] Although Obama's campaign denied these allegations, the concern that Colbert might actually
siphon votes from an African American candidate with an equally youth-
and web-oriented voting demographic offers another suggestive snapshot
of the stakes of the 2008 presidential campaign for Democrats, as well as
one of the many contradictory ways that Colbert's campaign managed to
infiltrate the mainstream political arena.

In all, despite its failure to infiltrate actual electoral politics, Stephen
Colbert's fake campaign is significant for its ability to reiterate the power
of the fake campaign to comment on real political trends. Borne from the
impulse to talk back to false images of televisual politics, fake campaigns
not only satirize those images but also often work to provide a fundamentally different view of the world than the one offered by the pool of

available candidates at their respective moments. Pat Paulsen's campaign combined comedic ineptness with media savvy to instruct youth audiences of the 1960s on how to read "between the lines" of increasingly mediated versions of presidential politics. Similarly, Jack Tanner's fake bid for the presidency in 1988 turned television's "all-seeing eye" on itself in order to highlight the punishing scrutiny of 24-hour commercial news that eradicates "honest" politics. Finally, the resonance Stephen Colbert had—and continues to have—among mainstream media pundits and "cyber-counterpublics" alike signals a broadening of the public discussion surrounding the limits of our current version of American democracy.

## NOTES

1. Nancy Fraser, "Rethinking the Public Sphere: A Contribution to the Critique of Actually Existing Democracy," in *The Phantom Public Sphere,* ed. Bruce Robbins (Minneapolis: University of Minnesota Press, 1993), 14.

2. Ibid., 1.

3. David Culbert, "Television's Nixon: The Politician and His Image," in *American History/American Television: Interpreting the Video Past,* ed. John E. O'Connor (New York: Frederick Ungar, 1983), 184.

4. Ibid.

5. Aniko Bodroghkozy, *Groove Tube: Sixties Television and the Youth Rebellion* (Durham, N.C.: Duke University Press, 2001), 124.

6. *Pat Paulsen for President,* tape no. n.a., UCLA Film and Television Archive, Los Angeles, California (hereafter referred to as "UCLA").

7. Ibid.

8. *The Smothers Brothers Comedy Hour,* 11 February 1968, tape no. VA7728, UCLA.

9. Garry Trudeau uses the phrase "personality journalism" during his commentary on the Criterion Collection DVD of *Tanner '88,* 2004.

10. *Pat Paulsen for President,* UCLA.

11. Ibid.

12. Ibid.

13. "Balance on Resurrection City," *Time,* 5 July 1968, at http://www.time.com.

14. *Pat Paulsen for President,* UCLA.

15. *The Smothers Brothers Comedy Hour,* 27 October 1968, tape no. VA7744, UCLA.

16. Culbert, "Television's Nixon," 188.

17. *The Smothers Brothers Comedy Hour,* 3 November 1968, tape no. VA7754, UCLA.

18. *The Smothers Brothers Comedy Hour*, 10 November 1968, tape no. VA7751, UCLA. Paulsen continued to "campaign" as part of his comedy act until his death in 1997. For more on this, see his official website and memorial, at http://www.paulsen.com/.

19. Bodroghkozy, *Groove Tube*, 124.

20. Four more episodes of the series were made and released on the Sundance Channel in 2004.

21. Ethan Thompson, "Comedy Verite? The Observational Documentary Meets the Televisual Sitcom," *Velvet Light Trap* 60 (2007): 63–72.

22. Mary Ann Doane, "Information, Crisis, and Catastrophe," in *Logics of Television*, ed. Patricia Mellencamp (Bloomington: Indiana University Press, 1990), 225.

23. *Tanner '88*, "The Dark Horse," Criterion Collection DVD, 2004.

24. Jürgen Habermas, *The Structural Transformation of the Public Sphere*, trans. Thomas Berger (Cambridge: MIT Press, 1989), 141–51, 181–96.

25. Thomas McCarthy, introduction to Habermas, *Structural Transformation of the Public Sphere*, xii.

26. *Tanner '88*, "Conversation with Garry Trudeau and Robert Altman," Criterion Collection DVD, 2004.

27. Bill Nichols, *Representing Reality: Issues and Concepts in Documentary* (Bloomington: Indiana University Press, 1991), 110.

28. Stephen Colbert, "I Am an Op-Ed Columnist (And So Can You!)," *New York Times*, 14 October 2007, at http://www.nytimes.com/2007/10/14/opinion/14dowd.html.

29. For more on the history of these developments in "political television," see Jeffrey P. Jones, "From Insiders to Outsiders: The Advent of New Political Television," in *Television: The Critical View*, 7th ed., ed. Horace Newcomb (New York: Oxford University Press, 2007), 408–37.

30. CNN Political Ticker, "Colbert Campaigns in S.C., Edwards Camp Attacks Doritos Link," 29 October 2007, at http://politicalticker.blogs.cnn.com/2007/10/29/colbert-campaigns-in-sc-edwards-camp-attacks-doritos-link/; Peter Hamby, "Obama Supporters Pressed Officials to Keep Colbert Off Ballot," CNN, 6 November 2007, at http://www.cnn.com/2007/POLITICS/11/06/obama.colbert/index.html.

|||||||||||||||||||||||||||||||||||||||||||||||

# Part II

# Fake News, Real Funny

III

# And Now . . . the News?

## *Mimesis and the Real in* The Daily Show

### *Amber Day*

Four nights a week, anchor Jon Stewart holds court in his studio, relaying and evaluating the day's news stories, debating the issues with politicians and pundits, and, oh, telling a fart joke or two. He is a comedian who traffics in complex policy discussion, a news host with a penchant for the absurd. Stewart's vehicle, *The Daily Show,* is a program that confounds genre expectations, resembling other examples of late-night comedy in form but involving a far more complicated and slippery relationship with the real political world. What is immediately striking about *The Daily Show,* in contrast to many of its variety and sketch comedy predecessors, is the extent to which it blends both the mimetic and the real. Rather than rely on impersonations, sketches based around politicians' personal foibles, or entirely made-up news items, the program works to blur the line between news and entertainment, recontextualizing and deconstructing current news footage and interviewing and engaging with actual public figures. It is a specifically performative form of parody and satire that injects the actors' bodies into the traditional political realm, as they physically interrogate and interact with the real, combining television's historic allure of "liveness" and immediacy with the tradition of comedic improvisation. Though the program is almost universally referred to as "fake news," that label obscures the show's more complicated relationship to "real" news programming, as well as the attraction it holds for fans frustrated with the compromised authenticity and relevance of straight news programming. Less a fictionalized imitation, the program acts as a comedically critical filter through which to process the suspect real world of reportage and debate.

Both the mimetic and the "real" are equally important components to the show, as the mimetic frame allows the stolen fragments of the real to

be satirically scrutinized and deconstructed, and even subsequently mobilized as a form of evidence in public debate. It is this blend of satire
and political nonfiction that enables and articulates an incisive critique
of the inadequacies of contemporary political discourse. The show then
becomes a focal point for existing dissatisfaction with the political sphere
and its media coverage, while Jon Stewart, as high-profile host, becomes a
viewer surrogate, able to express that dissatisfaction through his comedic
transformation of the real.

Of course, the term "real"—both seemingly transparent and metaphysi-
cally complex—can imply a host of different meanings. To clarify, on a fairly
basic level, I am using it to refer to nonfiction material—events and interactions that most would recognize as having a tangible existence outside of the
television show. For instance, I refer to *The Daily Show* making use of "real"
news clips, meaning that footage of a "real" press conference is not footage
of professional actors pretending that they are at a press conference but of
flesh-and-blood public figures whose words and actions are likely to have a
very tangible effect on the lives of individuals around the world. However,
this is not to overlook the fact that the "real" officials at the press conference are also, in a sense, actors playing their roles, wearing the appropriate wardrobe, speaking in the expected tone of voice, and often mouthing
memorized (or teleprompted) lines that have been scripted for them. "Real"
most certainly does not refer to an essential authenticity or lack of artifice.
Rather, it is precisely the importation of the "real" or nonfictional into the
mimetic frame of the program that can serve to call attention to the way in
which the "real" is itself constructed. One of *The Daily Show*'s primary targets, as I explore, is the lack of substance behind much political discourse—
the public-relations spin tactics used by politicians and corporations and
the lack of interrogation on the part of the news media. It is through this
act of pointing out the artificiality of real newscasts, press conferences, and
other forms of public discussion that, for many of its fans, this "fake" news
show actually comes closer to embodying the characteristics—like authenticity and truth—that we would normally associate with the "real."

## Mimesis and the Real

Clearly, as audience members, we are not to mistake Jon Stewart for a real
newscaster or view the show as a legitimate news broadcast. The structure and form of the program remains squarely within the mimetic realm.

Fig. 4.1. "Senior Political Analyst" Jason Jones
reports back to Jon Stewart on *The Daily Show*.

Mimesis, the representation or imitation of something, is the primary
function of theater, fiction film, television, and, of course, any form of parody. In Plato's foundational usage of the term, mimesis is to be viewed with
suspicion, precisely because it is an (inferior) imitation of the real, though
herein also lies its paradoxical appeal. As Tracy Davis argues in reference
to theatrical mimesis, "a mimetic act refers to an ideal 'real' which can
never quite be successfully invoked: theatre is doomed (or blessed) by this
failure."[1] Similarly, much of the pleasure of the parodic news show is derived precisely from this awareness of the mimetic act. Audiences are en-
tertained by seeing actors create impressions of a stereotypical news crew
on a stereotypical news set. It invokes all the tropes of the news genre, including the prominent anchor's desk, a slick background, and a television
monitor with iconic images and logos lurking over Stewart's shoulder.

These parodied tropes can function as punch lines in themselves,
pointing to perceived flaws in the practices of broadcast news, such as the
rotating, important-sounding, but vacuous titles given to the "correspondents," depending on the particular story they are covering (figure 4.1). In
most respects, though, the parodied markers function less as one-liners

and more as a vehicle for the performers. *The Daily Show* set and its trappings tend not to be overly exaggerated but are, instead, quite consistent with those of straight news programs. Anchor Jon Stewart plays a fairly believable news reporter, looking well groomed but not overdone and using a predominantly serious, well-measured tone. It is all the more pleasurable, then, when this respectable-looking newscaster throws a phrase like "douche bag" into his patter, reminding his viewers that he is only playing at respectability. Likewise, when Stewart segues to a report from a correspondent "on location," who is actually standing on set in front of a green screen, the studio audience erupts in giggles every time. Much of the comedy, then, derives from the audience's awareness of mimesis and appreciation for the mimetic skills of the performers.

Within this parodic universe, however, the show actively poaches from and draws in pieces of the real political world in a number of ways. Most obviously, it relies heavily on real, evolving news stories. As opposed to simply making up fanciful fake events, the show reports on the day's news as it is continuing to unfold. Stewart has become well known for his extended deconstructions of current events. Rather than joking about what theoretically could have happened around a particular issue, he spends several minutes of his opening monologue actively reporting an ongoing story, replaying footage seen on other news programs but with a decidedly comedic angle. As he explained in an interview with Bill Moyers, "we don't make things up. We just distill it to, hopefully, its most humorous nugget."[2] The comedy most often lies in him uncovering what he believes to be the real story behind a particular issue, breaking down the official rhetoric and media sound bites.

Stewart does this through strategies like highlighting particular statements within a longer exchange or speech, making faces of mock incredulity, or pretending that he believes the speaker is talking about something else as a means of throwing his or her logic or sincerity into question. For example, during the Terri Schiavo debacle of early 2005, Stewart ran a clip of a senator grandiloquently announcing that a society's commitment to life is measured by the extent to which its laws honor and defend its most vulnerable citizens. He then paused the tape, joyfully shouting, "Oh my God, we are getting universal healthcare!" He prefaced the next clip by asking "if you were wondering just how sick you have to be before Congress gives you healthcare," segueing to footage of Bush getting off a plane in Washington, answering that Bush had cut his vacation short so that he could sign a bill intended to prolong the life of the brain-dead Schiavo.[3]

While the straight news world simply reports statements and developments, the cast of *The Daily Show* is free to satirically compare and contrast, interrogate and mock, sometimes developing a deeper analysis of the story in question than the straight programs.

Within this humorous dissection of the day's news, the performers also provide editorials on current events through pointed comedic tirades. One of the topics the cast continuously returns to, for instance, is the quality of reportage in serious broadcasting. Stewart appears to become particularly incensed when journalists line up behind one another, all repeating the same assertions without investigation, or relying on "talking points" developed by politicians. One of the show's favored methods of disparaging this behavior is to create a montage sequence that both highlights and critiques the practice. In the lead-up to the 2004 election, for instance, Stewart did a piece ostensibly on how we arrive at conventional wisdom. In it, he focuses on the oft-quoted idea that presidential hopeful John Kerry and his running mate John Edwards are "out of touch with the mainstream." He muses over how it is that he remembers this piece of wisdom, remembering that TV drills it in. He then shows the audience a fast-paced montage of numerous commentators repeating phrases like "way outside the mainstream" and "second most liberal senator" over and over again, explaining that though we have no idea how these rankings are arrived at or who compiles them, we do not like the sound of them. He closes with the epithet, "talking points: they're true because they're said a lot."[4] It is through this type of stinging commentary on the world of real news broadcasting and political debate that the show paradoxically attempts to expose the artifice and scriptedness of that world.

In addition to the incorporation of real news footage and commentary, the program also interacts with the real political world in another important way: via interviews with politicians, newsmakers, and citizens. One of the forms this takes is the ambush on-location interview, in which the correspondents investigate local news stories (often those that appear trivial or absurd) and interview participants. Interviewees, some of whom are clearly unaware that they are speaking with a comedian rather than a reporter, are set up for maximum comic effect, often displaying a less than flattering side. For instance, during the show's coverage of the Republican National Committee convention in the lead-up to the 2004 election, correspondents Ed Helms and Samantha Bee interview Republican delegates. The montage of interview responses includes a woman answering a question about whether it could be seen as a conflict of interest to have Fox

News sponsor the convention, by stating simply and emphatically, "I think Fox News is absolutely awesome."[5] And when a man tells Bee that he is going to be exploring New York for the next few days, she inquires as to whether he has had his picture taken with a black person yet. He indicates that he has not, but would certainly be willing to do so, and cheerily agrees with a deadpan Bee that there aren't many of "them" in his home state of Montana. These interviewees thus unwittingly provide the evidence for existing critiques of the Republican Party as narrow, blindly ideological, and bigoted. The pleasure in the conceit is that real individuals (rather than caricatures) are drawn into their own satirizing. The victims' responses would not be nearly as entertaining were they fabricated by a scriptwriter.

In one more layer to the blurring of real and fake news, *The Daily Show* also includes lengthy (consensual) interviews with public figures taped in front of the studio audience. These interviewees are always fully aware of the type of show they are participating in. In fact, the program has become a highly sought-after stop on the interview circuit. Guests on *The Daily Show* are sometimes actors promoting a new movie but are also just as likely to be politicians, pundits, and journalists. The exchanges are conducted in a style somewhere between a straight news interview and a celebrity chat, with Stewart putting his guests at ease by cracking jokes and kibitzing about their personal lives, but also posing tougher policy questions, particularly when the interviewee appears to be relying on party talking points or is making broad statements without offering proof. Stewart is always congenial but never hides his own opinion, often relishing the opportunity for a debate.

For example, in an interview with Christopher Hitchens early in the Iraq war, Stewart began the discussion by asking Hitchens good-naturedly to "help me understand why I am wrong about Iraq." After a back-and-forth in which Stewart presses Hitchens on the urgency for invading Iraq in particular over a number of other countries, they move on to American dissent on the war. When Hitchens dismisses "liberals" as believing that terrorism has been created by the United States, Stewart vehemently retorts that such a conflation is disturbing to him, arguing "there is reasonable dissent in this country about the way this war has been conducted" that has nothing to do with a belief that we should "cut and run" or that terrorism is our fault. Hitchens then implies that Stewart has been ridiculing the president simply for not agreeing to withdraw from Iraq, to which Stewart responds that, to the contrary, he ridicules the president because "he refuses to answer questions from adults as though we were adults and falls back upon platitudes and phrases and talking points that does a disservice to the goals that he himself shares with the very people he needs in his defense." After this exchange, Stewart grabs Hitchens in mock aggression, comically defusing any animosity, then gives a quick plug for his new book and asks the audience to give Hitchens a round of applause.[6] Interviews such as these are certainly not "fake" or fictionalized, nor are they played entirely for laughs. Instead, light-hearted irreverence combines with a serious discussion of the issues of the day, further eroding the dividing lines between news, satire, and political debate, as the parodic, not-quite-news-host throws himself into the real political world.

While some of these interview segments are fluffier than others, many do present a more in-depth and transparent discussion of topical issues than can be found on a number of the straight news programs. And it is during the interview segments that Stewart makes his most obvious appeals for actual solutions to political woes. He generally has on politicians and pundits from all points on the political spectrum, and he attempts to have a genuine conversation about their ideas with all of them. Though he gets impatient with guests who seem to be repeating platitudes, the attitude he most often takes is of someone searching for solutions who is interested in what his guests think the answers are and in how political compromises and areas of consensus can be reached. One of his favorite themes is the desire to overcome entrenched political partisanship. Stewart generally approaches the exchanges not as a self-satisfied comic but as a citizen seeking answers to the questions that confound him, again ensuring that the interviews remain very much a part of wider political debate.

The interpenetration of the mimetic and the real on the show also allows for the manipulation of existing serious footage within the satiric frame with the intention of effecting broader discourse. The theses advanced by the show, based on their investigation and rearrangement of existing footage, become a part of the political record. For instance, in one episode focusing on the results of the 9/11 Commission report, Stewart, as anchor, plays footage of an interview Vice President Dick Cheney had recently given on CNBC, when he emphatically refuted the interviewer's assertion that he had once said that a meeting between one of the 9/11 hijackers and an Iraqi government official had been "pretty well confirmed." Stewart quickly segues from this footage of Cheney insisting that he absolutely never said those words to the original footage of him saying exactly that, handily exposing the blatant lie.[7] This segment, then, became a form of evidence within the real-world political discussion. In these instances, the program becomes performative, in that it creates that which it names and enacts in the moment. Of course, on this particular occasion, the revelation of the lie did not result in Cheney's firing or even in any sort of public reprimand, but it did become a part of the larger debate. And it is worth noting that, though both interviews were widely accessible, most straight news programs never bothered to show the two together. The intertwined nature of satire and serious political debate means that the newsworthy segments and exchanges that take place within the show are by no means safely cloistered in the realm of entertainment but are very much part of the general political discussion.[8]

In the end, both the mimetic and the "real" are equally important components to the form. The simultaneity of the two is a characteristic specific to performative parody. In most forms of textual parody, the parodist may allude to real people and events, poking fun at real world policy or personalities. However, his or her texts normally exist outside of and as commentary on the political world. Similarly, even in other performed parodies in which actors might create impersonations of public figures, these performances are typically separable from the day-to-day workings of public and political life, existing in a demarcated space of fictionalized entertainment that seems removed from the world of political fact (such as the often facile humor that tries to pass as satire on *Saturday Night Live;* see chapter 2 in this volume). *The Daily Show,* in contrast, works hard to blur the parodic with serious political discourse, as the cast physically interacts with the real, literally dialoguing with the day's news footage or interviewing the newsmakers themselves. Undoubtedly, there is something more potentially dangerous and unpredictable about this interaction than there is in a fictional send-up of a politician or other newsmaker. Here the hybridity of genre is inseparable from the performative. Viewers tune in to watch the cast comedically interrogate, critique, and transform the real. The pleasure in this transformation is, I believe, created through a melding of two traditions: comedic improvisation combined with what television theorists have pinpointed as the historic allure of television itself—the aura of "liveness."

## Improvisation and Dialogic Inquiry

From its inception, the television industry marketed its product by emphasizing its difference from cinema. Television programs were live and immediate, and, as Lynn Spigel has demonstrated, they represented a means of unifying newly dispersed suburban homes, allowing one a connection to the larger community, while remaining in the comfort and safety of one's living room.[9] From the very names of programs to their stylistic markers and genre conventions, television has claimed the concept of liveness. As Jane Feuer argues, "television's self-referential discourse plays upon the connotative richness of the term 'live,' confounding its simple or technical denotations with a wealth of allusiveness."[10] In fact, she explains, while television actually now involves less of an equivalence between time of event and time of transmission, "the medium seems to insist more and more upon an ideology of the live, the immediate, the direct, the spontaneous, the real."[11]

If there is one genre in particular that is built on this promise, it is, of course, the news show, which one watches with the understanding that one is receiving the most current information on world events as they unfold (regardless of how far in advance some of the pre-taped sequences have been filmed), witnessing the revelation of information among a community of viewers tuning in at the same moment. Though this community may be dispersed in space, they are united in time. To reassure the viewer that this is the case, news shows routinely provide markers of their liveness, including reference to the date and time, as well as a generalized format of "direct address," which Jérôme Bourdon defines as "the sequence where a person looks straight at the camera (as if at viewers) and addresses the viewers, using the appropriate deixis [proof of 'liveness']. The most evident part of this deixis is of course the personal pronouns 'I' (the host) and 'you' (the viewers at home)."[12] *The Daily Show* plays off these same markers, partially as a means of parody (imitating the tropes of the genre) and partially for similar reasons as the straight programs themselves. It also reports and reacts to events as they unfold, offering its redaction of the day's or week's stories. Audiences watch not simply for comedy but for its relevance.

This general reliance on topicality also importantly combines with the tradition of comedic improvisation. While related to much earlier folk theater traditions such as commedia dell'arte, modern stage improvisation became a codified performance tradition in the late 1950s. It is an unscripted form of sketch comedy in which actors create the material in the moment, sometimes based on suggestions from the audience or simply in collaboration with one another. It is a form from which *The Daily Show* draws heavily. With the ambush interviews in particular, the skills of the performer must be considerable in order to maintain their persona, while adapting to whatever their victim has to say, playing the straight man to the victim's unwitting comedy. Similarly, in the live interview segments, Stewart improvises both comedically and journalistically in his unscripted exchanges with his guests. As in watching stage improv, the audience takes pleasure in seeing something created on the spot, as the performer comes up with just the right provocations and responses to further the scene. While the ambushes are edited, both types of interview are unrehearsed. And with the exception of those on-location ambushes, the bulk of the show is filmed in front of a live studio audience, once again drawing on the aura of immediacy and community this creates. The monologues are written beforehand, but Stewart and his correspondents also ad lib in response to audience reaction, making the home audience feel as if they are part of the live performance (though they are not watching it in real time). *The Daily Show* has also made an occasional habit of doing "live" (real time) specials concurrent with particularly important events, such as after a presidential debate or on election night itself. These specials serve to further blur the line between satire and reportage, as the cast improvises their responses to the events simultaneously with the ranks of pundits providing their analyses on other channels.

Rather than sending up one particular program or newscaster, the show offers a broader satire of larger ills within the news genre, as well as hypocrisies within the day's news stories. Here the incorporation of nonfiction material serves to add an entirely new level to the unmasking abilities of parody and satire. In *A Theory of Parody*, Linda Hutcheon defines parody as a form of "inter-art discourse," arguing that what distinguishes parody from pastiche (mere similarity) is the use of "ironic transcontextualization" to provide critical distance from the original.[13] Hutcheon is clearly referencing more direct textual parodies within fine art and literature, offering such examples as the transcontextualization of Shakespeare's words into a new context in Tom Stoppard's play *Rosencrantz and Guildenstern Are Dead*. However, I would argue that the concept of transcontextualization is also a useful one for a program like *The Daily Show*. Rather than the transcontextualization of one fictional text or work of art within another, an official's real-world actions or words are transcontextualized within the frame of the show, so that the two texts or performances exist side by side: the original act, as well as the host's interpretation of that act.

The reason Stewart can get a laugh from simply playing a clip of President Bush at a press conference is not because Bush's statements were considered funny when he first said them, or even when they were aired on the evening news, but because they have been transcontextualized into a comedically deconstructive frame. Since the audience of *The Daily Show* is primed to watch the material with a critical eye, the original footage reveals a wealth of hidden meaning. Much of the audience's pleasure is derived from watching real, serious news material ironically transcontextualized and stripped down in front of their eyes.

Here parodic news does what the straight news cannot, which is to stage an ongoing dialogue with itself. As Geoffrey Baym points out in an incisive article on *The Daily Show,* while traditional news is monologic, presenting a closed, authoritative version of what the issues of the day are and why they are important, parodic news shows are dialogic, playing multiple voices against each other. While the straight news "claims an epistemological certainty, satire is a discourse of inquiry, a rhetoric of challenge that seeks through the asking of unanswered questions to clarify the underlying morality of a situation."[14] This becomes possible because parodic news is not beholden to the same industry standards as the straight news. Traditional news programs are expected to adhere to a type of dispassionate objectivity that frowns on any sort of subjective display on the part of the journalist. In the post-9/11 era in particular, this tenet has too often translated into a hesitancy to question the statements made by officials for fear of appearing partisan or "unpatriotic," meaning that a political party's public relations "talking points" become presented as fact without interrogation of veracity. This is a critique now frequently leveled at the mainstream media, and one that Stewart explicitly articulates, arguing "there are—should be—you know, truths, actual truths, and someone should be there to help arbitrate that, and it seems to be that media should be the forum for that."[15] His function as a parodic news host, then, is to act as comedic interrogator. In contrast to the seeming inadequacies of the broadcast news, Stewart, as comedian, is able to draw on a process of dialogical interaction, cross-examining the rhetoric of both public figures and standard news discourse.

Quite literally, he often stages a conversation between himself and the news footage he plays for his audience, stopping and starting the clip in question in order to provide his own interjections. For example, the day after the Iraq study group issued its assessment of the Iraq war in December 2006, Stewart did a piece on its reception, including footage of press secretary Tony Snow trying to downplay the critique. Snow is shown accusing one of the reporters at the press conference of being partisan, to which the reporter responds, "You are suggesting that by quoting the report, I am trying to make a partisan argument?" Stewart then stops the footage to say, "It's the way you quote it. You're quoting with a partisan inflection," adding with a comical voice, "the president's policies are not woooorrking." We are then returned to the footage, in which Snow is still responding, explaining, "The question is can you read this as anything but a repudiation of the president's policy, and the answer is yes, I can." Stewart retorts, "You absolutely can. It could be read as a nineteenth century comedy of manners," at which point he brandishes a copy of the report with a flourish, reading from it "pull out the majority of troops by 2008. Saucy!" Finally, Stewart closes with a short montage of Snow repeatedly answering questions by saying that he needs more time to "parse" the report. Stewart imitates Snow, adding, "I need time to parse, to split hairs. See, right now, you are not getting my top quality bull(bleep). It's not fair to you, the public I lie to."[16]

Stewart uses his own subjective responses to dissect the discourse of public officials and organizations. In so doing, he acts as the every-person stand-in. If a regular newscaster cannot roll an eye or arch a brow at a politician's statement, Stewart can fall off his chair doing so. Thus he is able to act as the viewer's surrogate, screaming at the television in frustration or summarily labeling someone "full of shit." As opposed to the average citizen, however, Stewart has an audience of millions at his command. For those of us without such a luxury, we can take vicarious pleasure in hearing our own opinions aired on national television. Indeed, this is an important component of the show's appeal. In one newspaper article on *The Daily Show*, a journalist interviews members of the studio audience, quoting a 78-year-old woman who explained her love of the program and of Jon Stewart in particular: "'He can really see through things and some of the shams that we're being fed,' she says. 'And I'm tired of the shams. I want a little truth to come out. I want somebody to see some of the things I see and Jon does that for me.'"[17] Stewart is still clearly recognized as a comedian, but as our stand-in he has also garnered a unique form of status and respect that is certainly not routinely granted to the average stand-up comic or sitcom actor.

## Sliding into Punditry

Because the program is so heavily reliant on and critical of contemporary political events and the evolving discourse surrounding them, it has itself become a fairly substantial presence within that discourse, while Stewart has been elevated to the status of legitimate political pundit. In

Fig. 4.2. Democratic presidential nominee
Senator John Kerry visits *The Daily Show.*

documenting the wider, growing genre of political entertainment on television, Jeffrey Jones notes that the hosts of new political television "have increasingly come to be seen as political commentators by fans and others within the television industry."[18] Indeed, Stewart is now one of the most well known and well respected of these new comedian commentators. When *The Daily Show* first began airing with Craig Kilborn as its host, it was much less focused on political critique and was often described as more of a spoof of *Entertainment Tonight* than of a serious news program. When Stewart took over in 1999, the show began to change, garnering a huge amount of attention over its coverage of the 2000 presidential election and becoming a full-fledged phenomenon by the 2004 election.

Leading up to the 2004 election, for instance, Stewart was featured in numerous magazines and television interviews, he and the show's other writers released an immediately best-selling book, and the program received a Television Critics Association award, not for comedy but for Outstanding Achievement in News and Information. Meanwhile, John Edwards announced his candidacy on the show, and Democratic presidential nominee John Kerry dropped by for an interview while declining offers from many news shows (figure 4.2). Suddenly, everyone was asking

Stewart's opinion on every nuance of the campaign and the media's coverage of it, while journalists speculated over what his influence would be on the election itself.

Finally, just a few weeks before the election, Stewart was invited on CNN's *Crossfire* to promote his book. It is a program he had previously criticized on his own show, using it as an example of political debate that has degenerated into a shouting match between characterized representatives of the left and the right rather than a discussion of facts. During his live appearance on *Crossfire,* he surprised everyone by dropping his comedic persona and dead-seriously begging the hosts to stop "hurting America," accusing them of engaging in "partisan hackery," and refusing to back down when asked to lighten up. News of the incident spread immediately, with hundreds of thousands of people downloading the footage and thousands of fans writing e-mails (primarily of support) to the Comedy Central network.[19] As a *Los Angeles Times* reporter put it, Internet buzz about the confrontation "universally hailed Stewart as a refreshing and clear-eyed critic of an increasingly trivial television news media and skyrocketed him to a new rank in his comedic career—from wry commentator to serious provocateur."[20] In that moment, Stewart took on legendary status as a heroic truth-teller, only increased by CNN's subsequent decision to drop *Crossfire* from its schedule. The point here is not simply that Stewart has become an extremely popular comedian, which he certainly has, but that, through his parodic commentary, he has achieved legitimacy as a political speaker, setting him apart from many predecessors. While at the helm of "Weekend Update" on *Saturday Night Live,* Chevy Chase was never asked seriously for his analysis of political events. Stewart, in contrast, is now sought out for his growing reputation as a media watchdog, while his show has gained a significant voice within political discourse.

Instead of conceptualizing the actions of Stewart and his correspondents as mere commentary on the political field from the jokers on the sidelines, it seems clear that their work functions as political speech in itself, affecting the direction of public discourse while elevating the parodist to the level of legitimate political expert. It appears that, while *The Daily Show* certainly takes comedic jabs at the conventions of television news, it also paradoxically borrows some of the authority imbued in those conventions. When Stewart appears on television to speak about current events with obvious knowledge and command (as well as irreverence), he absorbs some of the clout of real pundits and newscasters while simultaneously mocking those roles. Similarly, while the average comedian would presumably not normally be granted admittance to political functions, *The Daily Show* correspondents now routinely secure press passes to official events such as political party conventions, where they lampoon the authority and purpose of the real-world participants. One correspondent, Rob Riggle, has even gained access to the U.S. military, conducting a series of interviews on location in Iraq. In an interview with *Bust* magazine, correspondent Samantha Bee marvels over the fact that so many people have told her she could, in the future, get a job as a real newscaster if she wanted. She says, "I don't want to believe that it's true. But I almost do. Our impression is just good enough that we could be newsreaders. It's pretty sad. . . . It's ridiculous that we get the access we get. Why in the world would I be talking to Madeleine Albright? Why in the world would she stop to talk to me? It's crazy."[21] Far from remaining solely in the world of comedic entertainment—or "fake news"—*The Daily Show*'s parodic commentary has launched the show into the midst of the very real political sphere.

## Not Not Newscasting

Perhaps not surprisingly, however, the increased legitimacy of the program, combined with its slippery combination of the mimetic and the real, has also sparked some cultural anxiety. During the presidential campaign of 2004, a flurry of reports were produced on who was watching the show and for what reasons. The Pew Research Center for the People and the Press released a study in January of 2004 that reported that 21 percent of Americans aged 18–29 regularly learn about the campaign and the candidates from comedy shows like *Saturday Night Live* and *The Daily Show.*[22] The survey from which this data was gleaned asked respondents if they "regularly learn *something* from" (my emphasis) and then gave a list of various sources, including "comedy TV shows." In subsequent articles, this became redacted to statements such as *The Daily Show* was chosen as "the preferred election news source by one-fifth of surveyed Americans ages 18–29."[23] This dubious statistic soon became fodder for much hand-wringing over the idea of fans using the show for information.

In a spontaneous late-night exchange on the Democratic National Committee convention floor in 2004, Ted Koppel whined to Jon Stewart that "a lot of television viewers—more, quite frankly, than I'm comfortable with—get their news from the comedy channel on a program called *The Daily Show.*"[24] When Stewart appeared on Bill O'Reilly's Fox News program, O'Reilly infamously opined, "You know what's really frightening? You actually have an influence on this presidential election. That is scary, but it's true. You've got stoned slackers watching your dopey show every night and they can vote."[25] Fans of the show were vindicated when, within days of O'Reilly's comment, the National Annenberg Election Survey concluded that *The Daily Show* viewers were better educated and more affluent than the national average, and they were more knowledgeable about the presidential campaign than those who do not watch any late-night television.[26]

Much of the rhetoric about *The Daily Show* functioning as a news source has taken on a familiar tone. Like condemnations of soap operas or tabloids, the anxiety is over a perceived "other" (in this case, young people) who might be unable to tell the difference between truth and fiction, entertainment and real life. Writing on tabloid television, Kevin Glynn addresses the destabilization caused by the blurring of news and entertainment. He argues, "tabloid television disturbs not only the figure of the traditional anchorman . . . but equally the definitions of truth, seriousness, and authority that he embodies," a disturbance that undoubtedly accounts for at least some of the revulsion it engenders.[27] Jason Mittell also points out that genre mixing, in general, often creates a certain amount of controversy. As he argues, many generically mixed programs "face a particularly tumultuous cultural life, easily buffeted by competing contexts of reception."[28] In this case, the mixture of comedy with news and political commentary, of the mimetic and the real, creates anxiety in some that the show will somehow be read as straight news by others.

What detractors don't understand is that *The Daily Show* would have very little appeal were it to be simply a slightly hipper version of the straight news. The program is not attempting to become another incarnation of the existing real but to hold the real up for scrutiny, an operation that requires that audience members remain aware of its deliberate use of artifice. In fact, if Stewart and his cast are to maintain legitimacy as *satiric* newscasters, it is important that they continue to appear to be obviously playing a role. Stewart, in particular, must retain the aura of a cheeky journalistic outsider throwing stones rather than seeming like a part of the political establishment he critiques. His unique status stems from his ability to embody the authority of a pundit or newscaster while still being several steps removed from the profession. To borrow the terminology

Richard Schechner uses when describing performance, he will maintain this status as long as the audience knows that he is both not a newscaster and not not a newscaster.[29] It is worth noting that Stewart's physical being is also important to this operation. He is white, male, and middle-class looking, meaning that he does not appear out of place in the television expert's chair. However, he does make frequent reference to his Jewishness, allowing him to remain one step removed from the mainstream and play up his outsider's eye for absurdity. Ultimately, it is through his incorporation and engagement with the real, without actually becoming identical to it, that he is able to critique the real.

For many fans, there is something about Stewart's playful manipulations and dissections of the real world of television news and political debate that end up coming closer to reality than the original itself. In a highly mediatized discursive landscape, earnestness can seem suspect. It is the very quality that politicians and other overproduced public figures bend over backward attempting to convey, while there is something about the unabashedly personal, ironic, tongue-in-cheek perspective that appears refreshingly authentic. Stewart presents himself as the everyman surrogate, one who can display his disgust and amusement on our behalf, one who responds as anyone would to the crazy situations at hand, speaking out loud what we are all thinking, if perhaps in a somewhat wittier manner than we are able. And, within the ironic, not-quite-real universe of the show, Stewart is able to effortlessly shape the real into evidence for the critique his audience has grown to crave.

It is important to note, of course, that while Stewart may play the everyman, he is not always voicing a majority opinion. To a great extent, he and his staff interrogate and analyze dominant perceptions and official policies, often articulating a perspective that is somewhat outside of the mainstream (though perhaps not radically so). It is a perspective that is distinctly critical of the status quo of political debate in the United States. In marshalling this critique, they have created a television program that functions as a focal point for many who hold similar opinions, opinions that are not necessarily reflected in much mainstream programming, allowing people to identify through the consumption of and interaction with a popular culture text, while providing an easily shared reference.

The program has certainly been developed for a fairly specific taste public, one that undeniably skews left of center, but the show's popularity has meant that, after generating enough momentum, the critique then trickles into broader discussion. Its combination of political nonfiction and satire happens to provide particularly fertile ground for the dissection of public discourse, producing a welcome outlet for many who are already critical of that discourse. In a historical moment when all sides of the political spectrum bemoan the flaws of straight news, *The Daily Show*'s brand of fake news has emerged as a trusted filter through which to engage with the debased real.

## NOTES

1. Tracy Davis, *Stages of Emergency: Cold War Nuclear Civil Defense* (Durham, N.C.: Duke University Press, 2007), 85–86.

2. *Now with Bill Moyers*, PBS, 11 July 2003.

3. 21 March 2005.

4. 3 September 2004.

5. *The Daily Show with Jon Stewart: Indecision 2004*, DVD (Paramount, 2005).

6. 1 December 2004.

7. 21 June 2004.

8. For coverage of Stewart's interview with Pakistani President Pervez Musharraf, see *Good Morning America*, ABC, 27 September 2006. For commentary on Stewart's interview with Wolf Blitzer, as well as the quality of Stewart's political analysis, see Antonia Zerbisias, "Stewart Gets Serious, Why Won't Reporters?" *Toronto Star*, 10 August 2004, D5. For a discussion of Stewart's *Crossfire* appearance used as an entree to further commentary on partisan politics, see Fareed Zakaria, "TV, Money, and 'Crossfire Politics'" *Newsweek*, 1 November 2004, at http://www.fareedzakaria.com/ARTICLES/newsweek/110104.html.

9. Lynn Spigel, *Make Room for TV: Television and the Family Ideal in Postwar America* (Chicago: University of Chicago Press, 1992).

10. Jane Feuer, "The Concept of Live Television: Ontology as Ideology," in *Television: Critical Approaches: An Anthology*, ed. Ann Kaplan (Frederick, Md.: University Publications of America, 1983), 14.

11. Ibid.

12. Jérôme Bourdon, "Live Television Is Still Alive: On Television as an Unfulfilled Promise," in *The Television Studies Reader*, ed. Robert C. Allen and Annette Hill (London: Routledge, 2004), 185.

13. Linda Hutcheon, *A Theory of Parody: The Teachings of the Twentieth Century Art Forms* (New York: Methuen, 1985), 2.

14. Geoffrey Baym, "The Daily Show: Discursive Integration and the Reinvention of Political Journalism," *Political Communication* 22 (2005): 267.

15. "Jon Stewart Discusses Politics and Comedy," *Fresh Air with Terry Gross*, National Public Radio, 30 September 2004.

16. 7 February 2006.

17. Kevin D. Thompson, "Faking News Alert! Faking News Alert! On the Set of Jon Stewart's 'Daily Show,'" *Palm Beach Post,* 29 October 2004, 1E.

18. Jeffrey P. Jones, *Entertaining Politics: New Political Television and Civic Culture* (Lanham, Md.: Rowman and Littlefield, 2005), 93.

19. Joe Garofoli, "Young Voters Turning to Fake Anchor for Insight," *San Francisco Chronicle,* 21 October 2004, A1.

20. Lynn Smith, "On the Other Side of the Desk, Stewart Puts the Jokes Aside," *Los Angeles Times,* 18 October 2004, E1.

21. Aileen Gallagher, "Queen Bee," *Bust,* December 2005, 72.

22. *Cable and Internet Loom Large in Fragmented Political News Universe,* The Pew Research Center, at http://people-press.org/reports/display. php3?ReportID=200 (accessed 10 April 2004).

23. Geoff Boucher, "Television and Radio: Stewart, Comedy Central Sign Deal," *Los Angeles Times,* 16 February 2005, E1.

24. Lisa de Moraes, "Seriously: Kerry on Comedy Central," *Washington Post,* 24 August 2004, C1.

25. "O'Reilly Discusses 'The Daily Show,'" Fox News, 17 September 2004.

26. Dannagal Goldthwaite Young, "Daily Show Viewers Knowledgeable about Presidential Campaign," National Annenberg Election Survey (Annenberg Public Policy Center), at http://www.annenbergpublicpolicycenter.org/naes/2004_03_ late-night-knowledge-2_9-21_pr.pdf (accessed 12 January 2005).

27. Kevin Glynn, *Tabloid Culture: Trash, Taste, Popular Power and the Transformation of American TV* (Durham, N.C.: Duke University Press, 2000), 233.

28. Jason Mittell, *Genre and Television: From Cop Shows to Cartoons in American Culture* (New York: Routledge, 2004), 178.

29. Richard Schechner, *Between Theater and Anthropology* (Philadelphia: University of Pennsylvania Press, 1985), 6.

5

|||||||||||||||||||||||||||||||||||||||||||||||||||||||||||

# Jon Stewart and *The Daily Show*
## *I Thought You Were Going to Be Funny!*

## *Joanne Morreale*

*The Daily Show* is a discursively integrated text that is part talk show, news, and comedy.[1] In a larger sense, it exemplifies the merging of politics, entertainment, news, and marketing in contemporary American culture. As Jon Stewart noted in an interview for the now-defunct *George* magazine, "The longer I'm doing this I'm coming to learn that entertainment, politics, and the media are really juggling the same balls. We're all going for ratings, so we function by the same rules. What's a political poll except a focus group for a television show?"[2] Stewart expressed his discomfort with this state of affairs during the infamous interview on CNN's political debate program *Crossfire* during the 2004 presidential campaign. He assailed hosts Paul Begala and Tucker Carlson for presenting their predictably partisan, polarized party line positions as if they were substantive debate. In Stewart's words, "You're doing theater when you should be doing debate. You have a responsibility to the public discourse and you fail miserably." When Begala and Carlson responded by criticizing *The Daily Show*'s own lack of substance, Stewart made a distinction between the standards to which a supposedly legitimate debate program should be held and his own by reminding them that his show "follows puppets making phone calls." At the interview's close, Carlson implicitly endorsed Stewart's view by expressing in frustration, "I thought you were going to be funny! Come on, be funny!"[3]

Stewart criticized Carlson and Begala for behaving as entertainers rather than public figures with a responsibility to promote civic discourse, while Carlson responded to Stewart's deliberative arguments by telling him to behave like an entertainer rather than a public figure. Both the *Crossfire* interview and *The Daily Show* itself indicate the blurring of boundaries that differentiate the political speaker, who urges a decision or action, and the entertainer, who aims to delight and amuse.[4] In this context I explore *The Daily Show*'s role in American politics and culture through the Aristotelian concepts of deliberative and epideictic rhetoric. While deliberate rhetoric uses logic and reasoning to influence future actions, epideictic rhetoric aims to increase the intensity of adherence to common beliefs and values that bind a community and, in so doing, prepares the ground for deliberative action. In modern times, deliberative rhetoric has been associated with politics and epideictic rhetoric with entertainment, though as with all forms and genres, their boundaries are not discrete. Throughout history, the orator at the rostrum and the performer on the stage have borrowed from one another to make deliberation entertaining or to give entertainment a political edge.

Considered through this lens, Stewart's refusal to play the entertainer on *Crossfire* was a protest against the increasingly epideictic nature of ostensibly deliberative public discourse. Furthermore, *The Daily Show* is itself epideictic rhetoric that has become increasingly deliberative. Yet, epideictic rhetoric involves more than just entertainment. Contemporary theorists view epideictic rhetoric as a mode of argument that is central to persuasion and political processes. It is about appropriate conduct and values and occurs in contexts where individuals are invited to evaluate their communities and institutions, as well as their own and others' roles and responsibilities within them.[5] *The Daily Show* puts the epideictic rhetoric of news, media, and politics on display and invites evaluation, but Jon Stewart also leads by example when he deliberates—and sometimes debates—with guests during interview sequences.

*The Daily Show* is unique in the way that it is a satirical mode of entertainment that combines epideictic and deliberative rhetoric, while also engaging in deliberative rhetoric in a nonsatirical manner. It is an epideictic form that argues the value of deliberation as it incorporates deliberative techniques. It thus works as a pedagogical tool that teaches critical thinking and judgment to provide the foundation for deliberation. Moreover, its epideictic rhetoric avoids the constraints of propositional argument imposed on deliberative rhetoric and puts the operations of power on display. It is both comic performance and sociopolitical critique that collapses the distinctions between news, politics, and entertainment. Accordingly, it offers both deliberative and epideictic rhetoric through humorous and playful satire, yet it also delivers incisive and serious political talk. As comedian and public figure, Jon Stewart serves as "epideictic orator," making deliberation entertaining as he teaches—and demonstrates—the process of critical reflection that is essential to participatory democracy.

## Satire as Epideictic Rhetoric

In the classical liberal-democratic tradition, all forms of public discourse were considered rhetorical and thus played a central role in shaping collective identity and motivating action. The ancient Greeks privileged deliberative and forensic rhetoric, associated with the assembly and the courts, because these genres employed practical reasoning and rational argument as means to an end. Epideictic rhetoric, associated with civic rituals, was less highly regarded. It focused on praise or blame and shaped collective identity by affirming the ideals and values that bound a community, but it did not argue for a specific action. Deliberative and forensic rhetoric, from antiquity to the present, has been regarded as essential to an informed, educated, democratic citizenry. But epideictic rhetoric, associated with performance and display, evolved into a highly figurative, even fictional, mode of discourse that primarily advertised a speaker's skill.[6] Through most of the twentieth century, scholars relegated epideictic to the realms of aesthetics and entertainment.

In the mid-twentieth century, Chaim Perelman and Kenneth Olbrecht-Tybeca's *The New Rhetoric* reformulated classical Aristotelian theory and emphasized epideictic rhetoric's central function as a form of argumentation aimed at strengthening an audience's adherence to communal values. They wrote that the purpose of epideictic rhetoric is to "appeal to common values, undisputed though not formulated, made by one who is qualified to do so, with a consequent strengthening of those values with a view to possible later action."[7] They argued that epideictic rhetoric is vital to political processes because it "stirs or strengthens in audience members a *disposition* to act, a disposition that will be made salient when confronted with deliberative or forensic arguments."[8]

From the vantage of a literary critic still immersed in traditional definitions of epideictic, Dustin Griffin's *Satire: A Critical Reintroduction* argues that satire, which involves performance and display, is epideictic rhetoric:

> When rhetoric is deployed in the agora, the forum, the law court, or the senate house, it serves as a means to an end—some practical decision. But to the extent that rhetoricians on the platform, or declamatory satirists, are

separated from decisions, they become entertainers. That rhetorical appeal becomes a kind of fiction; this in itself introduces the element of performance and display.[9]

This view does not explain how satire, or epideictic rhetoric, can prepare the ground for deliberative or forensic rhetoric, or how epideictic rhetoric can question or challenge rather than reaffirm values, or even how it may enable communities to imagine and bring about change.[10] Although he does not explicitly address this issue, Griffin suggests satire includes both epideictic and deliberative rhetoric. He argues that satire consists of the epideictic rhetoric of display and play, but that it facilitates critical thinking, speculating, evaluating, and imagining through the rhetoric of inquiry and provocation: "By conducting open-ended speculative inquiry, by provoking and challenging comfortable and received ideas, by unsettling our convictions and occasionally shattering our illusions, by asking questions and raising doubts but not providing answers, satire ultimately has political consequences."[11]

In the case of *The Daily Show,* inquiry and provocation are deliberative tools incorporated into an epideictic form to foster critical thinking and invite evaluation of aspects of the social and political world that might otherwise remain unquestioned. While display and play create meaning without regard for real world consequences, inquiry and provocation work to contest meaning. Bernard Duffy writes:

> The language of epideictic is prone to be least referential and most poetic because the facts themselves are not really at issue. Rather, the affirmation of ethical standards of judgment and behavior serves as the impetus to the creative use of language. . . . While the forensic and deliberative orator are essentially bound to the facts at hand, the epideictic orator need be less concerned with material realities than with the abstract propositions he aims to affirm.[12]

As epideictic rhetoric of display and play, satire relies on the figure of amplification to dramatize and interpret its subject matter, while the more referential rhetoric of inquiry is an "open-ended attempt to discover, explore, survey and clarify," and the rhetoric of provocation seeks to disorient and unsettle by "exposing or demolishing a foolish uncertainty."[13]

Stewart's opening monologue often demonstrates both the performative, playful rhetoric of epideictic and the rhetoric of inquiry as he explores and seeks to clarify the meaning of statements made by government officials. On a basic level, Stewart may explore contested definitions of terms and, in so doing, points to the slippery, rhetorically expedient nature of language. During the Senate confirmation hearings for Attorney General Michael Mukasey, for example, Stewart demonstrated the inconsistencies in public definitions of torture, thereby both mocking and proffering the idea that *The Daily Show*, like all epideictic rhetoric, is "a discourse a community uses to reveal itself to itself."[14] He began: "From time to time we have to have a national conversation with ourselves, ask ourselves tough questions about who we are, what we believe in, is our children learning? Do we in fact want fries with that? Do we torture? Which like any weighty question of ethics is actually a question of semantics."[15] Clips from "official" sources followed that provided different, and contradictory, definitions of torture. George Bush deferred to the U.S. Code, which, Stewart pointed out, defines torture as "an act specifically intended to inflict severe physical or mental pain or suffering." Cut back to George Bush, who said, "And we don't torture." Stewart then pulled a newspaper article from his makeshift codebook, which quoted a Justice Department memo that said, "We are allowed to head slap, expose people to extreme temperatures and simulate drowning." After a diversion where Stewart provided the liberal definition of torture, and a clip where Rudy Giuliani took the Bush administration's position, Mukasey defined torture as "behavior that shocks the conscience." The segment culminated when correspondent Rob Riggle argued that Marine boot camp fit the definition of torture. Throughout this piece, the search for clarification only amplified obfuscations, which was in fact the point. Stewart's ironic comment on waterboarding crystallized the argument: "See this is the trouble with not being barbaric. We always find ourselves in these gray areas. You'd be amazed at how much uncertainty there is in the realm of drowning."

In other cases, set-piece conversations with a rotating staff of comedians who perform as reporters illustrate both the rhetoric of inquiry and provocation in the context of *The Daily Show*'s epideictic frame. These take the form of in-studio discussions with Stewart, who plays the ingénue, the straight man who asks questions that are answered by the somewhat exasperated reporters, who follow a line of thinking to its absurd conclusion. To continue with the semantics of torture, when the Bush administration tried to overturn the Geneva Convention's prohibition against torture, *The Daily Show* played a clip of President Bush stating, "And that Common Article 3 says that there will be 'no outrages against human dignity.' It's very vague. What does it mean? That's a statement that's wide open to interpretation."[16] Stewart later called on "Senior Terror Linguist" John Oliver to explain the ambiguity:

> STEWART: The president is saying that the phrase "outrages against human dignity" is too vague, and he will be the one to interpret what that means. Is that correct?
>
> OLIVER: That's correct, Jon. The president in his never-ending quest for knowledge forces us to examine truths that would otherwise go unexamined. He truly is a philosopher-king. What is dignity? What is truth? If a man is beaten to the floor in a sound proof chamber, does he make a noise? These are the questions that keep men up at night . . . those and brutal sleep deprivation techniques.
>
> STEWART: Are we suggesting then that any interrogation technique could be allowed under the president's discretion under the right circumstances?
>
> OLIVER: You mean like affixing a leech to a man's eyeball, or forcing him to drink horse semen? Would those be torture?
>
> STEWART: Yes.
>
> OLIVER: Wrong Jon. They are scenes from the number one film in America, *Jackass 2* . . . You see Jon, sometimes torture is in the eye of the beholder.

Throughout the interview, Stewart's points take the form of questions, while Oliver's answers mock both George Bush, a president not known for introspection, and, through his illogical analogy to a classic philosophical conundrum, the logic of the Bush administration's position. The posing of questions and answers to get to a "truth" emulates the Socratic method of inquiry, although here the process makes Bush's comments appear ridiculous. Indeed, the entire dialogue mocks the assumption of truth that exists outside of discourse. Oliver's final turn to popular culture also undermines any easy assignment of blame. It is a kind of verbal play that provokes and unsettles the audience rather than provides closure.

According to Griffin, the paradox is a kind of provocation used in satire, conceived as an apparently self-contradictory statement or simply a challenge to received opinion.[17] When *Daily Show* "reporters" conduct pre-taped and edited interviews (their version of the special interest pieces on news), the results are often structured to create the appearance of contradiction. As with "real" news interviews, editors may cut extensive footage down to a few minutes. A common *Daily Show* strategy is to splice together one question with an answer to an entirely different one. For example, when reporter Samantha Bee met with Bush consultant Frank Luntz, the interview was set up to emphasize the use of political doublespeak.[18] When Bee asked him to provide his version of "Drilling for Oil," he replied, "Responsible Exploration for Energy," while "Logging" became "Healthy Forests." When she inquired about his definition of the word "manipulation," he responded, "Explanation and Education." The interview ended when she asked the meaning of "Orwellian," and the camera cut to a flummoxed Luntz. The edited sequence both constructed and exposed the way that politicians exploit the inherent deceptiveness of language. According to Cynthia Sheard, while the deceptiveness of language can be read as tragic in cultures that hold transcendent truths in high esteem, it can be read as "comic" in a culture that holds such truths as unattainable.[19]

The visual paradox is one of *The Daily Show*'s primary satirical techniques, meant to provoke by juxtaposing conflicting comments made at different points of time. *The Daily Show* often uses juxtaposition in a way that realizes both the satiric rhetoric of provocation and Robert Danisch's definition of epideictic rhetoric as "aesthetic practices of display that uncover what lay hidden.[20] In this way, *The Daily Show* disrupts and challenges received opinions by functioning as a kind of investigative journalism that is often missing in mainstream media. For example, when the Democratic Senate began their investigation of the Justice Department for firing nine Bush-appointed attorneys, several of whom were aggressively investigating Republican legislators, *The Daily Show*'s juxtapositions exposed evasions and contradictions in the testimony of Bush administration officials. During the proceedings that began on April 19, 2007, clips repeatedly showed Attorney General Alberto Gonzales responding to questions with "I don't know" or "I don't remember." Senator Patrick Leahy underscored *The Daily Show*'s influence in Washington when he stated on *Meet the Press* that Gonzales would be asked to testify again before Congress, but he didn't want "a string of 'I don't knows' to become fodder for *The Daily Show*."[21]

On July 9, Stewart reprised the story, then showed footage from March 15 where White House spokesman Tony Snow asserted that the firings were performance based and not political. Stewart then explained that confiscated e-mails had revealed "these guys were really pretty good." He wondered aloud, "I wonder how the White House is going to resolve this discrepancy?" The camera cut to a June 13 news conference, where a reporter asked Snow, "How will you reconcile that you . . . said on camera that politics was not involved, this was performance based?" Snow replied, "No, that is something . . . we have never said that." Stewart stared wide-eyed at the camera, then declared: "You'll reconcile it by LYING." The two clips were then replayed side-by-side, giving Snow's contradictory remarks their full unsettling effect. Throughout the Gonzales hearings, *The Daily Show*'s inquiry and provocation made the Bush administrations' evasions and distortions apparent by putting them on display. In this way, its epideictic frame facilitated viewers' critical judgment by "uncovering" the media's lack of critical scrutiny.

## Satire as Critique of Epideictic Politics and Media

*The Daily Show* puts the epideictic rhetoric of news and politics on display, particularly the verbal techniques that work to reaffirm common values. Repetition of familiar slogans, catchphrases, and formulaic terms are essential to epideictic rhetoric as a means to intensify adherence to values and create what Perelman and Obrecht-Tybeca refer to as agreement or "communion."[22] In the context of social and political affairs, particular words chosen are constitutive rather than descriptive; they work to create rather than represent reality. Thus the political strategy of repetition inundates the public with messages that are heard or seen so often they are accepted as true (a classic propaganda technique). By replaying clips of political talking points, *The Daily Show* illustrates the strategic use of repetition to construct reality and emphasizes the way that the media simply reproduce the "official" version of events. For example, when the Democratic Congress gave President Bush the funding he requested for a troop surge in Iraq, but held him to a definite withdrawal date, he took his case to the American Legion Post 177:

> BUSH (*April 17, 2007, to the crowd*): They're pushing legislation that would undercut our troops just as we're beginning to make progress in Baghdad.
> *Cut to January 2006, where Bush addresses another crowd:* That's progress and it's important progress, and it's an important part of our strategy to win in Iraq.
> *Cut to Bush, November 2005:* Iraq has made incredible political progress.
> *Cut to Bush, October 2005:* Iraqis are making inspiring progress.
> *Cut to Bush, September 2005:* Iraq has made incredible political progress.
> *Cut to Bush, April 2005:* I believe we're making really solid progress in Iraq.

*Cut to Bush, July 2003:* We're slowly but surely making progress.

*Cut to Bush, May 2003:* In the battle of Iraq the United States and our allies have prevailed.

Stewart's ironic commentary dissects the inverted logic of these re- marks. Irony, where one seeks to convey the opposite of what one says, is the engine of satire that works, according to Perelman and Obrecht- Tybeca, as indirect argument.[23] "Wait a minute," he said. "I've figured this out. We've been following the logic of time as it goes forward. What a classic mistake. Linear time is so pre-9/11!" Viewers obviously get the joke, while they are also made aware of having heard the same vacant claim for "progress"—time and time again. Bradford Vivian describes words such as "progress" as "the recitation of cherished terms"; these are "positively valued words whose constant evocation makes them integral resources of epideictic rhetoric."[24] Here Stewart's repetition of the repetition renders it powerless.

*The Daily Show* also uses the rhetorical figure of amplification to dem- onstrate the inanity of news coverage, particularly in the "Moment of Zen" that closes each show. Here a brief clip from a humorous or incongruous story may reappear, such as the staid John Ashcroft singing his own com- position, "Let the Eagle Soar" or the tightly wound Karl Rove doing a hip- hop dance at the 2007 Press Correspondents Dinner. Or particularly egre- gious examples of muddled logic are presented without comment, such as Fox reporter Laura Ingraham stating, "The average American out there loves the show *24* . . . in my mind that's as close to a national referendum that it's okay to use tough tactics against high level Al Qaeda operatives as we're gonna get."[25] These examples, presented to a community of like- minded viewers, use ridicule as argumentative tool to point to the absur- dity of what passes for discourse, political or otherwise. Perelman and Obrecht-Tybeca suggest that the ridiculous is what deserves to be greeted by "exclusive" laughter. They add: "Exclusive laughter is the response to the breaking of an accepted rule, a way of condemning eccentric behav- ior which is not deemed sufficiently important or dangerous to be con- demned by other means."[26]

Devices of amplification also parody the typical style and structure of news. Parody and satire often work together; according to Griffin, parody occurs when satire "invades" an already existing form.[27] To par- ody the news, *The Daily Show* relies on the viewer's familiarity with its iconography, style, and narrative structure, as well as *The Daily Show*'s excessive caricature of them. Parody shows the discrepancy between the "official" presentation of events and *The Daily Show*'s and implicitly critiques the way that news is itself an epideictic construction of spectacle rather than a way to provide an understanding, evaluation, and constructive critique of the democratic process. The "news update" provides one example: a screen behind Stewart's shoulder provides a "window on the world" that replays images while Stewart comments on them. Unlike the "real" news, however, *The Daily Show* may "play" by intercutting news footage and invented material or by digitally altering images for the sake of a joke. Instead of presenting one viewpoint, stories often consist of a montage of video clips taken from different news sources in order to demonstrate the media's complicity in coverage of orchestrated political events, or the way that news focuses on the sensational and spectacular. While news anchors simply recount events, *The Daily Show* makes media coverage of events its topic, thus illuminating the politically complicit nature of the news without making a deliberative claim to that effect.

One of *The Daily Show*'s classic parodic critiques concerned the media's intense focus on Terry Schiavo, a comatose woman whose husband wanted to discontinue the life support system that kept her alive, despite her parents' objections. When on March 24, 2005, the Florida Supreme Court supported Michael Schiavo's decision, Stewart announced somberly, "The Terry Schiavo feeding tube will soon be removed from the cable news networks. It will be difficult for them. Throughout this ordeal, CNN, Fox, and MSNBC have served as our nation's conscience, helping our saddened nation more fully understand this complex ordeal."

The Schiavo story illustrated the way that the dominant discourse on television attempts to manage collective emotions. According to Vivian, "in our so called society of the spectacle, public events . . . increasingly are organized to unite an otherwise fractured citizenry in a dynamic affective experience."[28] Stewart's metaphor amplified the news media's dependence on a sensational story and highlighted their attempt to direct sympathies in a way that depoliticized a political issue and excluded the need for deliberation. *The Daily Show*'s coverage made apparent the way the news uses epideictic rhetoric as argument, in this case to present the conservative pro-life position as natural and common sense. For example, magnified on the video screen behind Stewart, photographs taken from the news showed a live and vibrant Terry Schiavo rather than a hospitalized

woman in a coma. Stewart made no deliberative claims but allowed viewers to infer his position from his ironic comments. In a deadpan voice,
he announced, "The one thing I actually should say cable news does do is
help humanize the participants." Clips then featured various news pundits
blaming Michael Schiavo or the judge who supported him, without any
dissenting opinion. The piece culminated when John Edward, a psychic
medium from the television show *Crossing Over*, made an "expert" appearance on *FOX and Friends* and asserted that Terry Schiavo's soul could
see and hear everything. *The Daily Show*'s selection of these clips, leading to Edward's appearance, illustrated the rhetorical figure of reasoning
called the enthymeme. Jeffrey Walker defines the enthymeme as a climac-
tic increase of "emotively significant ideas (or images) that work to motivate a passional identification with the speaker's stance that would strike
audiences as an 'abrupt' and decisive flash of insight."[29] The buildup of images in this sequence, interpreted by Stewart's ironic remarks and asides,
elicited critical judgment about media bias while intensifying viewers' adherence to his position. The rhetorical enthymeme, which leads viewers
to an insight that is directed but seemingly their own, is *The Daily Show*'s
signature. Through its use, *The Daily Show* turns the epideictic rhetoric of
the media back on itself and fosters a community of critical viewers.

Throughout, *The Daily Show* parodied the news by presenting exaggerated, selective images to make a point. Unlike other forms of epideictic
rhetoric, *The Daily Show* used parody to fulfill the traditional epideictic
function of blame; it ridiculed and indicted both the news media and the
official discourse the media reiterated. It critiqued the idea that this was
news rather than exploitation, while enabling the audience to get the argument. It highlighted both the media's complicity with the Bush administration's conservative agenda and the extent to which the media would
go to turn a tragic personal story into a media event that would capture
ratings. While the news reports merely invited viewers to participate as
spectators who could watch the drama play out (the traditional role for
audiences of epideictic rhetoric), parody served here as a constitutive epideictic technique that could create a community of like-minded viewers
dissociated from "official" discourse.

## *Jon Stewart as Epideictic Orator*

I have argued here that satire is an epideictic form that incorporates deliberative techniques. In the case of *The Daily Show,* the rhetorics of display, play, inquiry, and provocation work together to promote critical thinking and judgment. Yet *The Daily Show,* as an epideictic form, largely avoids making overt deliberative arguments. When Stewart does so, he breaks with the form and defies generic expectations. Most often, *The Daily Show* relies on inquiry and provocation to question or unsettle but not to proclaim, or relies on the humor and indirection of play and display to make its appeals. But satire has always been associated with both persuasion and performance. It is a mode of rhetorical argument and a display of wit and skill, and both satire and oratory depend on the speaker's (or satirist's) ability to make an argument convincing. Thus, a full account of how *The Daily Show* works as argument must take the "speaker" into consideration. Although a team of writers creates *The Daily Show,* and the faux correspondents take on some of the workload, Jon Stewart is the host who addresses and "stands in" for viewers; his wit and skill drives the program.

The figure of the jester, which has close associations with both satire and oratory, has often been invoked to describe Jon Stewart. Al Gore, on the show to promote his book *The Assault on Reason* (which argues that facts and reason no longer play a part in public decision-making), congratulated Stewart for taking on the role of the jester who "speaks truth to power."[30] Jeffrey Jones writes:

> Stewart gets to play the fool by using the words of those in power against them, revealing "truth" by a simple reformulation of their statements. Stewart, then, becomes the court jester, cleverly positioned on the public stage to question what the rulers have said through his "harmless" reassessment of what they (and their stenographers to power) have configured reality to be.[31]

Jesters, historically associated with epideictic rhetoric, have always used humor to manage deliberative or forensic settings or have used their position to make political points while given the freedom to speak what is otherwise forbidden.[32] Epideictic rhetoric is informed by an ethical sense grounded in *kairos* that compels an individual or group to say exactly what needs to be said when it needs to be said. Stewart is often commended for laying bare the absurdities that pass for common sense, and as a comedian, he is a master of the jest, which is both verbal play and an aggressive "barb." He uses many of the tropes associated with epideictic rhetoric, such as the rhetorical question, apostrophe, imaginary direct address to the audience, or the pronoun "we" to establish rapport and get the audience to actively participate.[33] Also, like the court jester, Stewart preserves decorum so that his words are not too threatening. He creates a feeling of inclusiveness with the audience. He appears as "one of us" who can't believe the absurdity of official discourse, while he also promotes civility by chastising studio audiences who vocalize their disapproval of guests. Even with guests with whom he disagrees, Stewart is apt to follow a sharp comment or probing question with a disclaimer to defuse a potentially uncomfortable situation.

Through Stewart's body language—the intonations, gestures, and facial expressions that mark him as a "clown"—and his self-deprecating humor that deflates any sense of self-importance, he disavows his own seriousness and suggests that he, too, might be thought silly, and he undermines his own claims to authority. When he presents the news, he breaks from the serious by mugging to the camera. He mimics (badly) the voices and postures of figures such as George Bush and Dick Cheney. He often stops in the middle of a bad routine, breaking frame as he shakes his head in disbelief. The evening after a fractious interview with former U.N. Ambassador John Bolton, he stated, "It turns out the theme of that interview was that I am . . . *frequently, ignorantly, woefully* . . . wrong. Now that's nothing I wasn't already aware of and told throughout my childhood and teenhood."[34] An audience reaction ensued, to which he responded, "Settle down . . . it's not my real life we're talking about, people. It's my *comedy* life." He delivers the lines with a congenial smile, managing to appear authentic by denying his authenticity. Or, when Stewart told Chris Matthews that his new self-help book was "a recipe for sadness," and later called it "fascist," Matthews angrily exploded, "This is a book interview from hell! This is the worst interview I've ever had!"[35] The next evening, in mock dialogue with Matthews, Stewart announced, "Sir, I'm not even sure you were the worst interview I'd done that week." He then showed a clip from an interview with a Blackwater private sector soldier who had been in Iraq. Stewart asked him, "What is the issue if somebody is an OK soldier and looking to make a little extra money? Why is that such a terrible thing?" He then criticized himself with clips from various news sources reporting, "Blackwater guards fired on civilians without being provoked" and "Eleven Iraqis were killed in a shootout with Blackwater contractors."

In this way, through self-deprecation and self-criticism, Stewart makes clear that he, too, is not to be trusted, that he, too, is not the source of authority, that his own vocabulary is not the final word. Like the wise fool, he is aware that no vocabulary can fully represent reality, that any selection is also a deflection. *The Daily Show* highlights the artificiality of all discourse. Stewart and his cadre of "correspondents" do not offer an alternative version of reality but leave open the possibility for its creation.

Interviews both on and off the show make clear that, despite Stewart's critique of politics and media, he aims to edify rather than destroy and to praise as well as blame. His mock history textbook, *America: The Book*, ends with a chapter that reminds readers that the American system, despite its flaws, is still the finest in the world. In his first show upon returning to the air after 9/11, a tearful Stewart declared that he saw his show as both a privilege and a luxury:

> This is a country that allows for open satire, and I know that sounds basic and it sounds as though it goes without saying—but that's really what this whole situation is about. It's the difference between closed and open. It's the difference between free and burdened and we don't take that for granted here by any stretch of the imagination and our show has changed. I don't doubt that. What it's become, I don't know.[36]

*The Daily Show* did, indeed, become more political after 9/11, with fewer celebrities and more political guests per week. But publicly, Stewart plays down his show as an agent of change and continues to insist that it is a comedy with no mission and no journalistic responsibility. He claims that the show is designed to interact with rather than replace news and that the role of satire is to provide cathartic relief rather than promote social change.[37]

Perelman and Obrecht-Tybeca write that in epideictic oratory, the speaker turns educator. He "deals with premises that are not controversial, and has been commissioned by a community to be the spokesperson for the values it recognizes, and as such, enjoys the prestige attached to his office."[38] But they add that he can "abuse" his position as educator and turn "propagandist" by advocating controversial positions and seeking to alter attitudes. While this charge may be leveled at FOX and other news stations that *The Daily Show* targets, Stewart is not a propagandist. But in a sense he does abuse his position as epideictic educator and turns deliberative. Stated less pejoratively, he "deforms" epideictic by incorporating deliberation. While deliberation is not controversial, and is assumed to be a fundamental democratic value, many critics argue that it is disappearing from the public sphere.[39] Stewart offers deliberation as an invitation and opportunity for engagement, as a means to link criticism and judgment with the possibility of change.

Stewart's role as educator who "deforms" the epideictic genre appears most clearly in the final segment of the show, which combines humor and serious discussion as Stewart interviews an author, celebrity, or public figure. This section of the show often features members of political, legislative, or journalistic establishments or their critics. In fact, *The Daily Show* is one of the few places on television where serious books are still promoted and discussed.[40] *The Daily Show* has become a requisite campaign stop for presidential candidates, and both John Edwards and Bill Richardson announced their candidacies on the show. Pakistan's President Pervez Musharraf was the first head of state to appear. *The Daily Show*'s satire covers both the left and the right, and guests include both Republicans and Democrats. According to Stewart, "People don't understand that we are not warriors in anyone's army. We're a group of people that really feel that they want to write jokes about the absurdity that we see in government and the world, and that's it."[41] Stewart's interviews are almost always about conversation rather than confrontation, about encouraging dialogue and allowing for a multiplicity of viewpoints. It is "strong" discourse that operates in the realms of "debate, discussion, dialogue, dispute," and it occurs "in an open context that aims to stir things up."[42]

Yet, as the political landscape has become more divisive, Stewart's challenging of supporters of the Bush administration has become more prevalent, more cutting, and less humorous. In an interview with former U.N. Ambassador John Bolton, their disagreements clearly revealed Stewart's political philosophy and his frustration with the Bush administration.[43] When Bolton claimed that the president ought to be surrounded by people who are philosophically attuned to his way of thinking, Stewart countered by asking, "What about Lincoln, who most people would agree was a great president? He chose people from varying points of view, that truly disagreed with him, and empowered them." The interview became uncharacteristically testy, turning from discussion to debate, as Stewart continually defended the value of listening to diverse viewpoints, and Bolton repeatedly told Stewart that he was mistaken or wrong. The interview disconcerted Stewart enough so that the following

Fig. 5.1. Jon Stewart and Senator John McCain debate
Iraq war policy on *The Daily Show*.

night he "phoned" Lincoln historian Doris Kearns Goodwin to confirm
the factuality of his remarks.

The next month, in an interview with Senator John McCain, Stewart
declared in characteristic fashion that they were going to go "mano y . . .
somewhat less of a mano."[44] Yet the interview was uncharacteristic in that
it exemplified Stewart's decision to shift from epideictic satire to deliberative debate. Stewart asked McCain to defend each of the Bush administration's talking points regarding the Iraq war (figure 5.1). When McCain refused to move beyond the administration's talking points, their discussion
became contentious when McCain used the argument that criticizing the
war was tantamount to not supporting the troops:

> STEWART: No one's saying that they shouldn't be proud of their service—
> this is a very unfair way to deal with this issue because—Let me explain it
> this way: what I'm saying is, it's less supportive of them—Settle down for a
> second!
>
> MCCAIN: No, *you* settle down. That they're fighting in a war that they lost.
> That's not fair to them.

STEWART: What I believe is *less* supportive to the good people who believe they're fighting a great cause, is to not give them a strategy that makes their success possible, and to not—

MCCAIN: We now have a strategy. Yes, we do.

STEWART: Adding 10,000 people to Baghdad—add 350,000, and you might have a shot.

MCCAIN: I don't *know* that that strategy will succeed, but we do have a new strategy. It's a fact.

STEWART: All I'm saying is, you cannot look a soldier in the eye and say, "Questioning the President is less supportive to you than extending your tour three months, when you should be coming home to your family." And that's not fair to put on people that criticize. And you know I love you, and I respect your service, and would never question any of that, and this is not about questioning the troops and their ability to fight and their ability to be supported, and that is what the administration does, and that is almost criminal.

In an ironic twist, the comedy show interview became a news story, reported on CNN and MSNBC. In an interview with Bill Moyers, Stewart admitted,

I do not particularly enjoy those types of interviews, because I have a great respect for Senator McCain, and I hate the idea that our conversation became just two people talking over each other at one point. But I also thought in my head that I would love to do an interview that just sort of deconstructed the talking points of Iraq, the idea that is this really the conversation we're having about this war?[45]

As the McCain interview indicated, sometimes deliberation calls for confrontation. But Stewart's public comments seem to reject the show's responsibility to politicize viewers or actively promote a constructive vision to replace its deconstruction of the world as it is. In reference to *The Daily Show*'s objectives, he has stated, "We'd love to be good and competent at attacking our world. We don't have a sense of a new world order and how we'd like it to be."[46] But it is clear that he is committed to the principles of participatory democracy, and *The Daily Show*'s epideictic rhetoric is a prelude to responsible critical judgment and action in the world. While the text of the show incorporates deliberation through the rhetoric of inquiry and provocation, the interview sequences, and Jon Stewart as public figure, often make deliberative arguments that promote beliefs if not actions. It would be bad faith to disconnect words and deeds; to praise deliberation without deliberating is practice without praxis.

## Conclusion

Overall, the categories of deliberative and epideictic rhetoric provide a means through which to understand, analyze, and evaluate *The Daily Show* as satiric epideictic that is both entertaining and a powerful critique of the epideictic rhetoric that constitutes news and politics in contemporary American culture. In a media landscape where most news, politics, and public affairs programs are epideictic spectacles, *The Daily Show's* deliberative rhetoric stands out in stark relief. While most contemporary political discourse uses epideictic rather than deliberative discourse as a means to discourage critical thinking, *The Daily Show's* satiric rhetoric both praises the value of critical thinking and blames the sociopolitical order. In so doing, it is both critical and educative. Through satire, parody, and irony, it reveals the contradictions, hypocrisies, and follies that shape our cultural milieu and counters the polemics and depoliticization that characterize social and political discourse.

While cynicism can be one response to satire, *The Daily Show's* combination of deliberative and epideictic rhetoric combats cynicism. Their interplay work together to produce a community of critical viewers who are poised for action in the world. It is both an artful rhetorical performance that impresses with its comedic wit, and incisive social criticism that teaches the skills of critical thinking and judgment that are essential to a participatory democracy. By leading through example, Jon Stewart and *The Daily Show* teach that deliberation is not a means to an end but an end in itself. Discussion, dialogue, provocation, and questioning are valued for their own sake—not because they lead to truth but because they foster a community able to discern untruth.

NOTES

1. Geoffrey Baym, "*The Daily Show:* The Discursive Integration and the Reinvention of Political Journalism," *Political Communication* 22 (2005): 259.

2. Allison Adato, " Anchor Astray," *George,* May 2000, at http://home.earthlink.net/~aladato/anchor.html.

3. Interview with Jon Stewart, *Crossfire* with Paul Begala and Tucker Carlson, 15 October 2004.

4. Dustin Griffin, *Satire: A Critical Reintroduction* (Kentucky: University Press of Kentucky, 1994), 71.

5. Cynthia Sheard, "The Public Value of Epideictic Rhetoric," *College English* 58 (1996): 771.

6. Ibid., 767.

7. Chaim Perelman and Kenneth Obrecht-Tybeca, *The New Rhetoric: A Treatise on Argumentation* (Notre Dame, Ind.: University of Notre Dame Press, 1969), 53.

8. Ibid., 50.

9. Griffin, *Satire,* 160.

10. Sheard makes this argument in "The Public Value of Epideictic Rhetoric."

11. Griffin, *Satire,* 160.

12. Bernard K. Duffy, "The Platonic Functions of Epideictic Rhetoric," *Philosophy and Rhetoric* 16 (1983): 90–91.

13. Griffin, *Satire,* 39, 52.

14. Sheard, "Public Value of Epideictic Rhetoric," 775.

15. 1 November 2007.

16. 25 May 2007.

17. Griffin, *Satire,* 53.

18. 19 April 2005.

19. Sheard, "Public Value of Epideictic Rhetoric," 778.

20. Robert Danisch, "Power and the Celebration of the Self: Michel Foucault's Epideictic Rhetoric," *Southern Communication Journal* 71, no. 3 (2006): 293.

21. 8 July 2007.

22. Perelman and Obrecht-Tybeca, *New Rhetoric,* 51–56.

23. Ibid., 207.

24. Bradford Vivian, "Neoliberal Epideictic: Rhetorical Form and Commemorative Politics on September 11, 2002," *Quarterly Journal of Speech* 92, no. 1 (2006): 9.

25. 20 September 2006

26. Perelman and Obrecht-Tybeca, *New Rhetoric,* 205–6.

27. Griffin, *Satire,* 102.

28. Vivian, "Neoliberal Epideictic," 15.

29. Jeffrey Walker, "The Body of Persuasion: A Theory of the Enthymeme," *College English* 51 (1989): 59.

30. 9 July 2007.

31. Jeffrey Jones, *Entertaining Politics: New Political Television and Civic Culture* (Lanham, Md.: Rowman and Littlefield, 2005), 113.

32. Chris Holcomb, *Mirth Making: The Rhetorical Discourse on Jesting in Early Modern England* (Columbia: University of South Carolina Press, 2001), 201.

33. Richard Graff and Wendy Winn, "Presencing 'Communion' in Chaim Perelman's New Rhetoric," *Philosophy and Rhetoric* 39, no. 1 (2006): 54.

34. 21 March 2007.

35. 2 October 2007.

36. 21 September 2001.

37. Michael Piafsky, "An Interview with the Writers of America," *Missouri Review* 28, no. 1 (2005): 95.

38. Perelman and Obrecht-Tybeca, *New Rhetoric,* 52–53.

39. G. Thomas Goodnight, "The Personal, Technical, and Public Spheres of Argument," in *Contemporary Rhetorical Theory: A Reader,* ed. John Lucaites, Celeste Condit, and Sally Caudill (New York: Guilford, 1998), 252.

40. Julie Bosman, "Serious Book to Peddle? Don't Laugh, Try a Comedy Show," *New York Times,* 25 February 2007, D3.

41. Interview with Jon Stewart, *Bill Moyer's Journal,* PBS, 27 April 2007.

42. Sheard, "Public Value of Epideictic Rhetoric," 787.

43. 20 March 2007.

44. 24 April 2007.

45. Interview with Jon Stewart, *Bill Moyers Journal,* PBS, 27 April 2007. Transcript available at http://www.truthout.org/article/bill-moyers-talks-with-jon-stewart.

46. Interview with Jon Stewart, *Charlie Rose Show,* PBS, 29 September 2004.

|||||||||||||||||||||||||||||||||||||||||||||||||||||||||

# 6

# Stephen Colbert's Parody of the Postmodern

## *Geoffrey Baym*

It wouldn't seem to be the usual fare for the late-night talk show, a point made more acute by the 1950s imagery of a June Cleaver-style home-maker—imagery that, to a twenty-first century mind, oozes with political incorrectness. Even more confusing are the guests that night—Jane Fonda and Gloria Steinem (neither the June Cleaver type), whom the host introduces as "two of the most special American ladies." The host, of course, is improv comic Stephen Colbert, the show his self-celebratory *Colbert Report*. Like most topics on his show, Colbert's salute to the American lady is complex—a multilayered satirical exploration of feminism in contemporary society that says many things, and maybe means some of them. The Fonda/Steinem interview is a particularly intriguing moment of political television. After his tongue-in-cheek introduction, Colbert describes the two as "activists, authors, icons of the women's movement," who are promoting their new talk radio network targeting women.

The interview begins in a serious posture, with all three sitting upright at the desk and Colbert asking them to explain their reasons for launching political radio for women. Before Steinem can answer the first question, though, Colbert interrupts her. "I don't mean to interrupt," he says, "but . . . let's go to the kitchen!" From there the segment shifts abruptly to a cooking set with the three of them now wearing aprons. As gentle music plays in the background, Colbert begins again. "It is fall," he says, "and what better time to explore the bounty of the American harvest than when there's a little nip in the air." This time, he continues, the ladies have joined him to make that "greatest of American deserts," the apple pie. The transition is remarkable: from a masculine form of television reminiscent of the Sunday morning public affairs talk shows to an overtly feminized tradition of programming, the weekday morning "breakfast TV" largely designed to give housewives helpful tips on keeping house. If the former represents television's attempt to facilitate the *public* sphere—that domain of politics, rational-critical discourse, and reasoned argument—the latter represents its efforts to celebrate the *private* sphere: the affective realm of the family and the home.[1] The play here on the gendered nature of televisual forms is further emphasized by the title card displayed on the screen: "Cooking with Feminists," which itself constructs a juxtaposition between seemingly incompatible terms.

The segment that follows crisscrosses the boundaries between masculine and feminine, public and private, reasoned and silly. Colbert alternates between instructing the two feminist "icons" on how to bake a pie and providing them a forum for the serious discussion of gender, feminism, and contemporary political discourse. "The polarizing, conflict-ridden, argumentative, judgmental tone of most talk radio now does not appeal to women," Fonda explains, just before Colbert asks her to knead the dough. The segment becomes further complicated when Steinem calls attention to Colbert's apron, which features a pair of red lips and the motto "kiss the cook." On cue, Fonda leans in and seductively kisses Colbert on the lips. To that, a befuddled Colbert replies: "I like you Fonda, you smell good." He regains his composure enough to ask Steinem if their radio network is "going to be Rush Limbaugh for the ladies." She responds: "There is no Rush Limbaugh for the ladies. Conflict is good, but it's not the entire world divided into two. There might be ten sides to an issue, or 24 sides to an issue." When Colbert satirically prods, "Don't we need to simplify the answers, don't we need to make it something that people can understand very easily?" she counters: "No, I think that people can handle complexity. Look, this is a complicated time, it's not just right or wrong."[2]

Steinem is right that these are complicated times, a point rarely clearer than when trying to make sense of *The Colbert Report,* Comedy Central's spin-off from *The Daily Show* in which the comedian plays the role of a ludicrous right-wing pundit who insists on the bright line between right (him) and wrong (anyone who might disagree). Working simultaneously on a number of apparently contradictory levels, the "Cooking with Feminists" segment illustrates *The Colbert Report*'s strategy of interweaving humor with serious talk, its dualities of form and discourse, and its complex discussion and performance of a wide variety of sociopolitical events, issues, and problematics. As such, it speaks to the complexity of an emerging kind of political TV that defies attempts to pigeonhole it into the generic categories that once ordered television and wider public political discussion, and as such, has become a new face of public affairs media in a discursively integrated media environment.[3]

My aim in this chapter is to explore how *The Colbert Report* works as an emergent form of political media and to consider its contribution to contemporary political discourse. To do that, I begin with the textual development of the Colbert character that emerges on *The Daily Show*. I then examine the intertextual parodic character of Colbert, which cannot be understood apart from Bill O'Reilly, the "real" right-wing pundit who provides the pretext for *The Colbert Report*. Finally, I explore Colbert's use of irony to critique a postmodern episteme that rejects reason and modernist knowledge claims and its corresponding politics of spectacle and spin.

## *"Ironically, I'm Stephen Colbert"*

In the midst of the 2004 Bush/Kerry presidential race, the faux correspondent Stephen Colbert found himself filling in for Jon Stewart as anchor of *The Daily Show*. He began that night with a brief but revealing introduction. "Welcome to *The Daily Show with Jon Stewart,*" he said, "Ironically, I'm Stephen Colbert. . . . If my presence here makes the fake news any less credible, I've done my job."[4] Although the *performer* Stephen Colbert has had a career dating back some 20 years, the *character* of Stephen Colbert—the enigmatically foolish and deeply ironic television personality whose blatant disregard both for accuracy and political correctness often results in piercing humor—was crafted during his seven-year tenure on *The Daily Show,* the program that honed the art of the so-called *fake* news. As I have argued elsewhere, though, the concept of fake news is inadequate in describing *The Daily Show* (see also chapter 4 in this volume).[5] Instead, I have suggested the program can be better understood as a kind of alternative journalism, one enabled by the ongoing collapse of boundaries, not just among news and entertainment or media genres and televisual forms but among *discursive domains* and the conceptual systems they produce.

In a discursively integrated media landscape dominated by various versions of local news happy talk, network "news lite," and cable TV punditry, "real" news has become harder to find or to define. If news was once expected to be the watchdog, the "hot light" of public accountability, in a post–September 11 environment, a docile, corporatized press corps largely has refused to confront an executive branch and its media guard dogs whose rhetoric most often is designed to manipulate mass opinion rather than inform public debate.[6] From such a perspective, *The Daily Show* can be understood not as fake but as *oppositional* news, one that uses humor to provide the kind of critical challenge that is all but absent in the so-called real news.

The character of Stephen Colbert took shape in this context. There he often played the role of reporter-qua-cheerleader for the Bush administration. As such, he appears in the midst of the 2004 Abu Ghraib torture scandal to address administration accusations that the problem lay not with torture but with a press corps that would dare report it. Colbert suggests that it is unfair to blame "a few bad apples":

> The journalists I know love America. But now all anybody wants to talk about is the bad journalists, the journalists who hurt America. But what they don't talk about is all the amazingly damaging things we haven't reported on. Who didn't uncover the flaws in our pre-war intelligence? Who gave a free pass on the Saddam-Al Qaeda connection? Who dropped Afghanistan from the headlines at the first whiff of this Iraqi snipe-hunt? The United States Press Corps. That's who.[7]

Here one sees the ironic approach that comes to define Colbert's humor. His speech is double-layered; his praise for the journalists who "love America" quickly becomes scathing condemnation of the press's refusal to engage in critical inquiry. But its meaning lies below the surface, or between the lines—it is nonliteral speech whose critical edge always exists at a measure of interpretive distance.

The idea for an entire show based on this Colbert character grew out of a series of spoof commercials *The Daily Show* aired in August of 2004. These promised an "exciting new *Daily Show* spin-off," a program to be hosted by an angry, know-it-all Colbert, crafted in the image of Fox's Bill O'Reilly. The first fake promo features a sequence of split screens in which Colbert appears to be interviewing newsmakers—John Edwards, John McCain, and Donald Rumsfeld—and in each one ordering the imaginary production crew to "cut his mic," a jab at O'Reilly, who can only tolerate disagreement up to a certain point before he either orders his guests to "shut up" or turns off their microphones so they can no longer speak. In the second fake promo, Colbert promises to "tear the news a new one" and concludes that, "right or wrong, I'm right, and you're wrong."[8] With the conceptual seed thus planted, and encouraged by Comedy Central executives who wanted a vehicle to further capitalize on the increasing popularity of *The Daily Show*, *The Colbert Report* went on air in October 2005 to an audience that has consistently remained well over 1 million people each night.

### "Make Me a Spaniel at Thy Gate, Bill"

Although the aesthetic of *The Colbert Report* has changed drastically since its first conceptualization on *The Daily Show*, its central premise remains Colbert's parody of O'Reilly, the archetypical right-wing pundit who, like Colbert, once played the role of reporter on a hybrid news and entertainment program—in this case, the early tabloid show *Inside Edition*. Now, of course, O'Reilly, whom Colbert glowingly calls "Papa Bear," is the flagship commentator for Fox News, itself another variation of discursively integrated reality-based TV. Colbert insists that he is crafted in O'Reilly's image, patterning his verbal performance and nonverbal mannerisms after him. This is most evident on the evening of the "Pundit Exchange," when the two appear as guests on each other's program. On the *O'Reilly Factor*, Colbert showers "Papa Bear" with praise, insisting that it is "an amazing honor" to be "at the foot of the master. Make me a spaniel at thy gate, Bill," he proclaims.[9] Later that evening, he tells his own audience that because O'Reilly finally is a guest on the *Report*, he now "gets to open the last door on my Bill O'Reilly advent calendar!" Colbert here proudly displays a fabricated advent calendar: a nativity scene populated by Fox News personalities, with an image of Colbert's face affixed to the Virgin Mary and O'Reilly's to the baby Jesus.[10]

Be he Papa Bear, the master, or perhaps Jesus himself, O'Reilly is the "pretext" for *The Colbert Report*, to which the parody continuously refers. To understand the Colbert character, one must begin with the O'Reilly character, a made-for-television construct that proclaims itself to be a "culture warrior" in the fight against liberalism. His interview with Colbert during the Pundit Exchange was part of his ongoing segment titled "Culture War," which he explained to Colbert later on the *Report* is a struggle "between secular progressives such as yourself . . . and traditionalists like me"[11] (figure 6.1). The self-appointed title of "warrior" might be an overstatement, but O'Reilly undoubtedly is a propagandist in the traditional sense of the word. Research from Mike Conway and his colleagues has

Fig. 6.1. On The Colbert Report, Stephen Colbert's "Papa Bear,"
Bill O'Reilly lectures Colbert on being a culture warrior fighting against
the danger of "secular progressives" such as Colbert, while Colbert insists
that he would follow O'Reilly blindly anywhere.

revealed that in his "'lalking Points Memo," O'Reilly constructs a fearful
and simplistic world of heroes and villains fighting over some imagined
American way of life. His most recurrent villains—the evildoers—are, of
course, terrorists and illegal immigrants, but the bad people in O'Reilly's
world also include academics, non-Christians, and both left-leaning and
politically neutral media. By contrast, he insists the virtuous are the right-
leaning media, Republicans, the Bush administration, Christians, and a
vague notion of the American people.[12] As such, his ironically titled "No
Spin Zone" functions as a key circuit in the generation of what Murray
Edelman refers to as "political spectacle": a form of right-wing political
artistry that imagines problems and invents enemies to sell a predeter-
mined, but often undisclosed, political and economic agenda.[13]

    In turn, Colbert parrots O'Reilly's rhetoric and his techniques. He
plays the role of the megalomaniacal and xenophobic demagogue who insists he is objective while regularly offering proclamations such as, "We
have a very simple system in America. Republicans believe in God, and

Democrats believe in a welfare state where we tax the rich."[14] Often *sounding* like O'Reilly, Colbert regularly refers to him, quotes him, and replays clips from his show. Thus O'Reilly explains to his audience the night of the Pundit Exchange that Colbert "owes everything to me," that he "tries to convince people that he *is* me."[15] What O'Reilly fails to acknowledge, however, is that the imitation is *parody,* a critical examination that targets the absurdities of its referent and invites its audience to "examine, evaluate and re-situate the hypotextual material."[16] Lest there be any confusion about his parodic intentions, Colbert ends the Pundit Exchange in revealing fashion. He proudly displays a microwave oven he says he stole from O'Reilly's "green room." He then holds up a DVD that he says contains the two interviews, now preserved for posterity. For "safe keeping," he puts the DVD in the microwave and then turns it on. The camera zooms in on the microwave as the DVD begins to spark and finally blows up—a dramatic gesture that confirms that, at least in this case, imitation is not always flattery.[17]

The juxtaposition between Colbert's praise of O'Reilly and its metaphoric destruction serves as an exemplar of the duality that runs throughout *The Colbert Report.* If political satire is the art of juxtaposition between apparently incompatible propositions, Colbert's ironic performance is continuously double voiced—his literal language always placed in juxtaposition with its implied meaning. This technique is most evident in Colbert's "Word" segment, an explicit parody of O'Reilly's "Talking Points Memo." The Word mimics the form of the Talking Points, with Colbert appearing in close-up on one side of the screen, his finger regularly wagging at the camera, while the other side of the screen displays key words from the monologue. But unlike O'Reilly's Talking Points, in which the on-screen text simply repeats his argument, on Colbert's Word, the written text provides an unspoken voice, a second level of meaning that often contradicts, challenges, and undermines the spoken words (figure 6.2).

One sees this in his exploration of then–Virginia Senator George Allan's proposal to replace the word "will," as proposed by a Democrat, with the word "shall" in an upcoming piece of legislation. Colbert suggests that there are "red words and blue words. 'Shall' is a red word, strong and authoritarian, like the Republicans. "I shall return" *{To Gay-Bashing in Election Years}.* Shall embodies traditional Republican values, like stick-to-itness and telling people how to live *{In Fear}.* "Though shall not kill" *{Except By Lethal Injection}.*[18] In the spoken words, Colbert sounds much like O'Reilly, insisting that the Republicans are strong and authoritarian, the

Fig. 6.2. Stephen Colbert admonishes President Bush for insisting that he's "flexible and open-minded": "If we had wanted that, we would have elected Al Gore," he says, while The Word responds.

party of Jesus. But the on-screen text turns monologue into dialogue, inviting its audience to critically deconstruct the sensibilities of the monologue's literal content. To put the point differently, the written text functions as an ironic "corrective," a textual device through which an "assumed or asserted fact is shown not to be true, an idea or belief to be untenable, an expectation to be unwarranted or a confidence to be misplaced."[19]

## "Where Do You Come Down on Gays Having Driver's Licenses?"

If this ironic duality shapes Colbert's monologues, it likewise frames his interviews, which comprise a significant portion of the show. During the first block of the show, Colbert often interviews authors and activists about contemporary issues. He also regularly interviews sitting members of the House of Representatives in his segment "Better Know a District."[20] Finally, the traditional late-night talk show interview that fills the third block of the show features an unpredictable array of guests drawn from the domains of celebrity, politics, journalism, social activism, and academia. Those interviews begin with Colbert's now-familiar inversion of the traditional late-night celebrity chat form. Rather than introducing his guests and watching them as they walk on set, Colbert instead gives a brief introduction and then celebrates himself as he makes his way to the interview set. This both invites the audience to celebrate along with him and makes another jab at O'Reilly, enacting the self-centered megalomania that characterizes the *Factor* and O'Reilly's self-presentation elsewhere.

Although his guests are often liberals who rarely are granted exposure elsewhere on television, Colbert does provide an open forum for conservative authors, activists, and politicians.[21] In all of his interviews, Colbert plays the role of the foil—the antagonist who struggles against the interviewee and forces the exchange into a form of dialectical tension. Against his conservative interviewees, Colbert often tries to "out right-wing" them, confronting their ideologies with his own absurdities. Thus, he tells Georgia Republican Phil Gingrey that "it's so nice to be talking with someone I agree with," after Gingrey explains that his opposition to gay marriage is rooted in his faith in the inerrancy of the Bible. Immediately, however, Colbert pushes Gingrey, asking him, "Where do you come down on gays having *driver's* licenses?" and arguing with him when Gingrey admits, "They have every right" to drive a car.[22] Likewise, when conservative pundit Jed Babbin throws out a series of mean-spirited barbs aimed at Democrats and liberals, Colbert responds by trying to force him to declare his unconditional support for George Bush, a verbal move even Babbin was unwilling to do.[23] The humor here pushes the conservative guests toward the center. Colbert's role of foil plays a moderating function, driving the guests to step back from their more stringent positions, or at least exposing the problematic endpoints of their "reasoning."

In place of moderation, confrontation is Colbert's primary approach in his interviews with liberals. One sees a revealing example of this in his interview with Dr. Michael Oppenheimer, an expert on global warming and the lead author on the most recent reports from the Intergovernment Panel on Climate Change. As Oppenheimer suggests strategies individuals can pursue to reduce greenhouse gasses, Colbert argues against him in every way possible. "Do you have a dishwasher?" Oppenheimer asks. Colbert responds: "I have four. I have one for just glasses, one for just silverware, and one I just run." Oppenheimer, however, is not derailed, and instead laughs and suggests, "When you get the fifth, look for the Energy Star symbol."[24] Oppenheimer understands Colbert's real strategy of *playing* the foil but not actually *being* the foil. This ironic duality serves a narrative function, crafting a domain of verbal conflict that harnesses the dramatic appeal of antagonism. As such, it creates an agora-like setting, a Socratic interrogation of sorts, in which the guests are forced to articulate and defend their ideas.[25] But because he is only playing, as opposed to O'Reilly or Limbaugh, whose game is anger and verbal attack, the guests often delight in the exchange. Laughter punctuates the discussions, and they become moments of playful engagement. In turn, the guests grant Colbert greater latitude to throw more and more absurd verbal roadblocks in their way, until he leaves the domain of rationality altogether and the guests no longer are obligated to respond seriously.

In a rare moment out of character, Colbert has explained his strategy:

> I say to all my guests, "you know I'm playing a character, you know I'm an idiot. I'm willfully ignorant of the subjects I talk about, disabuse me of my ignorance. Don't try to play my game. Be real, be passionate, give me traction I can work against." It's the friction between the reality, or the truly held concerns of the person and the farcical concerns that I have, or my need to seem important as opposed to actually understanding what's true . . . where those two things meet is where the comedy happens.[26]

That point of intersection between the "truly held concerns" of the guests and Colbert's farcical absurdity is also often a point of comedic subversion. This is evident in the remarkable "Metaphor Off" he holds with actor and liberal activist Sean Penn, the culmination of Colbert's week-long treatment of a speech Penn gave in which he accuses George Bush and the "smarmy pundits in your pocket" of bathing "in the moisture of your soiled and blood-soaked underwear." Colbert picked up the story from Fox's Sean Hannity, who, of course, was outraged at Penn's comment, and in parodic outrage of his own, invites Penn on the program to see who is the better metaphorist.

Coinciding with National Poetry Month, the Metaphor Off is a game-show-like competition, moderated by former National Poet Laureate Robert Pinsky, in which Colbert and Penn have to make up metaphors relating to "randomly" selected topics. The first question orders the contestants to come up with metaphors for "Dick Cheney." After Colbert stumbles through his, Penn recites: "Dick Cheney is the spinster left at the altar looking out her dirty window at the happy lives of the laughing girls in their calico prints, knowing her only pleasure will be the evening bath that she draws from the moisture of George Bush's soiled and blood-soaked underwear." Despite the uproarious delight that bursts from the audience, Pinsky informs Penn that he is "wrong." Quoting from Shelley's sonnet "Ozymandias," a commentary on the hollowness of a tyrant's lust for power, Pinsky insists the "correct" metaphor is "Dick Cheney is a shattered visage half sunk in the sand, Whose frown and wrinkled lip and sneer of cold command, Tell that its sculptor well those passions read."

From there, every one of Colbert's metaphors is terrible, and every one of Penn's ends with the phrase "soiled and blood-soaked underwear." Finally, in the last challenge, the contestants are shown a doctored photograph of George Bush, who appears to be wearing a pair of blood-soaked underwear. Pinsky asks, "What is *this* a metaphor for?" To that, Penn looks at the camera and succinctly declares: "The president's responsibility for a mishandled war based on lies." At that point, as the audience cheers, Pinsky awards Penn the title of metaphor champion and Colbert bursts into tears. In one last moment of comedic subversion, Penn hands Colbert a handkerchief that appears to be a pair of "blood-soaked" underwear.[27]

This is powerful and perhaps unprecedented television: highly literate and sharply satirical theater that pretends to be antagonistic but in actuality creates a forum for the circulation of oppositional rhetoric. Colbert plays the role of foil—in this case, intentionally poorly—not to confront his guests but to *enable* them in creative ways that transcend the familiar zero-sum "I'm right, you're wrong" approach that characterizes most political talk on television. Thus the Metaphor Off functions simultaneously as brilliant television, a venue in which Penn can amplify his political criticism, and as a pointed rebuke to Sean Hannity, who, like O'Reilly, uses his media soapbox to stoke outrage at the "secular progressives" of Hollywood and the "liberal media."

## *"I Give People the Truth, Unfiltered by Rational Argument"*

Underlying the metaphor-off and its accusation that the Iraq war was "based on lies" is the ethos of Colbert's parody: its recurrent exploration of truth and lies, reality and wishful thinking, and its consistent demand for reason in public discourse. That was the central critique Colbert offered in his much-discussed address at the 2006 White House Correspondents Dinner, in which he explained "every night on my show, *The Colbert Report,* I speak straight from the gut, OK? I give people the truth, unfiltered by rational argument. I call it the 'No Fact Zone.' Fox News, I hold a copyright on that term." Colbert suggests that Fox News is willfully uninterested in fact, a critique he extended to the president himself. "We're not members of the factanista," he says at the White House dinner, "we go straight from the gut. Right sir? That's where the truth lies—right down here in the gut."[28]

Colbert here articulates his concept of "truthiness," Merriam-Webster's 2006 "word of the year" and the central theme of the show. Colbert introduces the concept on his debut program, suggesting that the country is divided, not between "red and blue" but between "those who *think* with their heads, and those who *know* with their heart." From the start, he insists which side he is on:

> Anybody who knows me, knows I'm no fan of dictionaries or references books. They're elitist. Constantly telling us what is or isn't true, or what did or didn't happen. Who's Britannica to tell me the Panama Canal was finished in 1914? If I want to say it happened in 1941, that's my right. I don't trust books. They're all fact and no heart.

Finally he explains his goal for the *Report*. "The truthiness is," he says, "anyone can *read the news to you*. I promise to *feel the news at you*."[29] From the start, then, Colbert constructs a dichotomy between head and heart, fact and opinion, reasoned knowledge and intuitive inclination. Of course, in the multilayered world of Colbert, the concept of truthiness functions as challenge to those who would disregard fact to preserve belief.

The critique here runs deeper than simply pointing fingers at those who privilege opinion over fact. Rather, *The Colbert Report* confronts the wider postmodern deconstruction of the very grammar of fact. Thus Colbert challenges PBS's Jim Lehrer, who insists his *NewsHour* presents factual information without bias. "Doesn't information itself have a liberal bias?" Colbert asks, rejecting the fundamental premise of journalism and, indeed, scientific inquiry itself: that reality exists independent of human perception and can be objectively assessed.[30] He invokes the postmodern argument that objective reality is inaccessible and that facts themselves are social constructs, more the products of human institutions and cultural practices than reflective of any a priori reality.[31] He continues in this vein in his interview with MoveOn's Eli Pariser. When Pariser cites opinion polls that find a majority of Americans have turned against the Iraq war, Colbert dismisses the argument. "I don't accept your statistics," he says, "even if it's true, I don't accept them." He then engages directly with the question of the ontological basis of fact. "A majority of Americans thought Hitler was a great guy," he insists. "That's a fact. I just made up that fact, but that doesn't keep it from being a fact."[32] Colbert problematizes the definition of "fact," rejecting any notion of correspondence between statement and actuality and, instead, proposing that a fact is simply that which one (loudly) proclaims it to be.

If he makes up his own facts, Colbert also gleefully manipulates numbers, challenging the logic of mathematical reasoning. During the 2006 midterm election primaries, his Word segment explores Connecticut Senator Joe Lieberman's suggestion that his opponent Ned Lamont was "out of touch" with the mainstream of the Democratic Party because he opposed the Iraq War. Colbert agrees that Lamont's opposition is "so extreme that only 86 percent of Democrats agree with it {17/20th—A Fraction}." He then rejects the "Poll-stapo" who would insist that 86 percent is a majority, and instead commends Lieberman for siding with the "14 percent pro-war majority."[33] Likewise, in his interview with Nebraska Senator Ben Nelson, Colbert refers to a report that Iraq had met only eight of 18 congressional benchmarks, which he insists is "wonderful progress." When Nelson questions his logic, Colbert explains: "If you round eight to 10, and add that to the original eight, that is *all* of the original benchmarks. Grant me that," he concludes, asking Nelson to affirm the validity of his reasoning. Nelson responds confusedly, "but that's beyond fuzzy math."[34]

Well beyond fuzzy math, Colbert also questions the value of science as an avenue to truth. In his discussion of climate change with Michael Oppenheimer, he mimics those who continue to insist that global warming is a myth. When Oppenheimer references "the very serious science" of climate change, Colbert invokes the few remaining scientists who argue otherwise and asks, "Why are your scientists better than my scientists?" Showing disregard for both scientific method and consensus, Colbert challenges not only the science of climate change but also the credibility of the wider scientific enterprise. "In the 1970s when I was a kid," he explains, "all of the reputable scientists in the world believed that the Aztec pyramids were actually bomb shelters built by ancient astronauts."[35]

The ironic twist here, of course, is that as Colbert plays the foil, he gives Oppenheimer a public platform and offers critique of the simultaneous suspicion toward and politicization of science common during the Bush presidency. Colbert's ethos of truthiness thus calls into relief the postmodern inclination to reject modernity's privileging of empirical inquiry, reasoned discourse, and technocratic expertise. Colbert readily conflates expertise with a vague concept of "elitism," lashing out an elite "who reads books and knows things"—the elitist "who says he knows more than I do."[36] Underlying the humor here is commentary on a *postmodern episteme* that celebrates individual perception over objective truth, emotional inclination over rational knowledge, and political expediency over reasoned argument.

## *"Bringing Democracy to Knowledge"*

Colbert's concerns for the nature of truth and the function of expertise also underlie a second of his key terms: *wikiality*—the postmodern world in which "we can create a reality we can all agree on." Wikiality, of course, is enabled by the online, user-generated encyclopedia Wikipedia, which Colbert describes as "the encyclopedia where you can be an authority, even if you don't know what the hell you're talking about."[37] "What I love about it," he tells its creator Jimmy Wales, "is it brings democracy to information. For too long, the elite, who study things, got to say what is or isn't real."[38] Here Colbert appears to celebrate Wikipedia's, and perhaps the Internet's, decentering of modernity's institutions of knowledge production and its relocation of epistemic expertise, as Henry Jenkins has described, from recognized academic authorities to a form of electronically networked collective intelligence.[39] In the interview, Wales likewise endorses the power of "the community" to transcend traditional top-down epistemic structures.

Colbert regularly calls on his audience to change the content of Wikipedia pages, part of his larger strategy to activate the audience, to encourage them to become creative participants, not just passive recipients. His continued attempts to manipulate Wikipedia, however, illustrate his deep skepticism of wikiality. In the interview with Wales, he worries about the susceptibility of "group think" to control and manipulation.[40] The horizontal power of any knowledge community, Jenkins has noted, is always in tension with the top-down power "the nation-state exerts over its citizens and corporations within commodity capitalism exert over its workers and consumers."[41] In that vein, Colbert reports on the development of "wikiscanner" software that revealed that corporations are some of the most avid editors on Wikipedia. He notes that Pepsi had deleted a section on its page addressing "long-term health effects" and Exxon had added content to its page insisting there had been "no negative long-term effects" from the Valdez oil spill. To that, Colbert suggests that "if Exxon Mobil wants to present itself as a friend of the environment, well they have the right to that online fantasy."[42]

Most important, here, Colbert calls attention to the Bush administration's cooption of wikiality: its continuous campaign to manipulate public perception. In an age of wikiality, he argues, "you may come from generations of Connecticut bluebloods, and have gone to the finest prep schools out east, but if you clear brush and talk with a Texas twang, you *are* a cowboy."[43] Indeed, Colbert's original bit on wikiality focuses on the administration's skill at "information management." He highlights the systematic efforts to create the "knowledge" that Saddam Hussein did, in fact, have weapons of mass destruction by circulating *insinuations* that he did: "insinuations that have been repeated over and over again on cable news for the past three and-a-half years *{24,000 Hour News Cycle}*." As a result, he suggests, "18 months ago only 36 percent of Americans believed it. But 50 percent of Americans believe it now."[44] Colbert concludes that wikiality is "bringing democracy to knowledge," but that, too, is ironic critique— a warning that democracy demands knowledge, and both have become harder to find in an age of truthiness and wikiality.

## "Nothing I'm Saying Means Anything"

At the heart of *The Colbert Report* lies a consistent concern for the vitality of democratic practice in a postmodern age. His notions of truthiness and wikiality provide a modernist point of agitation against dominant political inclinations to reject objective inquiry and intellectual engagement in favor of hollow political spectacle. Thus Colbert delights in amplifying White House Press Secretary Tony Snow's suggestion that the problem with the apparently endless occupation of Iraq is that, "so far, we have very few visuals that confirm what Americans *want to believe.*"

In response, Colbert's Word that night is simply a smiley face. Once again articulating the core critique of truthiness, he endorses Snow's suggestion that "what Americans want to believe is more important than what's actually happening." He then puts a picture of a destroyed mosque on the screen and notes that "*this* is *not* what we want to believe." When the picture of the mosque is replaced by a YouTube video of a kitten falling asleep, Colbert continues: "*This is*," and asking: "How could kittens fall asleep in a world where Iraq is *not* on its way to becoming a democracy?" But Colbert recognizes, as does Tony Snow, that "visuals are not enough." He then quotes from Snow again, this time suggesting that what supporters of the Iraq war need is "a surge of new facts," the kind of truthy "facts," Colbert concludes, "that confirm what America wants to believe."[45]

Such "facts" might be the verbal equivalent of the smiley face, the intellectually vacuous sign without referent, one marked by its lack of concern for any actually existent state of affairs. Such "facts" might be, in the words of philosopher Harry Frankfurt, *bullshit*. In his essay titled *On Bullshit*, Frankfurt explores that subset of speech that lacks any "connection to a concern with truth"—those statements that "avoid, elude, dissuade questions of accurate representation." Bullshit, Frankfurt argues, both displays an "indifference to how things really are" and obscures the true intentions that lie behind it.[46] It is speech aimed not at representing reality or trying to reach consensus but entirely at generating a response or achieving an effect. As such, bullshit lacks "everything nutritive" and "cannot serve the purpose of sustenance or of communication."[47]

As the fake right-wing pundit, Colbert's fundamental premise therefore may be that O'Reilly and his brand of political speech is, ultimately, bullshit. That is the subtext of his Word segment titled "Jacksquat," a term quite similar to bullshit. Colbert uses it here to critique the ways in which the right-wing punditry are dealing with their complicity in the Iraq war:

> I didn't get where I am today by thinking about anything *{Ignorance Accomplished}*. I got here by feeling about everything. And what I'm feeling about Iraq is angry. I've done everything I could to solve this Iraq problem *{Kept Shopping}*. I have tried saying there isn't a problem . . . not reporting the news that could lead one to believe there might a problem . . . saying there is a problem, but we've solved it *{The Lie-Fecta}*. Nothing seems to help.

Noting the eventual ineffectiveness of prowar propaganda to mask reality, Colbert suggests that the next step is to find a scapegoat. "I blame the Iraqi people," he says, "all of them. Just like Papa Bear Bill O'Reilly said to Uncle Bear Geraldo Rivera . . ." Here Colbert's monologue is intercut with a clip from the *Factor*, in which O'Reilly barks at Rivera: "The Iraqis have got to step up and at least try to fight for their democracy, instead of being this crazy country. Shia wants to kill Sunni . . . [throws his hands up in a gesture of frustration] I mean, I don't ever want to hear "Shia" and "Sunni" again." Exposing O'Reilly's deep disinterest in reality—indeed, his unwillingness to acknowledge that which does not conform to his world view—Colbert concludes insightfully: "Nothing I'm saying means anything. For it to mean something, I would have had to have thought about it. And I don't play that game *{Thinking Makes Terrorists Win}*. I and every pundit who have supported this war have the right to stop hearing about it. We've done all we can *{Jacksquat}* . . . and that's the Word."[48]

## *"If You're an Act, Then What Am I?"*

For Colbert, "jacksquat" becomes a term of equal importance to the better-known truthiness and wikiality. It captures the essence of his critique of contemporary political speech: that so much of it is empty, hollowed out of informational content, vacant of propositional weight. He suggests that nothing seems to mean anything, that so much public speech is simply hot air—itself a phrase that Frankfurt notes is akin to bullshit. All of these—hot air, bullshit, and Colbert's jacksquat—are effects of postmodernity, Frankfurt argues. The "contemporary proliferation" of BS, he writes, is inseparable from the

> various forms of skepticism which deny that we can have any reliable access to an objective reality, and which therefore reject the possibility of knowing how things truly are. These "antirealist" doctrines undermine confidence in the value of disinterested efforts to determine what is true and what is false, and even in the intelligibility of the notion of objective inquiry.[49]

In the absence of any belief in a coherent or knowable reality, Frankfurt suggests and Colbert would likely agree, bullshit becomes the primary form of public discourse and the bullshitter becomes the central occupant of the halls of public power.

From such a perspective, O'Reilly himself is equally a product of a postmodern episteme. One suspects he is a spectacle created for the screen, a simulacrum that draws few connections to an actually existent reality, and actively works to obscure the reality that lies beyond his speech. Like the Colbert character, he says many things, and it is equally difficult to imagine that he, unlike Colbert, actually means what he says. He offers little trace of self-consciousness when he claims that his rabidly polemical program is, in reality, a "no-spin zone." Nor does he appear to recognize the irony of his Talking Points Memo—the talking point, of course, the core rhetorical device in the circulation of spin. As such, O'Reilly may be the *real* ironist here—the fundamentally ironic character whose speech not only does *not* mean what it says but *cannot* mean anything at all. He becomes the epitome of Wayne Booth's "unstable" irony, the character whose speech is untethered, free-floating in a discursive realm marked by a deeply cynical belief in the foolishness of "all linguistic characterizations of reality."[50]

With that in mind, we can return one last time to the Pundit Exchange, which wraps up on the *Report* in an unexpected manner. Colbert pushes O'Reilly on his media image as the angry warrior, asking him who would win in a fight between him and that other Fox News warrior, Sean Hannity. "Hannity could kick my butt," O'Reilly jovially insists. He then continues: "I'm effete, I'm not a tough guy. This is all an act. I'm sensitive." Like so many moments on *The Colbert Report,* this is a powerful instance of television, with O'Reilly suggesting what many have long suspected—that he is, ultimately, "all an act," an ironic invention whose agenda has far more to do with self-promotion and financial accumulation than it does with fighting the good fight. Or perhaps he is still speaking ironically here, not meaning a word that he says. Either way, the moment is not lost on Colbert, who instantly cuts him off and ends the interview by asking: "If you're an act, then what am I?"

Here then, we have reached the crux of the matter. If the pretext O'Reilly is an act, then what exactly is Colbert? He appears to be a parody of a parody—perhaps, more precisely, a parody of a more postmodern kind of pastiche, which like parody is the "wearing of a linguistic mask," but a mask that is "amputated of the satiric impulse, devoid of laughter."[51] Colbert is indeed a fiction, but one that functions to deconstruct another, far more problematic, fiction. Like the pretext he apes, Colbert enacts a postmodern cultural form that effaces boundaries among traditional discursive domains, delights in fragments and fractures, and rarely says anything that it might actually mean. But Colbert's postmodern *style* exists in ironic tension with its deeper and decidedly modernist *agenda.* If bullshit is an effect of postmodernism, parody is a modernist textual device, one defined by its critical edge and its unyielding faith that beyond the mask, there is some kind of linguistic normality—that words can, *and should,* mean something. Colbert's parody thus functions to pierce the O'Reillyan simulacra and to provide an antidote of sorts to the kind of "mystification" that is woven by so much contemporary political speech.

In the end, *The Colbert Report* does many things. It functions as an unfamiliar kind of public affairs show that grapples with an impressive range of issues, provides a televisual forum for alternative and at times oppositional politics, and employs a variety of comedic techniques to generate a laugh. Perhaps most important, though, it is, in the words of Murray Edelman, a "liberating form of political expression" with the power to "estrange" its audience from "conventional assumptions and conventional language," such that they can "see their inherent contradictions and recognize alternative potentialities."[52] The "conventional language" that Colbert's parody targets, ultimately, is the language of postmodernism itself—its ontology that equates individual perception with reality and its epistemology that dismisses knowledge as an effect of power, a product of unjust cultural conventions. At his most absurd, and he certainly has mastered the art of absurdity, Colbert helps us realize the implications of a postmodern episteme: he constructs a powerful view of what public speech and democratic politics may have already become if we truly have abandoned modernity's commitments to objectivity, rationality, and accountability.

### NOTES

1. Jürgen Habermas, *The Structural Transformation of the Public Sphere* (Cambridge: MIT Press, 1989); Craig Calhoun, ed., *Habermas and the Public Sphere* (Cambridge: MIT Press, 1992).

2. 10 October 2006.

3. Geoffrey Baym, "*The Daily Show:* Discursive Integration and the Reinvention of Critical Journalism," *Political Communication* 22 (2005): 259–76; Geoffrey Baym, "Crafting New Communicative Models in the Televisual Sphere: Political Interviews on *The Daily Show*," *Communication Review* 10 (2007): 93–115; Geoffrey Baym, "Representation and the Politics of Play: Stephen Colbert's *Better Know a District*," *Political Communication* 24, no. 4 (2007): 359–76; Jeffery P. Jones, *Entertaining Politics: New Political Television and Civic Culture* (Lanham, Md.: Rowman and Littlefield, 2005).

4. 6 July 2004.

5. Baym, "*The Daily Show*."

6. James W. Carey, "The Mass Media and Democracy: Between the Modern and the Postmodern," *Journal of International Affairs* 47 (1993): 1–21.

7. 11 May 2004.

8. 4 August 2004, 19 August 2004.

9. 18 January 2007.

10. Ibid.

11. Ibid.

12. Mike Conway, Maria Elizabeth Grabe, and Kevin Grieves, "Villains, Victims and the Virtuous in Bill O'Reilly's 'No-Spin Zone': Revisiting World War Propaganda Techniques," *Journalism Studies* 8 (2007): 197–223.

13. Murray Edelman, *Constructing the Political Spectacle* (Chicago: University of Chicago Press, 1988).

14. 5 March 2007.

15. 18 January 2007.

16. Simon Dentith, *Parody* (New York: Routledge, 2000), 16.

17. 18 January 2007.

18. 11 January 2006; the italic text in curly brackets appears on screen over the spoken word.

19. Douglas C. Muecke, *The Compass of Irony* (London: Methuen, 1969), 23.

20. Baym, "Representation and the Politics of Play."

21. By early 2008, Republican presidential long shot and avowed conservative Mike Huckabee had appeared on the program three times.

22. 16 April 2006.

23. 31 January 2007.

24. 12 February 2007.

25. Claire Colebrook, *Irony* (New York: Routledge, 2004).

26. *A Conversation with Stephen Colbert,* Institute of Politics, Harvard University, at http://video.google.com/videoplay?docid=5550134133036374310 (accessed 26 January 2007).

27. 19 April 2007.

28. *2006 White House Correspondents Dinner,* at http://video.google.com/video play?docid=-86918391775857487 (accessed 12 May 2006).

29. 17 October 2005.

30. 27 November 2006.

31. For example, Richard Rorty, *Philosophy and the Mirror of Nature* (Princeton: Princeton University Press, 1979); Mary Poovey, *A History of the Modern Fact: Problems of Knowledge in the Sciences of Wealth and Society* (Chicago: University of Chicago Press, 1998).

32. 10 August 2006.

33. Ibid.

34. 16 July 2007.

35. 12 February 2007.

36. 16 August 2007.

37. 29 January 2007.

38. 24 May 2007.

39. Henry Jenkins, *Convergence Culture: Where Old and New Media Collide* (New York: New York University Press, 2006), 254; see also Peter Walsh, "That Withered Paradigm: The Web, the Expert and the Information Hegemony," in *Democracy and New Media,* ed. Henry Jenkins and David Thorburn (Cambridge: MIT Press, 2004), 365–72.

40. 24 May 2007.

41. Jenkins, *Convergence Culture,* 245.

42. 21 August 2007.

43. Ibid.

44. 30 July 2006.

45. 18 July 2007.

46. Harry G. Frankfurt, *On Bullshit* (Princeton, N.J.: Princeton University Press, 2005), 33–34.

47. Ibid., 44.

48. 26 November 2007.

49. Frankfurt, *On Bullshit,* 64–65.

50. Wayne C. Booth, *The Rhetoric of Irony* (Chicago: University of Chicago Press, 1974); Hayden White, *Metahistory: The Historical Imagination in Nineteenth-Century Europe* (Baltimore: Johns Hopkins University Press, 1973), 38.

51. Frederick Jameson, *Postmodernism, or, The Cultural Logic of Late Capitalism* (Durham, N.C.: Duke University Press, 1991), 17.

52. Edelman, *Political Spectacle,* 126.

*Part III*

||||||||||||||||||||||||||||||||||||||||||||||||||||||||||||||

# Building in the Critical Rubble
*Between Deconstruction and Reconstruction*

# Throwing Out the Welcome Mat
## Public Figures as Guests and Victims in TV Satire

## Jonathan Gray

Heavy electricity [is] caused by particle accelerators sending huge jolts of power into domestic power lines. These knock the electricity back into its wild state, which is much heavier due to flattened electrons. The devastating result is that huge masses of heavy electricity start randomly falling out of wires and crashing onto anything below. . . . In the Sri Lankan village of Upuveli, inhabitants are suffering heavy electricity attacks even as I speak. Can we stand around and eat pies, while they're being flattened like flies, swatted by the tail of a mad invisible horse? Of course not. [We] must contact the Sri Lankan embassy now and let them know just how shoddy this all is. If you're in any doubt, just shut your eyes and imagine a child you know being hit on the head by a ton of invisible lead soup.

Heavy electricity is regularly flattening cattle in Sri Lanka. Afterwards, the poor beasts look like giant fur-covered slugs thrashing about on their backs and made of what scientists call "wobbly matter." It's caused by "sodomized electrons," which rush to the cow's head end. Now just apply that to a young girl human. It's an appalling thought, isn't it? Geeta is 15 years old, and now because of heavy electricity, she's only eight inches tall. Now just imagine that. She can't speak, but she must feel quite dreadful.

The above quotations read as parodies of public service announcements (PSAs) by erstwhile public figures trying to "make a difference." The science is ludicrous ("flattened" and then "sodomized" electrons, "wobbly matter," electricity in "its wild state"), the metaphors overreaching (as with the mad invisible horse), the willingness to believe in the foreign abnormal worrying, the calls for pathos with the notion of children being hit by "lead soup" and reduced to a mere eight inches tall overdone, and the editorial comment that Geeta "must feel quite dreadful," a clear tipping point . . . if one was needed. Both are indeed taken from a television parody, the 1997 spoof news journal *Brass Eye*, aired on Channel 4 in the United Kingdom. However, both represent parody with a satiric twist, since both were offered by public figures—actor Richard Briers and BBC reporter Nick Owen, respectively—who were led to believe that heavy electricity was *a real problem* requiring political action. Their calls for such action, while scripted by *Brass Eye* creator Chris Morris, were delivered in earnest and in faith. In short, Morris was using Briers and Owen here as pawns, not only to parody the format of the PSA but also to launch a satiric attack on the abuses of celebrity and public image, mocking the frequency with which those in the public eye will lend their voice and image to political or humanitarian causes, regardless of how little research they have conducted into the issue.

The inclusion of public figures in television parody and satire has rapidly become commonplace. *Saturday Night Live* invites a celebrity or politician to sit in with the cast each week. *The Simpsons* regularly invites public figures to voice themselves in one-off episodes. *TV Nation* and *The Awful Truth* allowed Michael Moore to hone his skill of pouncing on unprepared public figures. *The Eleven O'Clock Show* and *Da Ali G Show* followed in Morris's and *Brass Eye*'s footsteps, as Sacha Baron Cohen interviewed the famous in character, asking ludicrous and satirically leading questions. *The Daily Show with Jon Stewart* includes an interview with an in-studio public figure each night, and its beat reporters regularly set public figures up for a well-edited fall. *The Colbert Report* sees host Stephen Colbert interviewing guests as the Bill O'Reilly wannabe character. And Canadian *This Hour Has 22 Minutes* and *Rick Mercer Report* have used various strategies to interview prominent Canadian and American politicians. Some of these programs require that public figures come willingly and knowingly, some willingly and unknowingly, and some programs simply show up with camera rolling.

My task in this chapter is to analyze how these various strategies work as satiric comment on the nature of celebrity, public image, and their mobilization in mediated discussions of the political. Satire can support public figures and advance their political platforms. But I also chart the significant dangers for public figures of playing with the heavy electricity that is a guest spot on television satire. Ultimately, satirical play with public figures stands to construct new relationships between these figures, politics, and the viewing public, frequently victimizing and "shrinking" the public images of its guests, while surgically interrogating the celebrification of politics in general.

## Image Construction and the Celebrification of Politics

Whether politics and celebrity were ever separate is debatable, but their current collusion in contemporary politics is clear.[1] On one hand, politicians have turned to "political marketing" that mimics the strategies of Hollywood's publicists and Madison Avenue's branding gurus.[2] Many a critic of politics has bemoaned how politics has become increasingly centered on personalities and performance in a post–John F. Kennedy televisual era.[3] Numerous prominent political figures in particular have sealed the union between politics and celebrity, as, for instance, Ronald Reagan and Arnold Schwarzenegger parlayed their star capital into attaining political office; Bill Clinton fashioned a presidential path that involved important stops along the way at *The Arsenio Hall Show,* MTV, and, eventually, the *National Enquirer;* British novelist-politician Jeffrey Archer blurred the line between tawdry politics and tawdry fiction;[4] and the Dutch Pim Fortuyn made performative and lifestyle politics the only sorts of politics in town, even unwittingly in his death (to some, a John Lennon-esque martyrdom).[5] Meanwhile, on the other hand, celebrities have themselves become important players in politics. Martin Sheen, Bruce Springsteen, Michael J. Fox, Barbara Streisand, Ashton Kutcher, Curt Schilling, and countless others have stumped or voiced support for their respective parties or candidates, turning party conventions and political speeches into glamorous affairs. Rooting for a particular cause or party or simply being seen as "political" have become vital parts of many a star's image. Thus, for instance, in the run up to the 2004 American presidential election, Michael Moore and Mel Gibson served as lightning rods for political sentiment,[6] Eminem released a music video encouraging a voting mosh for John Kerry, and the Dixie Chicks' dissociation with President Bush at a concert in London attracted significant levels of both anti-fandom and fandom.

The urge by politicians to celebrify and by celebrities to politicize their respective images speaks to their desires to rid their personal aura of the common trappings of their professions. John Street cites Dick Pountain and David Robins's definition of "cool" as displaying narcissism, ironic detachment, and hedonism, all of which, as Street notes, "would seem to capture exactly what politicians are not, indeed what they cannot afford to be."[7] Most politicians in most countries appear desperately out of touch with regular people and especially out of touch with youth. Thus while to become truly cool would be an impossible feat for a politician, most want to *appear* cool. To do so, many draw from the sphere of celebrity, branding themselves as personable, accessible people, at once "just like you" yet also marked as special. Celebrities, meanwhile, may wish to appear as more than vacuous placeholders for the latest corporate-constructed image associated with their latest project, and thus the realm of politics offers a deep pool of authenticity from which to draw in order to seem connected to their audiences' world and its issues. While both politics and celebrity are frequently coded as inauthentic in and of themselves, many politicians and celebrities alike have nevertheless hoped that the sobriety and earnestness of politics and the magic and allure of celebrity will combine to produce the ultimate authentic individual.

Some politicians are simply "big characters," their personality and performance a quintessential part of who they are. And some celebrities have realized the discursive power that being a celebrity gives them, and they capitalize on that power to enhance their value as citizens.[8] Thus, while the celebrification of politics has been accompanied by a heightened cynicism on the part of citizens and audiences, a sign of just how tired of the publicity-seeking techniques of both camps most of us are, a certain degree of the connection between politics and celebrity is understandable. In addition, several critics have pointed out that personality and performance politics may not be as debased a discursive sphere as is often alleged, and therefore we might see the joint realm of political celebrity and celebrity politics as one that energizes certain functions of a democratic system. John Hartley writes of the popular press and lifestyle writing as playing a vital role in the development of modernity, noting that "the decisive political events of the day are as likely to be imagined (and imaged) in the dispersed and apparently depoliticized arenas of 'style' or 'consumer' journalism, as in the first few pages of the 'quality' daily broadsheet."[9] For example, he observes that environmental politics and civil rights are frequently discussed in more complex and engaging ways in lifestyle reporting. Dick Pels also notes how the celebrification of politics amounts to a deauraticization of high culture and hence to the opening up of politics to all citizens, not simply the bourgeois.[10] While not mindlessly celebrating the celebrification of politics, he echoes others' comments on the need for sentiment in political deliberation,[11] on the value of "fannish" engagements with politics,[12] and on the value of political gut reactions and "emotional rationalism,"[13] arguing that performance-driven politics may allow a large number of citizens not only to access politics and political discussion but to do so meaningfully and thoughtfully. Turning to satirical television in particular, Jeffrey Jones notes how celebrity involvement in political discussions on shows such as *The Daily Show* and *Politically Incorrect* or *Real Time with Bill Maher* can render politics more accessible, translating it out of the insider-speak usually employed to discuss politics on television and into everyday vernacular.[14]

However, political celebrification also has its public costs, producing most significantly a plethora of bullshit. Often politicians and celebrities' forays into the other realm are closely scripted by publicists and campaign strategists, based on audience research and public opinion polls, and crafted to win sales or votes. Emotional rationalism and gut reactions have their place in political deliberation, but savvy marketers can obfuscate such faculties, hijacking them with cynical ploys and calculated performance. The result, as we have seen, is a president whose bumbling grammar, Texan drawl, sly winks, and frat-boyish ways convinced many that he is a man of the people, yet whose administration proved one of the least responsive to the people in American history. Celebrities, meanwhile, might be wearing political causes like new jewelry, doing so as much for the sake of image construction as for personal conviction. Yet precisely because celebrity works in part by encouraging identification, empathy, and affect from audiences,[15] just as celebrity endorsement of products in advertisements aims to shift sentiment toward those products, celebrity endorsement of political causes aims to or can shift political sentiment. Political and mass communication theory has long charted the role and importance of "opinion leaders," with Paul Lazarsfeld, Bernard Berelson, and Hazel Gaudet offering their famous two-step flow of communication, wherein politics and ideas flow from the media to audiences through opinion leaders.[16] When celebrities wax political, they can easily slip into the role of opinion leaders, and thus we must interrogate not only their political motivation but also their political intelligence regarding the issue at hand, for they might be ushering citizen-fans to political causes of which neither star nor citizen-fan know much about.

Ultimately, as Street notes, today's politicians are commodities, but cultural goods, not simple consumable items.[17] In short, they are *texts*. And as many scholars of celebrity have noted, stars are also texts.[18] A key question therefore becomes, how are these texts authored, and with what political ramifications? But by being texts, they are also open to authoring from audiences and from other texts, since textuality is always open and active.[19] Rather than turn to production analysis to see how public figures are constructed at their start point, or to audience analysis to see how they are consumed, in the remainder of this chapter I examine the role that parodic-satiric television can play in *reauthoring* public figures, both in specific instances and as a group. As the introduction to this volume argues, parody and satire are profoundly dynamic, dialogic entities that bring together various discourses, frequently defamiliarizing them along the way and provoking (renewed) reflection.[20] Thus I now turn to parodic-satiric television as one site among many of the construction of political celebrity, focusing specifically on those moments when celebrities or politicians appear on the shows in person.[21] At such moments, how are we invited to make sense of them and of their political platform?

## *Strapping on Tony Blair's Jetpack: Satire's Guests*

Parodic-satiric television programs have become a key location for the celebrification of politics. As simultaneously smart and funny, cerebral and cool, and often blessed with wealthy, young, and intelligent potential voters and audiences, they offer both politicians and celebrities a seemingly ideal venue for image management. As I argue here, and as authors in other chapters in this book discuss, such shows are often also at the forefront of challenging and critiquing politics, celebrity, and various mixes thereof. But the promise to a politician is considerable. As John Corner notes, politicians' mediations tend to take one of three forms: (1) political publicity, managed by the politician and his or her staff; (2) interactive news-making, where politicians and the news media work together or at odds to craft the politician's image; and (3) journalistic revelation, where the politician loses any semblance of control. Corner offhandedly offers a fourth form of "the less news-based opportunities for politicians to project themselves on the public stage,"[22] but I contend that even such mediations subdivide into one of the other forms. Politicians clearly appear on parodic-satiric shows because they imagine that the opportunity is one for pure contained and managed "publicity," or at the least "interactive news-making," as do celebrities, whose mediation operates along a similar (if less *New York Times*-, more *People*-flavored) spectrum.

A key act of "interactive news-making" for many a public figure has been to appear on satiric shows to be interviewed as scheduled guests. After Bill Clinton's masterful stunt of playing the saxophone on *The Arsenio Hall Show* in 1992, American politicians have proved especially eager to appear on late-night talk shows, including *The Daily Show*. In the 2004 and 2008 presidential campaigns, for instance, several Democratic candidates appeared on *The Daily Show*, with John Edwards even choosing the venue to announce his candidacy in 2004. Over the years, Stewart's guests have also included heads of state of Pakistan, Iraq, and Bolivia, along with American senators, house representatives, and former cabinet members. Aside from the occasional photo shoot while fishing, a visit to *The Daily Show* has become one of the few situations in which politicians may discard the jacket and tie and even slouch a bit in the chair. *The Daily Show*'s list of celebrity guests is considerable, too, with many taking advantage of the opportunity to talk politics away from *Entertainment Tonight*. Public figures who appear on satirical television such as *The Daily Show* can use the site to perform a sense of humor and to come off as though they are approachable individuals, still "with it" enough to know what's cool and to take part in it. Importantly, too, they can aim to associate their image with that of the show, potentially borrowing from its countercultural edge and attaching those qualities to their own image. If the media is a site wherein public figures lay claim to power and posit themselves in the "cultural center" of society,[23] on one level, satiric television aids them toward this goal. Hence, for instance, in 2008, on the eve of the important Ohio and Texas Democratic primaries, Hillary Clinton went not to a rally in Cleveland or Houston but to Manhattan to appear on *The Daily Show*.

Jay Leno, David Letterman, and Conan O'Brien rarely challenge their guests with more than a playful joke here or there, and though they will wax satirical elsewhere on their shows, satire is rarely part of their interviewing techniques. *Saturday Night Live*'s political coverage also tends to be weak, more often ranging from the feckless to the fawning (as when, in spring 2008, the show became a cheerleader for Hillary Clinton, leading some to jokingly dub it *Hillary Night Live*). Even Jon Stewart and

*Daily Show* alum Stephen Colbert, though, commonly direct their satire at forces that beset their guest, rather than at the figure and his or her image. For instance, when Stewart interviewed John Kerry during the 2004 presidential election, much of his satire was directed at Kerry's critics and their unethical tactics, thereby largely allowing Kerry a chance to reestablish a glowing public image that was at the time being tainted by attack ads from the Swift Boat Veterans for Truth. In this and multiple other interviews, Stewart aids the figure by saying what they cannot—usually in a profane language that they cannot use and usually to the delight and raucous cheers of his live studio audience, hence creating a significant bond between himself, the interviewee, the live audience, and the assumed home audience. Stewart's remarks often represent lone breaths of fresh air in an otherwise toxic media environment, illustrating the degree to which satire is often required to *recuperate* public image in an age of attack campaigns and of a punditocracy's "aesthetic totalitarianism"[24] and to reauthor the text of a public figure.

*The Daily Show* has also become famous for its beat reporters' in-character humorous interviews and subsequent creative editing, a style that spawned the spin-off success of Stephen Colbert with his *Colbert Report,* and that can also be found in the satire of Sacha Baron Cohen. As described by Geoffrey Baym (chapter 6) in this book, Colbert's act consistently mocks the spectacularized demagoguery of the physically absent yet parodically invoked Bill O'Reilly and fellow right-wing pundits. In taking the role of ass in many interviews, Colbert commonly gives his guests space to improve their public image by rendering them the sane, rational one in the discussion. That said, the star and attraction of the show is Colbert, and so a questioning of the nature and value of interviewers' public image is perhaps more often subjugated to the general sense of carnivalesque play and to its satiric-parodic attack on absent public figures such as O'Reilly.[25]

A similar dynamic is present in the work of Sacha Baron Cohen, who in *The Eleven O'Clock Show* and then *Da Ali G Show,* created the interviewer personas of suburban gangsta wannabe Ali G, Kazakhstani journalist Borat, and Austrian culture reporter Bruno. Cohen's three creations offer considerable scope for satirically questioning hegemonic constructions of masculinity, race, ethnicity, and class, but, like Colbert, Cohen's characters are frequently the key or even lone site of satirical play, especially given their outrageous questions. When the comedy is not centered around Cohen's antics, though, as with Stewart and Colbert, Cohen offers some guests the opportunity to bolster their public figure and political platform. When, for instance, Ali G asks Professor Sue Leetch of the U.K.'s Center for Gender Research, "would you feel safe if you knew a woman was flying your plane?" and "Do you think all girls should try feminism at least once?," Cohen plays patsy to Leetch, making her case for her, placing her in relatively safe territory while making Ali's sexist mindset the satiric target. Similarly, when Ali G asks Major General Ken Perkins if he ever considered changing sides in World War II, likening the act to changing one's support for Manchester United to Arsenal when the former plays poorly, or when he asks why England does not simply carpet bomb Northern Ireland, only Ali looks stupid. At such moments, satirists such as Cohen can pick their spots to bolster a public figure's image if it is tied to politics that the satirist finds agreeable. Clearly, satirical television can often help public figures author their image.

At the same time, however, satirical television can prove to be a highly volatile, unpredictable space. Regularly, the price of admission for public figures is an openness to subversive counterauthorings, and in a battle of wits, politicians have often shown themselves ill-equipped to take on a wily satirist. Thus, for instance, when British Prime Minister Tony Blair appeared on an episode of *The Simpsons,* he and his public relations team would have hoped that this would endear him to the British populace (a particularly fervid ground of *Simpsons* fandom), but the scene including Blair mocks him as much as it flatters him. As with *Saturday Night Live,* *The Simpsons* seemingly offers the safest of environments for public figures within the realm of satirical television, since it is scripted, thereby allowing public figures and their public relations teams the right to screen the context of inclusion beforehand. Nevertheless, when Blair meets the Simpsons family at the airport in England, and, eager to win their love, gives them some money to spend as tourists before he speeds off on his jet-pack to meet a Dutch couple arriving off another flight, the scene mocks Blair's eagerness to please others (the United States or the European Union) before his own people, along with his willingness to hand over British money to non-Brits. Then, when he speeds away, Homer expresses amazement that they met Mr. Bean, hence recoding Blair as Rowan Atkinson's bumbling fool, while also suggesting his utter irrelevance (despite gifts of money and assistance) to the average American.

It is interesting to speculate whether Blair and his staff understood the satire in play. Since his welcoming of the Simpsons also includes a spiel on the wonderful attractions of the United Kingdom, and since his mode of exit and his exit music are evocative of a James Bond film, perhaps the subversive readings may have been lost on them, and perhaps they simply felt the short vignette would be "good for tourism" or that it playfully suggested Blair was a superhero figure. Or perhaps we should give them more credit, for maybe they felt the overarching message that Blair was willing to take part in such self-mockery coded him as a relaxed man who could take a joke. Speculation as to why Blair's PR team allowed him to proceed, of course, does not give us an answer. But speculation will nevertheless be required of any given viewer, not simply those analyzing the scene in a book chapter. While speculation that Blair and company actually got the joke may convince viewers that his participation thus makes him a "fun" guy, speculation that he wasn't in on it suggests a stupid and out of touch politician. The vignette itself offers either reading, hence showing that even in the seemingly controlled environment of scripted satirical inclusion, a public figure is not necessarily safe; rather, agreeing to appear as a "guest" on a satirical show always carries with it the gamble of being a victim. In Corner's terms, the apparent "interactive news-making" can always carry with it the risk of satiric "revelation." Moreover, regardless of one's assumptions of public figures' foreknowledge, audiences may also regard the figures' participation cynically, as a desperate ploy for attention.

### Don't Eat the Cake: Public Figures as Dupes and Victims

Stewart, Colbert, Cohen, and *The Simpsons* have all used their characters to help guests advance political positions, but they have also proven wholly capable of turning guests into victims with remarkable speed and skill. Even when offering to play patsy to their interviewees, satirists frequently make them appear wholly out of touch and removed from everyday life and popular culture. Cohen's characters, for instance, all require that the interviewees shift linguistic register to an everyday vernacular. Consequently, while many likely agreed to be interviewed in order to appear responsive to "regular people," they often appear anything but. Ali G asks Conservative MP Sir Rhodes Boyson if he believes kids should be "caned" in school (referring to a British slang term for being high on marijuana), leading to a lengthy discussion on how Boyson was himself caned in school and how the cane must be good. Later, Ali again hoodwinks Boyson with drug double-entendres, asking him why schools teach kilos and grams, "when you should really deal in ounces." Elsewhere, he convinces the clueless former U.S. Attorney General Richard Thornburgh to discuss plot points of a porn film entitled

Fig. 7.1. Stylist Tiffany and Bruno share a laugh at the poor's inability to afford fashion inspired by them, on *Da Ali G Show*.

*Barely Legal 3,* that Thornburgh eventually agrees he should see. With such exchanges, Cohen quickly turns some guests into victims, shifting the comedy away from his own carnivalesque character and squarely onto their utter distance from the assumed viewer.

Moreover, Ali G, Borat, and Bruno's performances of sexism, racism, and elitism have often lured interviewees into showing their own discriminatory values, as when Borat finds a Cambridge professor agreeing with him that women are not as intelligent as men. Ali G's suggestion to English Circuit Court Judge James Pickles that women shouldn't serve on juries because PMS is likely to affect their judgment produces an awkward moment when the judge considers the proposition quite seriously. Bruno, meanwhile, reveals a rank elitism in the fashion industry when asking a stylist about a fashion show whose "philosophy" was trailer trash (figure 7.1):

BRUNO: What is trailer trash?
TIFFANY: Backwoods, from, like, middle of nowhere, kind of poor, dressing
    with whatever you have around.
BRUNO: Ah so, they are kind of primitive, rubbish people?

TIFFANY: Kind of, yeah.

BRUNO: So tell me, do you hope that these white trash, trashing people will buy the clothes?

TIFFANY: I don't think they can afford it.

BRUNO: Ha! They are too poor! [both laugh heartily] We take the clothes from the homeless people and we sell them in the shop.

TIFFANY: And jack up the price.

BRUNO: The homeless people cannot buy them.

TIFFANY: Definitely, definitely.

BRUNO: That is the beauty of fashion.

TIFFANY: Yeah.

Similarly, as Baym in this volume notes, Stephen Colbert's interviews with right-wingers often playfully trap them within their own rhetoric, as when Colbert one-ups Georgia Republican Phil Gingrey's bigotry by satirically posing that homosexuals should not be allowed driving licenses, leaving Gingrey squirming for a way out and rendering him a fool in the process.

Stewart's interviewing style can also prove remarkably disarming. He can at one moment be a charming, friendly comedian making silly faces and can then prove one of American television's most intelligent and well-informed interviewers, willing to pounce and requiring thoughtful answers. Filmed in front of a live studio audience, *The Daily Show* offers public figures the *possibility* to appear authentic in a way that lending one's voice to a *Simpsons* script cannot allow, but the tradeoff is a situation in which the satirist gains more power. Stewart is known for at times adopting a more combative style, as is particularly evident in his interview/argument with former ambassador to the United Nations, John Bolton. In a case of sad irony, public figures can often be more sure of red carpet treatment, pleasantries, and easy-to-fool interviewers on established news programs than on *The Daily Show*. When Stewart does attack his guests, the presence of the live studio audience places the guest in the position of outsider: not only has the crowd come to see Stewart, virtually assuring their political allegiance, but also Stewart has established a performer's bond with them by the time the guest steps onto the set. Since American politicians and celebrities have often proven so successful at buffering themselves from any citizens but loyal voters and fans, *The Daily Show*'s comic space offers a rare zone in which audience members can jeer and boo public figures or register their displeasure through cheering Stewart's cutting remarks made at their expense. A key value of *The Daily Show*, as such, is that it provides, however small and limited in nature, a space for a range of American citizen-politician interactions and communication in which public image is anything but stable. Guests on *The Daily Show* are left trying to balance the appearance of being relaxed, calm, and personable, while also guarding themselves against a possible blow. At once a better test of their claimed authenticity, then, and a less sure site for the boosting of public image, the space is again a dangerous zone for public figures.

Michael Moore has similarly proven adept at catching public figures unaware, dragging them into the picture as victims less than guests. His technique, honed in *TV Nation* and *The Awful Truth*, of showing up at a public figure's office or home, camera rolling, provides for many the representative image of guerrilla interviewing, notable for providing a rare moment at which a public figure is wholly unprepared and unscripted. The prospects for revelation are once again high here, especially since Moore's questions, while edgy, are frequently ones that many citizen-viewers would like asked of public figures. Thus, this tactic holds with it the power to challenge the individual public figure's image, at the same time as it launches a parodic-satiric attack on journalism's velvet glove treatment of public figures that rarely demands answers to truly provocative questions.

While Moore, Stewart, Colbert, and Cohen are more familiar to American readers, one of guerrilla interviewing's greatest practitioners and innovators is the English satirist Chris Morris. Morris shot to fame with his radio news parody, *On the Hour,* and six-episode television news parody, *The Day Today,* aired in 1991 and 1994, respectively. Then came *Brass Eye,* a six-episode series aired in 1997.[26] Though *Brass Eye* stood out for being superb news parody, and for satirizing moral panics, it also became famous for Morris's interview technique. Each episode focused on a particular social issue, such as "Moral Decline," and, among other contents, each involved Morris creating a bogus social problem, an equally bogus interest group dedicated to fighting this problem, and, ultimately, Morris, acting as front man for the group, obtaining public service announcements from public figures. Thus, for instance, "heavy electricity" was the problem of the moment in the "Science" episode, while the closing credit sequence of the "Animals" episode ran audiotape of Morris informing *Baywatch* star Alexandra Paul of a case of "zoochosis" in a German zoo. He explained that Carla, an elephant, had become so depressed in captivity that she had placed first her trunk in her own backside and proceeded to ingest herself, then her head. Paul implored listeners to "help me get Carla's head out of her guts now, before she explodes," before Morris cranked the wheel further by informing Paul that he had just received word that a vet had managed to remove the head, "but it had shrunk, and it was now small and smooth and white . . . about the size of a man's head." Paul could only express shock at first, before recommending that Morris "get this out over the wire" to other news outlets so that something might be done about it.

Morris's most famous stunt occurred in the episode on "Drugs." The fictitious social problem was a new drug from Czechoslovakia called Cake that resembled a luminous yellow giant cake of cheese, while the interest group formed to fight it was "Free the United Kingdom from Drugs, incorporating British Opposition to Metabolically Bisturbile Drugs" (FUKD and BOMBD). Armed with a laughable set of symptoms and scientific data, Morris managed to record public service announcements from multiple public figures. Famed Australian entertainer Rolf Harris warned viewers of how the drug causes "Czech neck," whereby one's neck swells up "to engulf the mouth and the nose" (figure 7.2). English stand-up comedian Bernard Manning warned that Cake had led to one young child crying all the water out of his body and to a girl throwing up her own pelvis bone. Margaret Thatcher's press secretary Sir Bernard Ingham contextualized the knock-on dangers by noting that "several people have actually been brained by saucepans thrown out of tower-blocks used to make this kind of Cake," before asking viewers to "Use your cheese-box and say no, never." Radio and television personality Noel Edmonds explained that Cake

> has an active ingredient, which is a dangerous psychoactive compound known as dimesmeric anson-phosphate. It stimulates the part of the brain known as Shatner's Bassoon, and that's the bit of the brain that deals with time perception. So a second feels like a month. Well, it almost sounds like fun . . . unless you're the Prague schoolboy who walked out into the street, straight in front of a tram. He thought he'd got a month to cross the street.

Later, addressing the camera, Edmonds closes, "Thank you for listening to me, take care, and I really do mean, take care."

Morris's coup de grace, however, lay in convincing Conservative MP David Amess to lend his voice and image to the fight against Cake. Seething righteous indignation at "the filth" that sells Cake to the "poor user, or 'custard gannet' as the dealers call them," Amess described how Cake could make a two-second blip sound like four hours of cacophonic industrial techno (figure 7.3). Then Amess offered to push in Parliament for the illegalization of Cake, leading to a bizarre scene in the July 24, 1996,

Figs. 7.2 and 7.3. On *Brasseye*, Rolf Harris shows viewers Cake, the dangerous new drug taking Prague by storm, while Member of Parliament David Amess warns of its killer side effects.

parliamentary debates where Amess asked the Secretary of State for the Home Department what was being done about Cake. When Amess later complained to the country's broadcasting watchdog, the Independent Television Commission, the ITC rejected the complaint, pointing out that Amess should have been tipped off by any number of the ludicrous statements provided by Morris.[27]

Brass Eye thereby led to the public humiliation of these figures as their episodes aired. All encounters were scheduled, not spur-of-the-moment requests, so in theory the figures could have had time to research the imaginary problems. As a result, while we are laughing at the silliness of descriptions of Cake or heavy electricity, our laugh is doubled by the stupidity and gullibility of the public figure. Their indignation and concern would seemingly demand even the most cursory attempt at research, but, instead, Morris illustrates how ignorant many public figures are of the political issues that they champion and that they carelessly present to citizen-audiences. His victims no doubt imagined that they would be working for a good cause, and be acknowledged as good Samaritans and citizens by viewers, but, instead, they were reduced to objects of ridicule, their public image forever tainted by the "remember the time when . . . ?" comments that inevitably haunt them and their Wikipedia entries.

As true satire should, then, Morris's play with public figures can thoroughly defamiliarize the process by which public figures create and manicure their image. If any of these figures could be convinced to campaign for nonsensical causes, one is forced to wonder what else they could be duped into supporting, from political parties to platforms. Furthermore, since the cause of Brass Eye's social problems is always posited as foreign—Czech drugs likely to invade England, German zookeepers, or the Sri Lankan government—Morris's satire points to the Othering and racial or national vilification that often accompanies moral panics, to which public figures can thoughtlessly subscribe. As opposed to a public figure's appearance on The Simpsons or during an interview with Jon Stewart on The Daily Show, where, as has been said, public figures gamble on whether their image will benefit or be harmed, here Morris works solely to attack public image, so that the erstwhile PSA makes its speaker appear stupid.

Alongside Brass Eye, we can place several other satires that similarly involve either offering silly information to a public figure or editing the interview after the fact to produce a version that ridicules the figure. Of the former instance, Serra Tinic's contribution to this volume (chapter 8) discusses how Canadian satire This Hour Has 22 Minutes's Rick Mercer

hoodwinked numerous American politicians into betraying their ignorance in on-the-spot interviews in his "Talking to Americans" segment.
Then-Governor George W. Bush could not correct Mercer when he incorrectly named the Canadian Prime Minister; Iowa Governor Tom Vilsack
congratulated Canada on finally moving from a 20-hour to a 24-hour
clock; and Arkansas Governor Mike Huckabee congratulated Canadians
on preserving their National Igloo, supposedly the nation's capitol building built with ice. Turning to edited interviews, *The Daily Show* and *The
Colbert Report* have specialized in reconstituting interviews after the fact,
often with blatantly obvious cuts and edits that highlight their strategy
but that nevertheless can render the interviewee a patsy, once more allowing the possibility of a bump in public image from being seen as a good
sport but also offering the possibility of ridicule.

## Conclusion: The Dangers of Heavy Electricity

Two concurrent processes are at work in such shows and satirical play
with public figures: on one level, such shows frequently mock and undercut the figure being interviewed. Bush not knowing who leads Canada reveals remarkable ignorance, just as David Amess falling for the Cake setup even to the point of appearing in a FUKD and BOMBD t-shirt hurts
his public image. If celebrity or performance politics offers publicists the
chance to author the public figure as text by using details of their (supposed) personality to serve as metonymic to their political value, good
satire can reauthor the figure, "infecting" their image, and centering it on
stupidity and gullibility.

But a second-level attack is also made at the very concept of public
figure inclusion in politics and at their role as would-be intermediaries.
In the case of *Brass Eye*, for instance, the viewer is served a clear message
about the potential misuse of celebrity, and, as does all satire, *Brass Eye*
calls for a corrective. The show gouges at public figures' images, both to
send a loud and clear message to public figures to actually know what they
are talking about and to send an equally loud and clear message to audiences to be wary of assigning extra value or significance to any political or
social cause simply because a public figure implores one to. Of course, a
risk here is that audiences' prior identification with particularly well liked
figures will determine their loyalty as such, producing a defensive reading that sees the satirist's antics as unfair, rude, and manipulative. Viewers

might, in other words, simply feel sorry for the figure, a criticism that has often been lodged at Michael Moore's invasive interviewing style in particular. Satirical attacks on a beloved figure will galvanize some viewers rather than amuse or educate. Even in such cases, however, the viewer focuses on the ease with which public figures can be manipulated. In either situation, one is asked to reflect on public figures' relationships to both the causes they champion and the individuals and interests behind such causes. We are also invited to reflect on the artifice of media culture more generally, and on the public figure as a particular node of artifice within that culture, as satirists perform an inversion of public figure authority and authenticity in truly carnivalesque, up-ending manner.

Granted, we must be careful not to overvalue the critical potential of satirical attacks on the nature of celebrity politics. While all of the shows here have enjoyed cult status, and some have enjoyed large audiences, they face formidable opposition in the form of multiple magazines, entertainment news programs, celebratory news programs and cable channels, and so forth that peddle and build up the celebrification of politics in uncritical ways and that are vulnerable to a decent public relations expert's moves. Moreover, much of this satiric attack risks perpetuating a notion of politics as being peopled and controlled by individuals, not institutions per se. While these shows have at other times lodged important attacks on political institutions, the focus of their attacks on public image can reify the notion of political will and power being embedded in the individual—in other words, the very notion that serves as bedrock for today's celebrification of politics.

Nevertheless, as I have argued elsewhere, satire has a viral quality that aids in satirists' attempts to speak to a larger audience, allowing it to broadcast via networks of online video-sharing sites and everyday discussion.[28] Undoubtedly, today's television satirists could go further at times, and it is also no surprise that some of the form's most unapologetically Juvenalian satirists have courted considerable controversy, attack from public figures, and, simply, short-lived shows. But when, for instance, Rick Mercer can capture presidential hopefuls thinking that Canadians convene Parliament in a giant igloo, or when Chris Morris can capture Thatcher's press secretary unaware, viewers are treated not only to funny television but also to a public interrogation of public figures' mediation of politics, as well as media culture's mediation of these figures. Politicians and celebrities flock to television satire in hopes of friendly, image-enhancing treatment, but many risk heavy electrical shock, figuratively reducing them to eight inches tall. The easy joke would be to say that these victimized public figures "must feel quite dreadful," but the satirists' skill is often such that their targets hardly even notice, ensuring yet more victims on the next show and yet more satiric media and political literacy instruction regarding the celebrification of politics.

NOTES

1. Liesbet van Zoonen, *Entertaining the Citizen: When Politics and Popular Culture Converge* (Lanham, Md.: Rowman and Littlefield, 2005), 72.

2. John Street, "The Celebrity Politician: Political Style and Popular Culture," in *Media and the Restyling of Politics*, ed. John Corner and Dick Pels (Thousand Oaks, Calif.: Sage, 2003); Joseph Schumpeter, *Capitalism, Socialism and Democracy* (London: George Allen and Unwin, 1976).

3. For instance, Stuart Ewen, "Marketing Dreams: The Political Elements of Style," in *Consumption, Identity, and Style: Marketing, Meanings, and the Packaging of Pleasure*, ed. Alan Tomlinson (New York: Routledge, 1990); Bob Franklin, *Packaging Politics: Political Communications in Britain's Media Democracy* (London: Edward Arnold, 1994); Nicholas Jones, *Sultans of Spin: The Media and the New Labour Government* (London: Victor Gollancz, 1999); Neil Postman, *Amusing Ourselves to Death: Public Discourse in the Age of Show Business* (New York: Penguin, 1986).

4. John Corner, "Mediated Persona and Public Culture," in *Media and the Restyling of Politics*, ed. John Corner and Dick Pels (Thousand Oaks, Calif.: Sage, 2003).

5. Dick Pels, "Aesthetic Representation and Political Style," in *Media and the Restyling of Politics*, ed. John Corner and Dick Pels (Thousand Oaks, Calif.: Sage, 2003).

6. G. Thomas Goodnight, "*The Passion of the Christ* Meets *Fahrenheit 9/11*: A Study in Celebrity Advocacy," *American Behavioral Scientist* 49, no. 3 (November 2005): 410–35.

7. Street, "Celebrity Politician," 96; Dick Pountain and David Robins, *Cool Rules: Anatomy of an Attitude* (London: Reaktion, 2000), 26, 171.

8. P. David Marshall, *Celebrity and Power: Fame in Contemporary Culture* (Minneapolis: University of Minnesota Press, 1997).

9. John Hartley, *Popular Reality: Journalism, Modernity, Popular Culture* (London: Arnold, 1996), 84.

10. Pels, "Aesthetic Representation."

11. George E. Marcus, *The Sentimental Citizen: Emotion in Democratic Politics* (University Park: Pennsylvania University Press, 2002).

12. Van Zoonen, *Entertaining the Citizen.*

13. Andrew Samuels, *The Political Psyche* (New York: Routledge, 1993); Andrew Samuels, *Politics on the Couch: Citizenship and the Internal Life* (London: Profile, 2001).

14. Jeffrey P. Jones, *Entertaining Politics: New Political Television and Civic Culture* (Lanham, Md.: Rowman and Littlefield, 2005), 173–77.

15. Richard Dyer, *Stars* (London: British Film Institute, 1998); Marshall, *Celebrity and Power*; Richard Schickel, *Intimate Strangers: The Culture of Celebrity* (Garden City, N.Y.: Doubleday, 1985); Graeme Turner, *Understanding Celebrity* (Thousand Oaks, Calif.: Sage, 2004).

16. Paul F. Lazarsfeld, Bernard Berelson, and Hazel Gaudet, *The People's Choice: How the Voter Makes Up His Mind in a Presidential Campaign* (New York: Columbia University Press, 1944).

17. Street, "Celebrity Politician," 92.

18. Dyer, *Stars;* Marshall, *Celebrity and Power;* Cornel Sandvoss, *Fans: The Mirror of Consumption* (Malden, Mass.: Polity, 2005).

19. Mikhail M. Bakhtin, *The Dialogic Imagination,* trans. Caryl Emerson and Michael Holquist (Austin: University of Texas Press, 1981); Roland Barthes, *S/Z,* trans. Richard Miller (Oxford: Basil Blackwell, 1990); John Fiske, *Understanding Popular Culture* (Boston: Unwin Hyman, 1989).

20. See also Jonathan Gray, *Watching with* The Simpsons: *Television, Parody, and Intertextuality* (New York: Routledge, 2006).

21. Regarding caricature, see Jones, chapter 2 in this volume.

22. Corner, "Mediated Persona," 77.

23. Nick Couldry, *Media Rituals* (New York: Routledge, 2003).

24. Geoffrey Baym, "Representation and the Politics of Play: Stephen Colbert's *Better Know a District,*" *Political Communication* 24, no. 4 (2007): 359–76.

25. On the carnivalesque, see Gray, Jones, and Thompson, chapter 1 in this volume.

26. A seventh episode, "Paedophilia," was broadcast in 2001, mocking moral panics with raw, uncomfortable humor and ironically creating its own moral panic, fast becoming the most complained about show in British television history.

27. Paul McCann, "Brass Eye Wins Over Watchdog," *Independent* (19 May 1997), at http://findarticles.com/p/articles/mi_qn4158/is_19970519/ai_n14107835 (accessed 26 August 2007).

28. Gray, *Watching with* The Simpsons.

*8*

<sup>||||||||||||||||||||||||||||||||||||||||||||||||||||</sup>

# Speaking "Truth" to Power?
## Television Satire, Rick Mercer Report, and the Politics of Place and Space

### Serra Tinic

In 2003, the *New York Times* published a front-page article proclaiming that the emergence of a distinctive Canadian identity, marked by a notably European sociocultural sensibility, was the foundation of the nation's increasingly fractious relationship with the United States.[1] The fact that the most influential newspaper in the United States had pronounced the resolution of the national identity crisis that had defined Canada since the end of British colonialism should have been remarkable in and of itself. More astonishing, however, was that the source of this revelation was Canada's "leading political satirist" Rick Mercer, who was interviewed after the following "editorial" from his weekly fake news comedy, *Rick Mercer Report*: "Being attached to America these days is like being in a pen with a wounded bull. Between the pot smoking and the gay marriage, quite frankly it's a wonder there is not a giant deck of cards out there with all our faces on it."[2] Although Mercer emphasized to the *Times* that his comment was merely "for laughs," he opened the door for more "official" sources—including Canadian academics, economists, and business analysts—to explain the growing breach between the two countries on issues such as sexuality, multiculturalism, militarism, drug use, and social welfare policies. The fact that Mercer's comedic quip about the continental drift in social values could provide the basis for a lead news story in the "national paper of record" provides a compelling insight into the contemporary role of political satire in both the televisual and public spheres in North America.

In many respects, the *New York Times* interview with Rick Mercer epitomizes Geoffrey Baym's conceptualization of the "discursive integration" that is characteristic of other fake news satires, such as *The Daily Show with Jon Stewart*, wherein the boundaries between the "discourses of news, politics, entertainment, and marketing have grown deeply inseparable."[3] As media genres become more fluid, new forms of political communication evolve and contribute to an arena in which previously unauthorized voices become participants in the debates of the day. The article also speaks to the broader communal dimensions and cultural specificity of satire as a mode of address. What is "news" to an American journalist is an easily recognizable joke to Canadian audiences—one that emanates from the sociocultural experiences of disproportionate power relations in the North American relationship.

In this chapter, I explore the cultural geography of political satire and the implications for the construction of national and regional identities through an analysis of the faux news comedy *Rick Mercer Report* and Rick Mercer's 2001 television special, *Talking to Americans*. It begins with a discussion of the place (in both literal and figurative terms) of satire within Canadian culture and, in particular, its inextricable link to the country's relationship with the United States. Specific consideration is given to the imperative of exploring sociohistorical context as a central component of satirical discourse, as well as power relationships and community building. Consequently, I conclude the discussion with an exploration of how Mercer's satirical commentary adapted to the geopolitics of the evolving Canadian-American relationship after September 11, 2001.

## Satire and Nation-Building in Canada

Satire is often defined as a moralistic mode of address that critiques the missteps and hypocrisies of those who wield cultural and political authority.[4] It is a tactic of resistance for those who sit outside the circles of power, and its success depends on the complicity of an audience of cultural insiders who are privy to the codes needed to "get the joke." Consequently, satire as a discursive form speaks specifically to issues of social cohesion and division rooted within the particular experiences of places and communities. And if a position of marginality is integral to this mode of critique, it is perhaps not surprising that satirical sketch comedies have proven to be among the most popular genres on Canadian television, as well as one of the few domestic formats that regularly generates large audiences cross-nationally.

The Canadian experience of postcolonial nation-building has been marked by concentric forms of domestic and international center-periphery relationships. In a regionally fragmented country, it is often only the shared sense of political and cultural subordination to the powers of central Canada and the United States that has provided the regions with a unified sense of community. And as Gerald Lynch notes, "Comedy is often born out of such conflicting impulses and emotions . . . the history of Canada has been the story of contending forces: French and English, liberal and conservative, England and America, Canadian nationalist and North American continentalist agendas, among others."[5] As an oppositional form of comedy, satire resonates profoundly with the negative sense of identity that defines the Canadian national self-consciousness—the tendency to define yourself by what you are not. From this perspective, the definition of Canada is always one of shifting centers and margins; it can only be articulated in opposition to the "other."[6] The other defines who an individual is as a Canadian at any given time, and thus identity is in a constant state of flux, depending on whether the other is the United States, Quebec, Ontario, or a different ethnic group or region. Herein, identity stands in relation to perpetually unsettled hierarchies of "us" and "them."

As a form of cultural bonding, satire, and its relationship to power and marginality, is particularly effective as a mode of symbolic resistance to the perceived power of the dominant other. As such, literary theorists have argued that satirical irony has long been a defining feature of Canadian cultural productions that attempt to negotiate the multiple forms of alienation that mark the national psyche:

> Obsessed, still, with articulating its identity Canada often speaks with a doubled voice, with the forked tongue of irony. Although usually seen as either a defensive or an offensive rhetorical weapon, irony—even in the simple sense of saying one thing and meaning another—is also a mode of "speech" (in any medium) that allows speakers to address and at the same time slyly confront an "official" discourse: that is to work within a dominant tradition but also to challenge it—without being utterly co-opted by it.[7]

And in the hierarchy of dominant others, Canada's superpower neighbor to the south has become the favored target of ironic critique. Indeed, the oppositional form of identity that derives from "not being American" has provided Canadians with the most efficacious other with which to overcome regional discontent and form the national imagined community.[8]

The political and cultural insecurity that accompanies the seemingly insubstantial border between the two countries provides perhaps the greatest sense of marginalization for most Anglo-Canadians. Because of this, the cultural and geographic proximity of the United States has probably provided Canadians with their strongest impetus to rally around the flag.[9] These connections between irony and marginalization, and their representation within the genre of satire, reaffirm the tension between inclusion and exclusion that underlies the maintenance of collective identities. And if we accept that the ironic voice is most adroit when performed by those who stand outside the spheres of power, then it is not surprising that the most successful Canadian satirical television comedies over the past 15 years have been created by a group of comedians, including Rick Mercer, from Newfoundland.

Newfoundland is not only one of the most marginalized provinces in the country, it is also the most reluctant member, after Quebec. With a small population inhabiting a rocky outcropping along the Atlantic Ocean, Newfoundland has supported itself through a precarious fishing-based industry and regional equalization payments—a form of national welfare subsidized by the wealthier provinces. The combination of underpopulation, isolation, and poverty placed Newfoundland in the unfortunate position of being the most ridiculed province in the country. The "Newfie joke" is a continuing national tradition that has provided Canadians from other regions with a source of superior sentiment that could be seen as masking their own feelings of subordination to central Canada and the United States. As popular culture critics Geoff Pevere and Greig Dymond explain, the ensuing sense of exclusion emanating from the experience of being the poor relation has provided Newfoundlanders with a keen and critical perspective of the country:

> Separated from the rest of Canada by a combination of factors which include geography, history, politics, economics, and culture, Newfoundland represents the virtual and actual outer limits of the Canadian experience. If one of the defining characteristics of Canadian popular culture is a sense of continental marginality, the Newfoundland experience exists on the margins of marginality. The outsider's outsider. Alienation squared.[10]

It is within this regional context that Newfoundland comedian Rick Mercer honed his talents as a satirist and eventually joined with three fellow Maritimers in 1993 to develop the most popular weekly fake news comedy in Canadian broadcasting history, *This Hour Has 22 Minutes.* Following the mise-en-scène of the nightly national newscast, the show's four characters reported the "news" to a live CBC (Canadian Broadcasting Corporation) studio audience. Filling the roles of both anchors and roving correspondents, the cast members combined interviews with fictional news sources and editorial commentary of actual news footage. Their satirical range reached a new height of political verisimilitude when, in character, they attended actual media scrums and scathingly interviewed real politicians. The show quickly gained a large and loyal audience and became so influential politically that the cast became known as the country's "unofficial opposition" in Parliament. And while Canadian audiences reveled in watching their politicians trapped in the contradictions of their own rhetoric and actions, the show's equally acerbic send-up of American culture and politics became one of the most popular features of the series. As the show's two primary political satirists, Mary Walsh and Rick Mercer consistently stressed the saliency of regional and continental marginalization as integral to the extent to which a national audience could see themselves inscribed within *22 Minutes* satirical sketches:

WALSH: I felt alienated from Canada. I learned a great deal of resentment for Canada and all things Canadian. Newfoundlanders went from being England's doormat to being Canada's laughing stock. Canadians do not know who they are. Newfoundlanders always knew who Canadians were: People who thought they were better than us. But what makes Canadians constantly think they're not as good as the buddy [Americans] next door? Why are we so ashamed of what shaped us? We have an identity. We're us. We have different voices.[11]

MERCER: I don't think there's a lot funny about being Canadian. I think one of the reasons why all of those [comedy writers] are successful is they know what's really funny about being an American. We speak the same, we look the same. Yet we're very different, so we have a good bead on America. And I think Newfoundlanders feel the same way about Canada. We're similar but we have this attitude that we're way out on the edge.[12]

These expressions of multiple experiences of inferiority are instructive to both the Canadian sociocultural experience and the nature of satire itself. Satire assumes the voice of moral superiority in the face of political, economic, and cultural subordination. This tends also to be a common Canadian narrative in the project to define a sense of national difference from the United States. In his final few years as a member of 22 *Minutes*, Mercer devoted many of his segments to the pursuit of the theme that, despite their nation's hegemonic global presence, Americans knew very little about world politics or other cultures, including that of their largest trading partner and neighbor: Canada. The 1996 U.S. presidential election provided Mercer with the material that would not only solidify his celebrity in Canada but also eventually lead to his role as a sought after commentator on North American relations. In his persona as reporter J. B. Dickson, Mercer went on location in Washington, D.C., to cover President Clinton's reelection to office. As part of his "foreign correspondent" activities, Mercer used a favored mode of Canadian satire vis à vis the Americans by encouraging them to show their lack of knowledge about Canada in their own words. Here, J. B. would stop Capitol Hill employees on their way to work and ask their opinion as to whether the upcoming meetings between President Clinton and Prime Minister Chrétien should be called the "Clinton-Chrétien Summit" or the "Chrétien-Clinton Summit." Playing on the assumption that even Washington insiders would not know the name of the Canadian prime minister, Mercer substituted the names of Canadian media personalities Ralph Benmergui and Peter Gzowski in the place of Chrétien. After none of the selected interviewees corrected the prime minister's name, J. B. closed the segment with the following response to an individual who had selected the Benmergui-Clinton Summit option:

J. B. DICKSON: Oh, alphabetical. Very diplomatic.
INTERVIEWEE: That's why I work in Washington.

These Washington segments were so popular with 22 *Minutes* audiences that they became regular segments called "Talking to Americans." Mercer's future "reports" included trips to other sites where the implication was that people who "should" know better actually did not. For example, Harvard professors and students were asked their opinions on nonsensical "facts" such as the cruelty of the seal hunt in the prairie province of Saskatchewan. Shortly before his departure from 22 *Minutes* in 2001, Rick Mercer completed a one-hour episode of *Talking to Americans*. The special drew 2.7 million viewers and still ranks as one of the highest-rated programs on CBC television, aside from *Hockey Night in Canada*.

## Making the News: Talking to Americans

In the opening scene of *Talking to Americans,* Rick Mercer stands in front of the White House and in direct address to the camera states to the audience: "You are in America. America the strong. America the free. America our next-door neighbor. They are our greatest friends, our strongest allies. They are kind. They are generous. They have an uncanny ability to go on at great lengths on subjects they know absolutely nothing about."[13] *Talking to Americans* achieved maximum ironic effect when the CBC deliberately aired the special on April Fools' Day. While the special included some of Mercer's best clips from his work on *22 Minutes,* the hour-long version provided Mercer with a broader satirical canvas as he traveled coast to coast formulating questions in cars and coffee shops with his producer as his sounding board. In the role of sardonic prankster, Mercer asked Berkeley students, known for their progressive social views, about their opinion of Canadian Prime Minister Jean Chrétien being the first black leader in the then-G7. The students were thrilled to hear this, and one noted that he hoped the United States would soon follow suit and elect an African American president. No one corrected Mercer on the fact that Chrétien was a white male. Similarly, at New York University, Mercer "Canadianized" an American phenomenon when he asked whether the "fact" that 70 percent of Canadian junior high school students could not identify their home "state" on an unmarked map, reflected a crisis in that nation's educational system. One outraged university student replied that he found it "disgraceful that people are that unaware of the world they live in." The irony of the student's lack of knowledge of both Canada and his own country's educational statistics is accentuated when Mercer later poses the same question to a mother and her young son, to which the little boy replies: "Hang on, Canada has provinces."

*Talking to Americans* illustrates the centrality of power to the practice of effective satire. To the extent that satire serves as an "attack on unwarranted pride, particularly when someone demands more respect than he or she should,"[14] Mercer's selection of Americans at prestigious universities and urban business centers heightened the comic value by exposing the insularity of the country's elite. Indeed, there is no humor in mocking those who lack the requisite forms of capital to lay claims to cultural, economic, or political authority. That is merely mean-spirited mocking. For the domestic audience back home, the punch line provided an intangible—and fleeting—sense of intellectual and cultural superiority that ensued from the perception that the "average" Canadian is more knowledgeable than the most "privileged" American.

The question that arises is whether such satirical discourse has any greater political impact than to temporarily unite a community against a perceived other. Dustin Griffin refers to this as the "special compensation of satire" in which the discourse "induces a gratifying sense of moral victory to compensate for [the satirist's and audience's] status as political underdogs or outsiders."[15] The momentary catharsis that results from laughing at a shared indignation may help "keep up the spirit of [one's] own side."[16] But to what effect? After all, a satirical statement that speaks to taken-for-granted Canadian assumptions cannot be expected to contribute to structural change in international relations. In this respect, the political potential, and limitations, of *Talking to Americans* corresponds with Mikhail Bakhtin's conceptualization of carnival wherein social hierarchies are temporarily overthrown and the masses are able to celebrate the recognition of themselves as a collective—united across class and other divisional lines in their mockery of those whose material power is far greater than their own.[17] Mercer, in the role of the carnival's insightful "fool," leads the domestic audience in an act of symbolic resistance that briefly accords them the upper hand culturally in their relationship with the United States.

*Talking to Americans* also underscores the critiques levied against the cathartic potential of Bakhtin's optimism for the political potential of carnival: namely, that it may operate with the sanction of those in power as it offers a release that alleviates the desire for actual rebellion. Herein, the emphasis on resentment against Americans deflects criticism from Canada's own politicians, who are largely accountable for the economic and political relationship between the two countries. Simultaneously, the continual emphasis on uniting against the external other detracts from the internal regional conflicts that mark the Canadian domestic sphere, which is the site within which Canadians actually have the capacity for material political intervention.

In the end, *Talking to Americans* proved that although satirical observation may not lead to revolutionary political or cultural change, the well-timed barb did hold the power to provoke an informed dialogue between the "knowledgeable outsider" and the target of the joke. Consequently, while Mercer's satire may have defused the need for a self-reflective dialogue about Canada's own national schisms, the timing and content of the comedy special engendered an unforeseen response of self-questioning within the American news agenda.

Mercer's American road trip was filmed during the 2000 presidential primary races and, surprisingly, the comedian managed to work his way into the media scrums surrounding the two top candidates, Al Gore and George W. Bush. Mercer caught up with Gore at the Iowa primary, where he pushed his way up to the Democratic candidate and tested his knowledge of national capitals:

> MERCER: Mr. Gore, a question from Canada. You know it's a tradition that newly elected presidents make their first foreign visit to the capital of Canada. Can we expect to see President Gore in Toronto in the New Year?
> AL GORE: Well, I'm just focused on the election.

To reinforce his point about the relative insignificance of Canada within American politics, Mercer turned to a Gore campaign supporter to determine if he would know that Ottawa was the actual capital of the country. When Mercer asked whether he thought it was significant that Gore knew that Toronto was the capital of Canada, the man shrugged and said, "Well yeah, if you think that's important." Gore, however, was spared the humiliation that awaited George W. Bush at the Michigan primary. While Gore could easily dismiss his error as a rushed and brief response in the confusion of a loud and bustling crowd, Bush made the mistake of responding at length to one of Mercer's favorite factual distortions: the name of Canada's prime minister.

> MERCER: A question from Canada, the Canadian Broadcasting Corporation. Prime Minister Jean Poutine said that he wouldn't endorse any candidate in this race and today he said that George W. Bush should be the man to lead the free world into the 21st century. How important is this endorsement?
> BUSH: Well I'm honored. I appreciate his strong statement. He understands I believe in free trade. He understands I want to make sure our relations with our most important neighbor to the north of us—the Canadians—is strong and we'll work closely together.

No one could fault Bush for not knowing that *poutine* is a Québecois side dish of french fries mixed with gravy and melted cheese curds. However, his failure to correctly identify the prime minister of his "most important neighbor" as Jean Chrétien was an egregious error, given the criticism he had recently faced in the American press when he was unable to name the president of Pakistan; particularly given his public statement that he could never be "stumped" again about the names of world leaders. And just to add emphasis to his gaffe, these facts both appeared in graphics as the lead-in to the Bush and Mercer segment in *Talking to Americans*.

Bush's blunder, in particular, drew the attention of the American press to both Mercer and his larger satirical project. Within due course, he was interviewed by the *Washington Post*, the *New York Times*, and news-radio stations throughout the United States. The line between fake news correspondent and real political commentator was blurred further when Mercer was invited to participate as a guest panelist on ABC's *Nightline* in July 2001. Here, Mercer found himself in the role of pundit on the topic of the problems of polling and public opinion, given his expertise in talking to Americans. Even the celebrity machine of the entertainment industry moved into action, and Mercer was offered the hosting role for the game show *The Weakest Link*, which he declined.[18] In an exemplary moment of discursive integration, the "outsider's outsider" had become an authorized voice on the subject of power politics in the center of North American power.

Genre and cultural positioning are important factors in this regard. The insights that Mercer, as a knowledgeable external observer, provided through the comedic framing of American insularity highlighted the incongruity of that nation's global status in a way that the insider discourses of domestic journalism were unable to accommodate. After all, the issues that Mercer brought to the surface were not startling revelations or breaking news. For years, the official voices of the American news media had reported on the educational crisis in the United States, as well as on the shortcomings of politicians, intellectually and otherwise. The implication, therefore, is that satire as a discursive form that emphasizes "the discrepancy between what is and what ought to be" brought into vivid relief the credibility of America's claim on the status of world power broker.[19] Although political satire may not lead to extensive structural transformation, it has the capacity to enter the larger sphere of public dialogue through provocation, whether by presenting an old argument in a new light or through the lens of alterity. This, in and of itself, can be a significant political intervention.

Moreover, Mercer's cultural positioning as the informed interloper speaks to the mutually reinforcing relationship between the center and the periphery in both the practice of satire and the formation of communal identification. As Jonathan Rutherford explains, the periphery actually contributes to the definition of the center by continually drawing attention to the issues of difference or "marking what the center lacks":

"It is in its nature as a supplement to the centre that the margin is also a place of resistance. The assertion of its existence threatens to deconstruct those forms of knowledge that constitute the subjectivities, discourses and institutions of the dominant hegemonic formations."[20] In this respect, *Talking to Americans* can be seen to act as a dialogue that both reinforces and disrupts the cultural dimensions of the Canadian-American relationship. Within the Canadian context, the satire worked to reaffirm dominant assumptions about the leaders and populace of the United States in a manner that supported the negative identity project of national unity. It contributed to a sense of collective smugness, based on the presumption of Canadians' greater awareness of the world at large, and thereby assuaged the sentiment of continental marginality. The reception of the comedy special within the United States, conversely, challenged the generalized idealizations of populist democracy wherein the assumption of an informed citizenry is an integral component of the power-endowment process of selecting those who will govern nationally and lead globally.

As with any mode of speech, however, the efficacy of satire is driven by sociohistoric context, and Mercer's moment as a participant in the center's questioning of itself was brief. The events of September 11th changed the boundaries of public discourse as the United States retreated into itself. External satirical critique was neither desired nor appropriate. In one of those twists of irony, *Talking to Americans* was nominated for two Gemini awards (the Canadian equivalent of the American Emmy) one week after the attacks on the World Trade Center. Mercer turned down the nominations and issued a public statement: "I feel that this is not a time to be making light of the differences between two nations but rather a time to offer our unconditional support to our neighbors, friends and relatives to the South."[21] Mercer's words echoed the sentiments of the majority of Canadians who responded with shock to the images of that day. September 11th brought home that the tensions between the two countries were akin to a sibling rivalry where the younger's resentment emanated from the feeling of being overshadowed by the bigger, stronger, overachieving older brother or sister. A familial sense of commonality rather than difference would define the continental relationship—temporarily, at least.

In 2001, Mercer departed from fake news and turned his satirical gaze to the entertainment industry in the weekly series *Made in Canada,* in which he played a ruthless television producer. Two years later, the world would change again. The ruling Liberal Party in Canada was mired in internal conflict, and the United States was preparing to invade Iraq. The public sphere was ripe for satirical intervention, and Mercer returned to the faux news genre with *Rick Mercer Report*.[22] However, the structure and tone of *Rick Mercer Report* departed, to a noticeable extent, from the emphasis on the other that marked *Talking to Americans* and therein corresponded with the changing power geography of Canadian-American relations in a post-9/11 world.

## Faking the News: Rick Mercer Report

When Mercer returned to the genre of fake news, he brought with him much of the repertoire that had established his career on *22 Minutes*. There were some noticeable differences, however. First, there was no longer an ensemble cast. *Rick Mercer Report* was a one-man show, and Mercer now played himself as opposed to the "reporter" J. B. Dickson. Second, Mercer did not revive his "Talking to Americans" shtick but, instead, traveled across Canada and participated in the quotidian practices and special events that marked the domestic cultural arena. These weekly segments showcased Mercer taking part in activities ranging from the mundane to the spectacular—from learning to drive a Toronto subway train, attending the Toronto firefighting academy (figure 8.1), exploring campus life at various universities, spending a day at Quebec's winter Carnivale, to flying as a passenger in an Air Force fighter jet. In an interesting reversal of tone and method, Mercer had begun a seemingly celebratory exploration of the interregional bonds of community in Canada, as opposed to the reification of a negative or oppositional sense of nationalism that marked *Talking to Americans*.[23]

If satire serves as a barometer of the temper of the times, then Mercer's glimpses into everyday domestic life seemed to indicate a maturation point in the Canadian national identity project. The aftermath of September 11th did mark a departure of the ways between Canada and the United States, as articulated in the *New York Times* article discussed at the beginning of this chapter. With the election of George W. Bush and the dominance of the social conservative movement, Americans found themselves increasingly divided ideologically. Canada's refusal to send troops to Iraq combined with a more socially liberal cultural and legislative attitude did, indeed, set the two countries apart. Satirists like Mercer no longer needed to overemphasize the differences between the two nations as these were demonstrated nightly on the national news. The juxtaposition of Mercer's

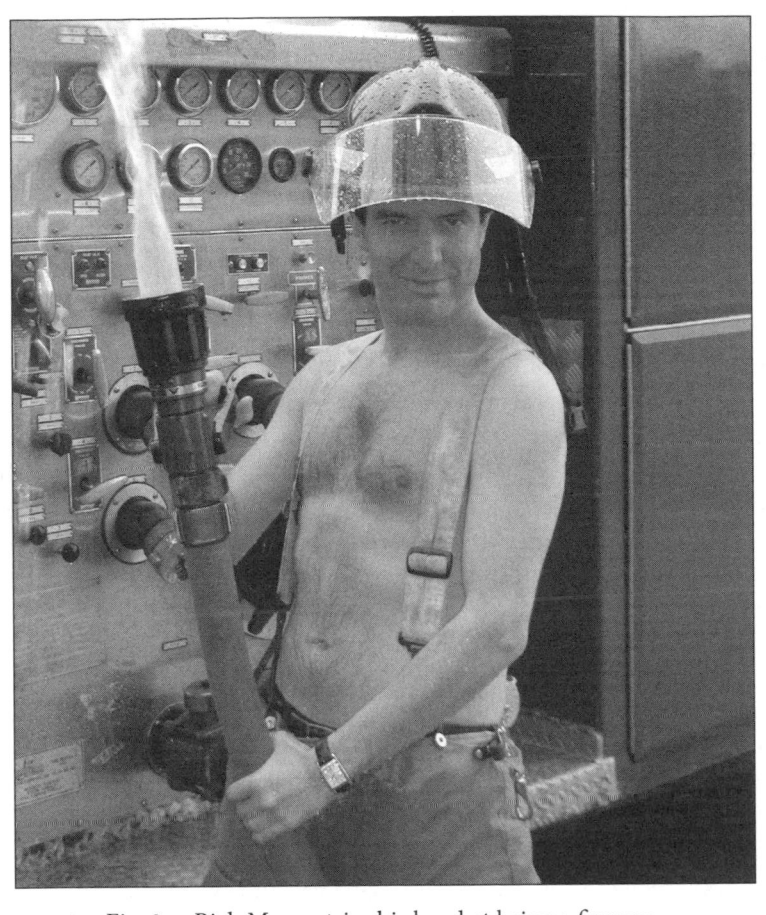

Fig. 8.1. Rick Mercer tries his hand at being a fireman,
on *Rick Mercer Report*.

segments of "ordinary" Canadian life with his fake news reports on continental politics served to reinforce this sense of cultural divergence.

In turning his attention away from the American lack of knowledge
of Canada, Mercer's reports and editorials increasingly focused on attacking the hypocrisy and perceived corruption of the U.S. administration, as
well as the networks of interest groups that sought to impose their ideological agenda on all Americans. This denunciative satirical turn closely
resembles the political tone and material of America's own *The Daily
Show with Jon Stewart*. Indeed, *Daily Show* viewers would immediately

recognize the discursive structure of *Rick Mercer Report*. With the exception of the cross-country cultural excursions, Mercer's faux news routines parallel those of *The Daily Show*. A typical half-hour episode of Mercer's show begins with an introduction of the major stories of the day and then moves to the "Front Page," a segment in which Mercer applies fictional backstories to news photos of politicians. Faux political and product advertisements are interspersed throughout the newscast, as are real interviews with Canadian politicians and celebrities.

Although inevitable comparisons can be made between *Rick Mercer Report* and its American counterparts *The Daily Show* and *The Colbert Report*, Mercer's work in the genre not only predates these comedies but also employs a wider array of satirical modes of address. His political commentary may best be described as an amalgamation of Jeffrey Jones's characterizations of the "court jester" (Jon Stewart) and "the mad prophet" (Dennis Miller).[24] Here, in his interviews and news analysis, Mercer moves between the "smirking disbelief" of the caring, yet mischievous, jester and the "enraged but bemused" prophet who rants about contemporary politics.[25] Indeed, every episode of *Rick Mercer Report* includes a "Rant" in which Mercer walks the streets of downtown Toronto giving a self-described "state of the union address." Mercer first introduced his rants (also called streeters) in *22 Minutes* and deploys them as a means of venting against the apparent outrages wrought by those wielding power. Canadian-American relations were frequently the focus of Mercer's *22 Minutes* rants. In *Rick Mercer Report*, however, Mercer's rants correspond with the cultural shift between the two countries. The United States features less frequently in his weekly diatribes, and when Mercer does rail against American politics, it is often on a topic unrelated to bilateral issues. Instead, the rants tend to center on the integrity of America's larger global policies or the contradictions between what is preached to other nations, compared with what is practiced at home.

For example, it is difficult to miss the irony in his rant about the moral crusade to censor television in the United States as the country fights a war in Iraq under the alleged banner of freedom, democracy, and secular governance:

I've always believed that in the United States there was a big difference between conservative and stupid. But boy, it's getting harder by the minute to prove that one. On Veteran's Day in America, the movie *Saving Private Ryan* was dumped by over sixty ABC affiliates. And why? Well apparently, it's against family values. And so a whole bunch of family values groups, they got together. And they decided that because they didn't want to watch this movie then nobody should be allowed to watch this movie. So they lobbied the FCC and they threatened to boycott any channel that would dare air this film. And it worked. The movie was censored in one-third of the country. And why? Because these people know it is immoral to celebrate Veteran's Day by watching a war movie if, get this, it contains violence, swearing or taking the Lord's name in vain. None of which of course happened in World War II. No. Because in World War II people were too busy getting killed trying to protect America from the type of person that would definitely tell you what you can and cannot watch. According to these people, everyone would be much better off celebrating Veteran's Day by just staying at home and watching another episode of *Touched by an Angel*. Thanks to family values, when it comes to freedom and personal choice, the wheels are off the bus in America. And let's face it—it was a pretty short bus to begin with.[26]

Unlike his interview style in *Talking to Americans,* where the subjects of his questions are presented as objects of amusement, Mercer's rants employ a direct mode of address through his gaze into the camera combined with his frenetic pacing and breathless banter. The result is a more engaged form of spectatorship that implies a personal dialogue with audience members, akin to the heated conversation that may arise between simpatico friends discussing the contemporary political landscape. Mercer assumes, in this particular rant, a shared cultural code in which the audience will recognize that their own national community is defined by a more tolerant social climate where freedom of speech is also defined as freedom from the policing by—or imposition of—another group's moral code. Here, the other is more subtly invoked, and in this structured absence the audience identifies with the differences between the two countries' understandings of history's lessons for the present and the fundamental principles of democratic governance.

Although Mercer only "ranted" about the United States in a handful of segments in the first four seasons of *Rick Mercer Report*, Canada-U.S. relations continued to be a dominant theme throughout every "newscast." The regularity with which American politicians, bureaucrats, and the Bush administration, in particular, appeared in the Front Page and video footage segments underscores the centrality of the association between the two countries. Moreover, Mercer's surveillance of the minutiae of American political follies assumed a complicit and well-informed domestic audience who could recognize the roles and names of even the most minor political figures. To some extent, the United States still served as a mirror—albeit of the funhouse variety—through which Canadians assessed themselves. It is also plausible that the increasingly evident and radical divisions within American society challenged the comic potential of any material beyond that provided by "official" actors. The United States no longer seemed to speak with a single voice, thus diminishing its image as the monolithic other. In any event, Canadian politicians were providing Mercer with more than sufficient ammunition for a weekly rant. The domestic news landscape was rife for mining between a party leadership convention, a federal election where no party could form a majority government, and the blurring of clear ideological boundaries separating the four major parties. In the competition for attention and image management, Canadian politicians became eager and willing to risk themselves as satirical targets in *Rick Mercer Report* interviews and guest segments.

The segment flow from the rant to the political interview is the clearest mark of Mercer's transformation from mad prophet to court jester. Mercer perfected the role of the sardonic reporter grilling the discomfited politician during his days as the character J. B. Dickson on *22 Minutes*. For an audience in 1993, the scene of a satirist "interviewing" a real politician read as a revolutionary act of both comedy and political dialogue. More often than not it looked like a hostage situation. Today, politicians and their media handlers have refined their self-presentation skills and are able to move more seamlessly between news and entertainment arenas. The ability to appear as a good sport on a fake news show is sound political currency, particularly when appealing to the younger television generation. And, unless fake news hosts represented themselves as caricatures—along the lines of Stephen Colbert—they, too, found it necessary to change their strategies in a way that allowed fakery to blend with real journalism without diminishing the comic impact.

Mercer's decision to dispense with the J. B. Dickson persona in *Rick Mercer Report* modified his "real" interviews in a manner similar to Jon Stewart's affable bantering. However, he went beyond the personable "conversational discursive space"[27] that defines Stewart's style and moved his political interviews out of the studio and into neutral territories where he and politicians appeared as friends casually chatting about issues of the day. Thus, rather than sitting behind a desk to interview then–Prime Minister Paul Martin, the two men went on a shopping trip to Canadian Tire

Fig. 8.2. Canadian Prime Minister Stephen Harper
reads a story to Rick Mercer on *Rick Mercer Report.*

to purchase tools to fix a broken door at the prime minister's official residence. To learn more about the platform of Liberal leadership candidate
Bob Rae, Mercer took the politician fishing, and the two men ended the
day by skinny-dipping in the lake. While Mercer's interviewing technique
allows for candid revelations similar to those generated by friends talking
over a cup of coffee, it is often difficult to distinguish art from artifice.
Thus, Bob Rae's comment (as he casts his fishing rod) that he hopes to
establish a government "that's not based on these crappy, right-wing ideologies" appears to be a genuine expression of intent. Conversely, Mercer's
slumber party with Prime Minister Stephen Harper—which included late-
night snacks and a pillow fight with the children and ended with Harper
tucking Mercer into bed and reading his proposed Accountability Act as
a bedtime story—seems designed to merely humanize one of the least ex-
pressive federal leaders in Canadian history (figure 8.2).

Mercer's persona as court jester, both in his celebrations of the cultural
life across the country's regions and in the structure of his political interviews, has garnered accusations that the comedian has abandoned subversive comedy. Even his friend and former *22 Minutes* cast mate Mary Walsh

publicly stated that he "had stopped being satirical."[28] Although Mercer himself has long described his relationship with politicians as a necessarily "mutually parasitic" one, recent observations claim that he has been "co-opted" by those in power.[29] What critics tend to overlook, however, is that in the same episode where Mercer pals around with politicians, he will simultaneously rake them over the coals in the "news" reporting segments.

At a broader level, however, these critiques speak to the larger implications of satire and its place within society. They assume that satire must be overtly oppositional and confrontational to achieve an intended political and social goal. But Mercer's capacity to exploit the subversive voice of satire stems not merely from a desire to constantly express indignation at contemporary power politics but also from his own stated goals to address the experiences of life in the periphery of both national and continental power. And in *Rick Mercer Report,* Mercer found a venue in which to explore the possibility of a newly emergent national self-confidence, one that need not only define itself by "not" being American. As the two countries appeared to be experiencing a cultural continental drift, Mercer consequently began to explore the potential to satirize the foibles of regionalism and nation-building from within the country's own borders:

> Canada has so many problems—and geography is often the root cause. For the size of the population we are simply too big. I can't count the number of times I've been in a situation where five people were busy complaining about what the problem was with another part of the country that they were too happy to admit they had never visited. . . . And sure, on the surface Canada may appear hopelessly dysfunctional, but the more I rant the more I realize that we are also spectacular. . . . Canada, for all its challenges, is worth ranting about.[30]

To this end, *Rick Mercer Report* and *Talking to Americans* reinforce the need to contextualize satire as a culturally specific discourse that is entrenched within a sociohistoric context of power relations informed by the politics of cultural geography. While *Talking to Americans* characterized the relative insecurity of the Canadian identity project, Mercer's work in *Rick Mercer Report* exemplifies the challenges facing the maturation of the country's sense of self, specifically, the need to take domestic responsibility for the nation's future agenda in light of the diminishing emphasis on an other to either blame or to measure oneself against.

In what is perhaps a liminal moment in the bilateral relationship, Canadians find themselves in an unaccustomed position of relative power continentally. The United States remains mired in the war in Iraq, and the trillion-dollar deficit combined with a domestic economic crisis has brought into question its role as a world superpower. For the first time in more than 30 years, the Canadian dollar surpassed the value of its American counterpart, and the domestic economy is defined by a record level of employment and overall growth. The gamble to follow an independent road politically and culturally appears to have benefited Canada for the time being. As both countries prepare for federal elections, however, we are reminded that power is transitory. As power shifts, so, too, will the nature of satirical commentary—and as Mercer's work indicates, satire provides the opportunity for self-reflection, as well as sustained critique.

NOTES

1. Clifford Krauss, "Canada's View on Social Issues Is Opening Rifts with the U.S.," *New York Times,* 2 December 2003, A1.

2. Ibid.

3. Geoffrey Baym, "*The Daily Show:* Discursive Integration and the Reinvention of Political Journalism," *Political Communication* 22 (2005): 259–76. For a similar and expanded argument, see Liesbet van Zoonen, *Entertaining the Citizen: When Politics and Popular Culture Converge* (Lanham, Md.: Rowman and Littlefield, 2005).

4. Jane Ogburn and Peter Buckroyd, *Satire* (Cambridge: Cambridge University Press, 2001).

5. Gerald Lynch, "Canadian Comedy," in *Comedy: A Geographic and Historical Guide,* Vol. 1, ed. Maurice Charney (Westport, Conn.: Praeger, 2005), 201.

6. Linda Hutcheon, *Splitting Images: Contemporary Canadian Ironies* (Oxford: Oxford University Press, 1991).

7. Ibid., 1.

8. This process is exemplified in the highly popular "Joe Canada" television commercial for Molson Canadian beer. In the advertisement, a man playing the role of the "average Joe" stands in front of a movie screen and adamantly corrects all of the stereotypes that are perceived to inform American understandings of Canada. The commercial is part of Molson's "I am Canadian" campaign and can be viewed on YouTube under "Joe Canada Rant."

9. The emphasis on Anglo-Canadians is important here. Buffered by linguistic and cultural differences, the Québecois have successfully fostered a Francophone popular culture that is not seen as under threat from American dominance.

10. Geoff Pevere and Greig Dymond, *Mondo Canuck: A Canadian Pop Culture Odyssey* (Scarborough, Ont.: Prentice Hall, 1996), 30.

11. Sid Adilman, "A Hilarious Hymn to Canada," *Toronto Star,* 8 December 1993, D2.

12. "The Creative Land: Out on the Edge," *Maclean's,* 1 July 1994, 38.

13. As of early 2008, *Talking to Americans* could be viewed on YouTube.

14. Harry Keyishian, "Satire," in *Comedy: A Geographic and Historical Guide,* Vol. 2, ed. Maurice Charney (Westport, Conn.: Praeger, 2005), 529.

15. Dustin Griffin, *Satire: A Critical Reintroduction* (Lexington: University Press of Kentucky, 1994), 156.

16. F. P. Locke cited in ibid., 155.

17. M. M. Bakhtin, *Rabelais and His World* (Bloomington: Indiana University Press, 1984).

18. Robert Ballantyne, "Inside the Mind of Rick Mercer," *Popjournalism,* 25 November 2004, at http://www.popjournalism.ca/magazine/.

19. Keyishian, "Satire," 529.

20. Jonathan Rutherford, "A Place Called Home: Identity and the Cultural Politics of Difference," in *Identity: Community, Culture, Difference,* ed. Jonathan Rutherford (London: Lawrence and Wishart, 1990), 22.

21. Quoted in Ballantyne, "Inside the Mind."

22. The first four seasons of *Rick Mercer Report* can be viewed at http://cbc.ca/mercerreport.

23. The emphasis on the Canadian-American relationship in this chapter should not overshadow the significant role that satire has played in mocking the interregional power struggles within Canada. For further consideration of this aspect of television culture, see Serra Tinic, *On Location: Canada's Television Industry in a Global Market* (Toronto: University of Toronto Press, 2005). Excerpts of that work have been revised and incorporated into this chapter.

24. Jeffrey P. Jones, *Entertaining Politics: New Political Television and Civic Culture* (Lanham, Md.: Rowman and Littlefield, 2005), 96, 110.

25. Ibid., 110.

26. 22 November 2004.

27. Geoffrey Baym, "Crafting New Communicative Models in the Televisual Sphere: Political Interviews on *The Daily Show,*" *Communication Review* 10 (2007): 93–115.

28. Janice Kennedy, "Funny You Should Ask," *Ottawa Citizen,* 20 May 2007, B6.

29. Ibid.

30. Rick Mercer, *Rick Mercer Report: The Book* (Toronto: Doubleday Canada, 2007), xii–xiii.

‖‖‖‖‖‖‖‖‖‖‖‖‖‖‖‖‖‖‖‖‖‖‖‖‖‖‖‖‖‖‖‖‖‖‖‖‖‖‖‖‖‖‖

# 9

# Why Mitt Romney
# Won't Debate a Snowman

## *Henry Jenkins*

Newscaster Anderson Cooper opened the CNN/YouTube Democratic Debate with a warning to expect the unexpected: "Tonight is really something of an experiment. . . . What you're about to see is, well, it's untried. We are not exactly sure how this is going to work. The candidates on this stage don't know how it is going to work. . . . And frankly we think that's a good thing."[1] The eight candidates would face questions selected from more than 3,000 videos "average" citizens had submitted via YouTube. Speaking on National Public Radio's *Talk of the Nation* a few days before, CNN executive producer David Bohrman stressed that the new format would give the American public "a seat at the table," reflecting a world where "everyone is one degree of separation away from a video camera."[2]

Afterward, most people only wanted to talk about the Snowman. One short segment featured a claymation snowman talking about global warming, "the single most important issue to the snowmen of this country" (figure 9.1). As the video showed Junior's frightened face, the Snowman asked, "As president, what will you do to ensure that my son will live a full and happy life?" The candidates chuckled. Cooper explained, "It's a funny video. It's a serious question," before directing the query to Dennis Kucinich. The serious-minded Kucinich drew links between "global warming" and "global warring," explaining how the military defense of oil interests increased American reliance on fossil fuels and describing his own green-friendly policies: "We don't have to have our snowmen melting, and the planet shouldn't be melting either."

Fig. 9.1. Billiam the Snowman asks candidates in the
CNN/YouTube Democratic Debate what they will do to
protect his son from global warming.

CNN ended the broadcast by announcing a future debate involving the
GOP (Republican) candidates, but the status of this debate was far from
resolved. By the end of the week, most of the GOP front-runners were
refusing to participate. Mitt Romney put a face on their discomfort: "I
think the presidency ought to be held at a higher level than having to
answer questions from a snowman." CNN's Bohrman deflected his criticism: "I think running for president is serious business . . . but we do
want to know that the president has a sense of humor."[3] Many bloggers
also argued that the Snowman demeaned citizen's participation in the
debates: "By heavily moderating the questions, by deliberately choosing
silly, fluffy, or offbeat videos to show the nation, CNN is reinforcing the
old media idea that the Internet entertains, but does not offer real, serious
discussion or insight."[4] There would be a CNN/YouTube GOP debate, but
behind the scenes, negotiations delayed it and substantially toned down
the content.

Here I use the Snowman controversy as a point of entry for a broader
investigation into the role of Internet parody during the pre-primary
season in the 2008 presidential campaign. This debate about debates

raises questions about the redistribution of media power, the authenticity of grassroots media, and the appropriateness of parody as a mode of political rhetoric. Parody videos, both produced by the public and by the campaigns, played an unprecedented role in shaping public perceptions of this unusually crowded field of candidates. This essay picks up where my recent book, *Convergence Culture: Where Old and New Media Collide,* left off: with a call for us to rethink the cultural underpinnings of democracy in response to an era of profound and prolonged media change.[5] The rise of networking computing, and the social and cultural practices that have grown up around it, has expanded the ability of average citizens to express our ideas, circulate them before a larger public, and pool information with each other in the hopes of transforming our society. A closer look at the role that parody videos played in American politics in 2007 may help us understand how we are or are not realizing the potentials of this new communication environment. Such videos give us an alternative perspective on what democracy might look like, though we have a long way to go before we can achieve anything like a new public sphere in the online world. As Anderson Cooper suggests, none of us know where this will take us—and for the moment, at least, that's a good thing.

Debates about digital democracy have long been shaped by the fantasy of a "digital revolution" with its assumptions that old media (or, in this case, the old political establishment) would be displaced by the rise of new participants, whether new media startups confronting old media conglomerates, bloggers displacing journalists, or cybercandidates overcoming political machines. This depiction of media change as a zero-sum battle between old powerbrokers and insurgents distracts us from the real changes occurring in our media ecology. Rather than displacing old media, what I call "convergence culture" is shaped by increased contact and collaboration between established and emerging media institutions, expansion of the number of players producing and circulating media, and the flow of content across multiple platforms and networks. The collaboration between CNN (an icon of old media power) and YouTube (an icon of new media power) might be understood as one such attempt to work through the still unstable and "untried" relations between these different media systems.

Far from advocating a digital revolution, CNN's Bohrman openly dismissed new media platforms as "immature" and questioned whether the user-moderated practices of YouTube would have been adequate to the task of determining what questions candidates should address, given how easily such processes could be "gamed." Bohrman often cited what he saw as the public's fascination with "inappropriate" questions: "If you would have taken the most-viewed questions last time, the top question would have been whether Arnold Schwarzenegger was a cyborg sent to save the planet Earth. The second-most-viewed video question was: Will you convene a national meeting on UFOs?"[6] Bohrman clearly feared the participatory culture's power to negate. Tongue in check questions about cyborgs and aliens allowed many to thumb their noses at the official gate-keepers and their anticipated dismay at being "forced" to put such content onto the public airwaves. Such gestures reflect a growing public skepticism about old media power, as well as uncertainty about how far to trust emerging (though still limited and often trivial) efforts to solicit our participation.

Some such material made it into the final broadcast but only as part of an opening segment in which a smirking Cooper lectured the public about the kinds of videos that did not belong on national television: "Dressing up in costume was probably not the best way to get taken seriously." Here, participatory culture's power to negate ran up against old media's power to marginalize. Old media still defines which forms of cultural expression are mainstream through its ability to amplify the impact of some user-generated content while labeling other submissions out of bounds.

Because the public openly submitted their videos through a participatory media channel like YouTube, the selection process leaves traces. Even if we can't know what happened within the closed door meetings of the CNN producers, we can see which submitted questions got left out, which issues did not get addressed, and which groups did not get represented.

Afterward, some who felt excluded or marginalized deployed You-Tube as a platform to criticize the news network. For example, anony-mousAmerican, a rotund man in a Mexican wrestling mask who speaks with a working-class accent, posted a video labeled "Fuck You, CNN." He describes his anger over the fact that CNN deployed his masked face but not his words: "This could lead the public to imagine that my question was insulting or irrelevant. We all know that CNN would never air anything insulting such as a host asking the only Moslem member of Congress if he's a terrorist or irrelevant like a very old man spending his show interviewing people like Paris Hilton." Links lead to the question he submitted (calling for the immediate withdrawal from Iraq) and other political videos concerning the Bush administration's crackdown on civil liberties. His mask allows him both to speak as an everyman figure and to represent visually the process of political repression. It also links his videos to the Lucha Libra tradition where Mexican wrestlers often used their masked personas to speak out against social injustice.[7]

## *The Birth of a Snowman*

Writing in *The Wealth of Networks,* Harvard Law Professor Yochai Benkler suggests, "What institutions and decisions are considered 'legitimate' and worthy of compliance or participation; what courses of action are attractive; what forms of interaction with others are considered appropriate—these are all understandings negotiated from within a set of shared frames of meaning."[8] As average citizens acquire the ability to meaningfully influence the flow of ideas, these new forms of participatory culture change how we see ourselves ("through new eyes—the eyes of someone who could actually interject a thought, a criticism, or a concern into the public debate") and how we see our society (as subject to change as a consequence of our deliberations).[9] Some participants were making their first videos, but many more had acquired their skills as media producers through more mundane and everyday practices, through their production of home movies or their participation in various fan communities, or through media-sharing sites. As such practices become more normalized, as we come to see ourselves as capable of expressing ourselves through the emerging media network, how will this affect citizenly discourse? The reliance on parody as a mode of political discourse might be understood as part of this transition process by which we move from participatory culture to participatory democracy.

The strange history of the Snowman illustrates this process at work. The Snowman video was produced by Nathan and Greg Hamel, two brothers from Minneapolis.[10] Their debate video repurposed animations from an earlier, less politically oriented, video showing a Samurai attacking Billiam the Snowman while his young child watched in horror. The name of the Snowman, his high-pitched voice, and the video's aggressive slapstick paid homage to the Mr. Bill videos originally produced by Walter Williams for *Saturday Night Live* in the 1970s. The Mr. Bill segments represented an earlier chapter in the history of the networks' relationship to user-generated content: Williams had submitted a Super-8 reel in response to *Saturday Night Live*'s request for home movies during its first season.[11] The impressed producers hired Williams as a full-time writer, resulting in more than 20 subsequent Mr. Bill segments, all maintaining the low-tech look and feel of his original amateur productions. Williams's subsequent career might have provided the Hamel brothers with a model for their next step—from broad slapstick toward political satire. Starting in 2004, Williams deployed Mr. Bill as a spokesperson in a series of public service announcements about environmental issues (specifically, the threat to Louisiana wetlands).[12]

Empowered by the media attention, the Hamels produced a series of other videos confronting Romney, the man who refused to debate a snowman. While these subsequent videos were not incorporated into the GOP debate, they did attract other media attention. When interviewed by CNN about a video in which Billiam tells Romney to "lighten up slightly," the Hamel brothers used their explanation to direct attention at a growing controversy within the blogosphere. During a campaign appearance in New Hampshire, Romney had been photographed holding a supporter's sign, which read "No to Obama, Osama, and Chelsea's Mama" (part of a larger effort to play on xenophobic concerns about Barack's "foreign sounding" name).[13] Another amateur videomaker had captured a confrontation at an Iowa campaign appearance where Romney told a critic of the sign to "lighten up slightly," insisting that he has little control over what his supporters might bring to an event.[14] Bloggers were circulating the video of what they saw as a disingenuous response. This Romney video fits into a larger history of footage captured by amateur videomakers that reached greater public visibility via YouTube and sometimes found its way into mainstream coverage. For example, one popular video showed John McCain joking with supporters, singing "Bomb, Bomb, Bomb Iran" in imitation of a classic rock and roll tune. The Hamel brothers were using their five minutes of fame to help direct the media's attention onto a brewing controversy that might further undermine Romney's credibility.

Over just a few weeks, the Hamel brothers progressed from sophomoric skit comedy to progressively more savvy interventions into media politics, demonstrating a growing understanding of how media travels through YouTube and how YouTube intersects broadcast media. As they did so, they formed an informal alliance with other "citizen journalists," and they inspired a range of other amateur producers to create their own snowman videos, including those which included a man wearing a snowman mask or which recycled footage from old Christmas specials, in hopes that they might get caught up in Billiam's media coverage.

CNN had urged the public to find "creative" new ways to express their concerns, yet the producers clearly saw many of the more colorful videos as the civic equivalent of *Let's Make a Deal*—as so many people in colorful costumes huckstering to get on television. Some certainly were hungry for personal fame, but others were using parody to dramatize legitimate policy concerns. In the case of the Snowman, his question about global warming was not outside the frames of the current political debate, but the use of the animated snowman as a spokesperson broke with the rationalist discourse that typically characterizes Green politics. The Snowman parody spoofed two of American politics' most cherished rhetorical moves. Snowmen are represented here as one more identity politics group; snowmen are made to "embody" larger societal concerns. We might compare Billiam's attempt to speak about the environment on behalf of snowmen with the oft-cited image of Iron Eyes Cody weeping as a native American over the littering of the American landscape during the Keep America Beautiful campaign produced for the 1971 Earth Day Celebration, or, for that matter, the ways that Al Gore deployed drowning polar bears to dramatize the threat of global warming in *An Inconvenient Truth*. The video also spoofs the ways both conservative and progressive groups make policy appeals in the name of protecting innocent children from some perceived threat.[15] We might link Billiam's frightened offspring back to the famous spot in the Lyndon B. Johnson presidential campaign, depicting a little girl plucking the petals from a daisy over the soundtrack of a countdown to a nuclear bomb blast.

Presidential candidates have long deployed animations as part of the rhetoric of their advertising campaigns, so why should voters be prohibited from using such images in addressing candidates? What's different, perhaps, is the way such videos appropriate popular culture content (Mr. Bill) as vehicles for their message. As Benkler notes, mass media has so dominated American culture for the past century that people are necessarily going to draw on it as a shared vocabulary as they learn how to use participatory media toward their own ends:

> One cannot make new culture ex nihilo. We are, as we are today, as cultural beings, occupying a set of common symbols and stories that are heavily based on the outputs of the industrial period. If we are to make this culture our own, render it legible, and make it into a new platform for our needs and conversations today, we must find a way to cut, paste, and remix present culture.[16]

Television commercials, for example, often provide simple, easily recognized templates for representing ideological concerns. Consider Bill Hope's parody of the Romney campaign, which juxtaposes the voice-over from a recent Jaguar commercial with news footage of the candidate: "Gorgeous deserves your immediate attention. Gorgeous makes effort look effortless. . . . Gorgeous has no love for logic. Gorgeous gets away with it. Everyone cares what gorgeous says. Gorgeous gets in everywhere. . . . Gorgeous was born that way. Gorgeous trumps everything." Each phrase evokes and reinforces the public perception of Romney's privileged background, slippery political stances, and matinee idol appearance, while the juxtaposition of advertising slogans and news footage mocks the repackaging of candidates for mass consumption. Similarly, a group called SmallMediaXL produced a series of spoofs on the differences between Republicans and Democrats modeled on a popular Mac/PC campaign—depicting Republicans as "very good at looking after the interests of big business" and the Democrats as "being better at the people stuff." No doubt, both producers were hoping to tap public familiarity with Madison Avenue iconography to expand the reach of their messages.

## Parody in High Places

In "The Spectacularization of Everyday Life," Denise Mann discusses the ways that early television deployed parody to signal its uncomfortable relationship to Hollywood glamour, positioning its technology—and its own stars—as closer to the public than their cinema counterparts.[17] Early television often spoofed the gap between Hollywood and reality, making fun of its overdramatic style and cliché situations, depicting television characters (such as "Lucy" in *I Love Lucy*) as fans who want but are denied access to film stars. In the process, these programs helped to negotiate television's emerging social status, stressing the authenticity and everydayness of its own modes of representing the world. Something similar has occurred as digital media has negotiated its own position within users' experiences. Amateur media makers often signal their averageness through parody, openly acknowledging the gap between their limited economic resources or technical means and more-polished commercial entertainment.[18] Through parody, they hope to invite people to laugh with them, not at them.

Hollywood stars often embraced self-parody when they appeared in early television, showing that they were also in on the joke and were able to make the adjustments needed to enter our homes on television's terms. Something similar occurs when presidential candidates embrace self-parody as a campaign tactic. In one famous example, the former president and first lady reenacted the final moments of *The Sopranos*. Here, "Hillary" and "Bill" seek to become more like average Americans, tapping a YouTube trend in the aftermath of the HBO series' wrap-up. Through this video's jokes about Hillary's attempts to control her husband's diet and Chelsea's difficulty with parallel parking, the Clintons hoped to shed some of the larger-than-life aura they gained during their years in the White House and to reenter the life world of the voters. A candidate, who was otherwise closely associated with a culture war campaign against media violence, sought to signal her own fannishness; a candidate often seen as uptight sought to show that she could take a joke. And the video itself was designed to call attention to the Clinton campaign's effort to get the public to pick a theme song for her campaign.

Or take the case of a Mike Huckabee campaign commercial, originally broadcast but also widely circulated via YouTube. The spot's opening promise of a major policy announcement sets up its punch line: action film star Chuck Norris is unveiled as the Arkansas governor's policy for securing the U.S.-Mexico border. The video does offer some serious policy statements, including a discussion of Huckabee's stands on gun rights and the Internal Revenue Service, but they are rendered over a western movie soundtrack and coupled with more playful statements: "When Chuck Norris does a push-up, he's not lifting himself up, he's pushing the earth down. . . . Chuck Norris doesn't endorse. He tells America how it's going to be." The video thus seeks to establish Huckabee's credentials as a man's man, even as it makes fun of his need to do so. The video both exploits— and spoofs—the role of celebrity endorsements in American politics.

CNN had asked the Democratic presidential candidates to submit their own "YouTube-style videos" for the broadcast debate. For the most part, they recycled existing advertising content, without much regard for the rhetorical strategies by which YouTube contributors signaled their distance from the commercial mainstream. A notable exception was the video submitted by John Edwards's campaign, a spot set to the song "Hair," which jokingly suggested that media coverage of the candidate's expensive haircuts displaced attention from more substantive issues. We might contrast this with Roger Rmjet's similarly themed "Feeling Pretty" video, which sets captured footage of Edwards's primping before doing a local news appearance to a highly feminized song from *West Side Story.* The first invites us to laugh with, the second at, Edwards. Read side by side, they reflect a moment where both top-down and bottom-up forces are deploying Internet parody for their own ends—though with different rhetorical consequences.

## *From Serious Fun to Barely Political*

Traditional campaign rhetoric stresses the seriousness of the choices Americans face, rather than the pleasures of participating within the political process. Both progressives and conservatives have displayed discomfort with the tone and content of popular culture, especially in the current "culture war" context. Most attempts to mobilize popular culture toward political ends are read contemptuously as efforts to dummy down civic discourse.

In a recent book, *Dream: Re-Imagining Progressive Politics in an Age of Fantasy,* Stephen Duncombe offers a different perspective, arguing that politicos need to move beyond a knee-jerk critique of popular entertainment as "weapons of mass distraction" and learn strategies for "appropriating, co-opting and most important, transforming the techniques of spectacular capitalism into tools for social change."[19] Playing on Noam Chomsky's critique of propaganda (*Manufacturing Consent*), Duncombe calls on progressives to learn new strategies for "manufacturing dissent":

> Given the progressive ideals of egalitarianism and a politics that values the input of everyone, our dreamscapes will not be created by media-savvy experts of the left and then handed down to the rest of us to watch, consume, and believe. Instead, our spectacles will be participatory: dreams that the public can mold and shape themselves. They will be active: spectacles that work only if the people help create them. They will be open-ended: setting stages to ask questions and leaving silences to formulate answers. And they will be transparent: dreams that one knows are dreams but which still have power to attract and inspire. And, finally, the spectacles we create will not cover over or replace reality and truth but perform and amplify it.[20]

Duncombe cites Billionaires for Bush as a primary example of this new kind of political spectacle. Billionaires for Bush used street theater to call attention to issues such as campaign finance reform, media concentration, and tax cuts for the wealthy. Seeking to dodge attempts by conservative critics to paint their efforts as "class warfare," the group adopted a more playful posture, dressing up like cartoon character versions of the wealthy, showing up at campaign stops, and chanting along with other Bush supporters. Similarly playful tactics were adopted by True Majority, an organization founded during the 2004 presidential campaign by Ben Cohen (of Ben and Jerry's Ice Cream). The group sought to increase voter participation and rally support behind a progressive agenda, in part by embracing what Cohen described as "serious fun." True Majority produced a mock preview for an episode of *The Apprentice* during which a disappointed Donald Trump fired George W. Bush for driving the economy into the ground, using lies to justify a war, and spending way over budget.[21]

As YouTube's cultural visibility has increased, more activists have followed True Majority's example, making parody videos as a more playful and pleasurable mode of political discourse. Save the Internet tapped the talents of diverse online media producers to help raise public awareness of impending policies that they argued threatened net neutrality. To dramatize the diversity of the current web community and thus the potential impact of the proposed policy changes, Save the Internet encouraged members to make and circulate their own videos explaining the issues to their own niche constituencies. Their website offered a central hub for distributing the videos, juxtaposing serious documentaries with more playful parodies, mixing commercially produced content (such as a Bill Moyer's PBS special or a segment from *The Daily Show*) with those by amateur and semiprofessional groups (such as *Ask a Ninja* and *This Spartan Life*, two of the more successful Internet comedy series). The *Ask a Ninja* series, created by Los Angeles improvisational comedians Kent Nichols and Douglas Sarine, featured a Ninja who speaks with a surfer dude accent. *This Spartan Life*, created by the startup Bong and Dern productions, stages a weekly talk show within multiplayer XBox Live sessions of Bungie Studio's first-person shooter video game, *Halo 2*.

One of the segments featured during the CNN/YouTube debate came from a similar source—*Red State Update*. Two west coast comics, Travis Harmon and Jonathan Shockley, have perfected the online personas of Jackie Broyles and Dunlap, two rednecks from Murfreesboro, Tennessee, who offer colorful commentary on the campaign and candidates. *Red State Update* receives upward of 3 million views on YouTube and 1.2

million more via MySpace; the segments are also syndicated through Salon and replayed on the DirecTV network.[22]

Most writing about the CNN/YouTube debates gets framed in terms of amateur media makers and a commercial network, overlooking how many videos were submitted by semiprofessionals (such as the web comedy troops referenced above) or even by editorial cartoonists for various newspapers and magazines. We might better understand the videos produced for the debates (or those circulated by Save the Internet) as emerging from the mixed media economy that Benkler describes in *The Wealth of Networks*. Media producers with different motives—government agencies, activist groups, educational institutions, nonprofit organizations, fan communities—operate side by side, using the same production tools and distribution networks. YouTube constitutes a shared portal through which these diverse groups come together to circulate media content and learn from each other's practices. In this shared distribution space, short-term tactical alliances between such groups are commonplace. On YouTube, it becomes increasingly difficult to distinguish between videos produced by fans as a playful tribute to a favorite media property, by average citizens seeking to shape the agenda of the campaigns, by activist organizations to promote a specific political objective, and by small-scale comedy groups seeking to break into the commercial mainstream. Content produced for and distributed through YouTube, then, might have complex and sometimes contradictory motives.

A case in point might be the series of *Obama Girl* videos. The initial video, "I Got a Crush . . . on Obama," was produced by advertising executives Ben Relles and Rick Friedrick in collaboration with actress and model Amber Lee Ettinger and singer-comedian Leah Kauffman. These media professionals wanted to use their sexy and irreverent content to generate a buzz that might draw attention to a newly launched on-line comedy site. In the original video, the scantily clad Obama Girl describes how she fell in love with Obama during his talk to the 2004 Democratic convention (figure 9.2), signals her growing passion for the man and his ideas through stroking his campaign posters, kissing his photograph on a website, and having the candidate's name printed on her panties. News commentators often reduce women's political interests to which male candidate is most attractive, reading them less as concerned citizens and more as groupies for the campaigns. The Obama Girl videos turn such representations around, transforming the candidates into beefcake embodiments of these women's erotic fantasies. The rapid-paced images and

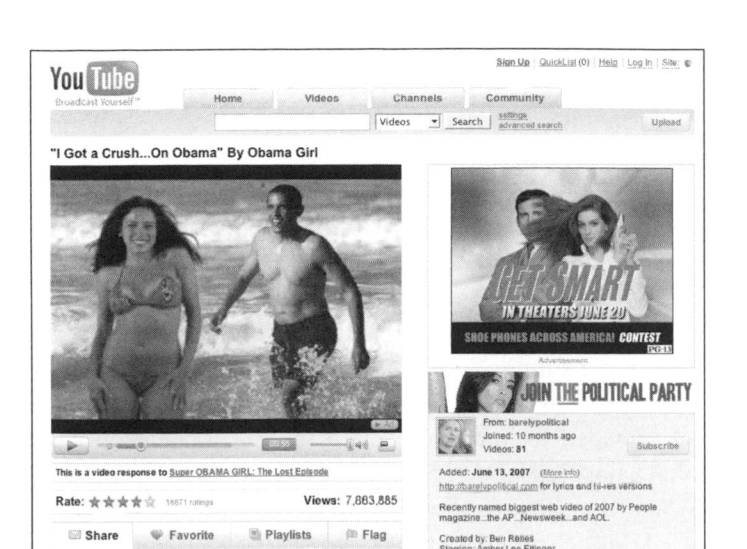

Fig. 9.2. Obama Girl sings of her crush on Barack Obama.

the multilayered wordplay reward careful decoding, requiring consumers to learn more about the campaigns in order to "get" the jokes. But like the other media "snacks" associated with YouTube, they may also be consumed on a more-casual level, and we cannot easily account for the range of meanings that emerged as these videos were spread within different online communities, passed between friends and coworkers, or mobilized by activist groups and campaign workers.[23] Politics, as they say, makes for strange bedfellows. The buzz pushed the giggling Obama Girl onto the cable news circuit, while the producers announced a partnership with Voter Vision, a multimedia political campaign marketing program that wanted to demonstrate the political value of "viral video." Somewhere along the way, the videos had moved from entertainment to activism, from a parody of the campaign into something that was explicitly intended for activist purposes. The slippery nature of such distinctions is suggested by the company's name—"Barely Political."

This hybrid media environment and the active circulation of content beyond its points of origin make it hard to tell where any given video is coming from—in both the literal and the metaphoric senses. Increasingly, we are seeing fake grassroots media being produced by powerful institutions or economic interests—what has become known as "Astro-turf." Consider the case of *Al Gore's Penguin Army*. This cut-up animation spoof of *An Inconvenient Truth* was first posted by a user named Tout-smith from Beverley Hills, but further investigation revealed that it was professionally produced by the DCI Group, a commercial advertising firm whose clients included General Motors and ExxonMobil; the firm also had historically produced content for the Republican Party.[24]

One of the best-known Internet parodies of the 2007 campaign season, a remix of Apple's "1984" commercial where Hillary Clinton stands in for Big Brother, has a similar dubious history. The video turned out to be the work of Phil de Vellis, an employee of Blue State Digital, an Internet company that provided technology to both the Bill Richardson and Obama presidential campaigns. De Vellis was forced to resign his job as both the company and the campaigns sought to distance themselves from his activities. He told the readers of the *Huffington Post*:

> There are thousands of other people who could have made this ad, and I guarantee that more ads like it—by people of all political persuasions—will follow. This shows that the future of American politics rests in the hands of ordinary citizens. The campaigns had no idea who made it—not the Obama campaign, not the Clinton campaign, nor any other campaign. I made the ad on a Sunday afternoon in my apartment using my personal equipment (a Mac and some software), uploaded it to YouTube, and sent links around to blogs. . . . The game has changed.[25]

The game has indeed changed, but it isn't necessarily clear what game is being played here or by whom. Will we see other such videos circulated by groups or campaigns that hope to maintain a "plausible deniability" about their roles in generating their content? Are the candidates losing some control over the campaign process?

## Parody as Pedagogy

We cannot reduce the complexity of this hybrid media ecology to simple distinctions between top-down and bottom-up, professional and amateur, insider or outsider, old and new media, Astroturf and grassroots, or even "serious fun" and "barely political." Grassroots and mainstream media might pursue parallel interests, even as they act autonomously. Consider, for example, a video that TechPresident identifies as one of the top "voter-generated videos" of 2007. The video starts with a clip of Joseph Biden joking during one debate appearance that every sentence Rudy Giuliani utters includes "a noun, a verb, and 9/11," and follows with a database of clips showing the former New York Mayor referencing 9/11. The video was produced and distributed by Talking Points Memo, one of the most widely read progressive political blogs. In many ways, all the parody does is amplify Biden's own political message, supporting his claims that Giuliani was exploiting a national tragedy for his own political gains. The ready access of digital search tools and online archives makes it trivial for small-scale operators, like the bloggers, to scan through vast amounts of news footage and assemble clips to illustrate their ideas in a matter of a few days. Such tactical raids on digital archives—for both serious and satirical purposes—would become commonplace during the 2008 political season, originating from campaign staffers and politically motivated bloggers alike.

Often, these playful tactics get described in terms of the needs to adopt new rhetorical practices to reach the "digital natives," a generation of young people who have grown up in a world where the affordances of participatory media technologies have been commonplace. Researchers debate whether these young people are, in fact, politically engaged since their civic lives take very different forms from those of previous generations. W. Lance Bennett contrasts two different framings of this data:

> The engaged youth paradigm implicitly emphasizes generational changes in social identity that have resulted in the growing importance of peer networks and online communities. . . . This paradigm emphasizes the empowerment of youth as expressive individuals and symbolically frees young people to make their own creative choices. . . . As a result, the engaged youth paradigm opens the door to a new spectrum of civic actions in online arenas from MySpace to World of Warcraft.

He might have added YouTube. Bennett continues:

> By contrast, the disengaged youth paradigm may acknowledge the rise of more autonomous forms of public engagement such as consumer politics, or the occasional protest in MySpace, while keeping the focus on the generational decline in connections to government (e.g., voting patterns) and general civic involvement (e.g., following public affairs in the news) as threats to the health of the democracy.[26]

The activist deployment of parody videos can be understood as an attempt to negotiate between these two perspectives. It starts with a recognition that young people have come to see YouTube as supporting individual and collective expression and that they often feel excluded by the policy wonk language of traditional politics and the inside the beltway focus of much campaign news coverage. Parody offers an alternative language through which policy debates and campaign pitches might be framed, one that, as Duncombe suggests, models itself on popular culture but responds to different ethical and political imperatives. The often "politically incorrect" style of Internet parody flies in the face of the language and assumptions by which previous generations debated public policy. Such videos may not look like "politics as usual," yet their goals are no different in many cases from traditional political advertising: the people who produced and circulated these videos want to motivate young voters to participate in the electoral process. Such a model sees Internet parodies as springboards for larger conversations—whether through blogs and discussion forums online or face to face between people gathered around a water cooler.

These parody videos bring the issues down to a human scale, depicting Bush as an incompetent reality show contestant, Romney as someone who is afraid to go man to man with a snowman, Giuliani as obsessed with 9/11, and Edwards as a narcissist with fluffy hair. Duncombe has argued that news comedy shows, such as *The Daily Show* and *The Colbert Report,* foster a kind of civic literacy, teaching viewers to ask skeptical questions about core political values and the rhetorical process that embody them: "In doing this they hold out the possibility of something else, that is, they create an opening for a discussion on what sort of a political process wouldn't be a joke. In doing this they're setting the stage for a very democratic sort of dialogue: one that asks questions rather than simply asserts the definitive truth."[27] We might connect Duncombe's argument back to Benkler's larger claim that living within a more participatory culture changes how we understand our place in the world, even if we never chose to actively participate. Yet, there is also the risk, as Duncombe points out, that such parody "can, just as easily, lead into a resigned acceptance that all politics are just a joke and the best we can hope for it to get a good laugh out of it all." Here, skepticism gives way to cynicism. Nothing ensures that a politics based in parody will foster one and not the other.

## Downsides of Digital Democracy

If this essay can be read as a defense of the Snowman as a meaningful and valid participant in a debate about the future of American democracy, it is at best a qualified defense. I have tried to move us from an understanding of the CNN/YouTube debates through a lens of digital revolution in favor of a model based on the ever more complicated interplay of old and new media and on the hybrid media ecology that has emerged as groups with different motives and goals interact through shared media portals. I have tried to move beyond thinking of the Snowman as trivializing public policy debates toward seeing parody as a strategy that a range of different stakeholders (official and unofficial, commercial and grassroots, entertainers and activists) are deploying toward their own ends, each seeking to use YouTube as a distribution hub and tapping social networks to ensure the broader circulation of their content.

While I believe very firmly in the potential for participatory culture to serve as a catalyst for revitalizing civic life, we still fall short of the full realization of those ideals. As John McMurria has noted, the democratic promise of YouTube as a site open to everyone's participation is tempered by the reality that participation is unevenly distributed across the culture. An open platform does not necessarily ensure diversity.[28] The mechanisms of user-moderation work well when they help us collectively evaluate the merits of individual contributions and thus push to the top the best content; they work badly when they preempt the expression of minority perspectives and hide unpopular and alternative content from view.

Chuck Tyron has argued that the speed with which such videos are produced and circulated can undercut the desired pedagogical and activist goals, sparking short-lived and superficial conversations among consumers who are always looking over their shoulders for the next new thing.[29] To put it mildly, the user comments posted on YouTube fall far short of Habermasian ideals of the public sphere, as was suggested by one blogger's parody of the CNN/YouTube debates. Here, the candidates interact in ways more commonly associated with the online responses to the posted videos:

SEN. CHRISTOPHER DODD: omg that video was totaly gay
SEN. BARACK OBAMA: Shut up Dodd thats offensive when u say gay like that.

FORMER SEN. MIKE GRAVEL: Check out my vids at youtube.com/user/grave12008.

REP. DENNIS KUCINICH: to answre your question bush is a facist who only wants more power. hes not even the president you knopw, cheny is. i would b different because i would have a vice presidant that doesnt just try and control everything from behind the seens/

SEN. HILLARY CLINTON: CHENEY CANT BE PRESIDENT BECUZ THE CONSTITUTION SAYS THE VICE PRESIDENT IS NOT THE PRESIDENT WHY DON'T U TRY READING THE CONSTITUTION SOMETIME??????!!!![30]

Here, YouTube is associated more with mangled syntax, poor spelling, misinformation, and fractured logic than with any degree of political self-consciousness or citizenly discourse. Yet, YouTube cannot be understood in isolation from a range of other blogging and social network sites where the videos often get discussed in greater depth and substance.

The insulting tone of this depicted interaction captures something of the no-holds-barred nature of political dialogue on YouTube. In an election whose candidates include women, African Americans and Hispanics, Catholics and Mormons, groups that historically have been underrepresented in American political life, online parody often embraces racist, sexist, and xenophobic humor, which further discourages minority participation or conversations across ideological differences. One popular genre of Internet parody depicts insult matches between Hillary Clinton and Barack Obama or their supporters (typically represented as women and minorities). One prototype of this style of humor was a MADtv sketch, which drew more than half a million viewers when it was posted online. The sketch ends with a Guiliani supporter clapping as the two Democratic campaigns rip each other apart, suggesting an interpretation focused on the dangers of party infighting. But, this frame figures little in the public response to the video, whether in the form of comments posted on the site (such as one person who complained about being forced "to pick between a Nigger and a woman") or videos generated by amateur media producers (which often push the original's already over-the-line humor to even nastier extremes). Here, "politically incorrect" comedy provides an opportunity for the public to laugh at the unseemly spectacle of a struggle between women and African Americans or may offer a justification for trotting out ancient but still hurtful slurs and allegations—women are inappropriate for public office because of, haw, "that time of the month"; African American men are irresponsible because they are, haha, likely to desert their families, go to jail, or experiment with drugs.

Another website posted a range of Photoshopped collages about the campaign submitted by readers, including ones showing Hillary in a yellow jumpsuit waving a samurai sword on a mocked-up poster for *Kill Bill*, Obama depicted as Borat in a parody that plays on his foreign-sounding name, and Obama depicted as a chauffeur driving around Mrs. Clinton in an ad for a remake of *Driving Miss Daisy*.[31] Such parodies use humor to put minority candidates and voters back in "their place," suggesting that women and blacks are inappropriate candidates for the nation's highest office. This problem may originate from the interplay between old and new media: the racist and sexist assumptions structured the original MADtv segment and may account for why Internet fans were drawn to it in the first place. The subsequent reactions amplify its problematic aspects, though the amateur responses stoop lower than network standards and practices would allow.

In such videos, Internet parody producers fall far short of the "ethical spectacles" that Duncombe advocates: "A progressive ethical spectacle will be one that is directly democratic, breaks down hierarchies, fosters community, allows for diversity, and engages with reality while asking what new realities might be possible."[32] By contrast, too many of the parody videos currently circulating on YouTube do the opposite—promote traditional authority, preserve gender and racial hierarchies, fragment communities, discourage diversity, and refuse to imagine any kind of social order other than the one that has long dominated American government. Speaking to a *Mother Jones* reporter, Lawrence Lessig explained: "If you look at the top 100 things on YouTube or Google it's not like it's compelling art. There's going to be a lot of questions about whether it's compelling politics either. We can still play ugly in lots of ways, but the traditional ways of playing ugly are sort of over."[33] All of this is to suggest that Romney would have faced things far more frightening than snowmen if he had ventured into the uncharted and untamed space of YouTube rather than the filtered and protected space provided him by CNN.

The advent of new production tools and distribution channels has lowered barriers of entry into the marketplace of ideas. These shifts place resources for activism and social commentary into the hands of everyday citizens, resources that were once the exclusive domain of the candidates, the parties, and the mass media. These citizens have increasingly turned toward parody as a rhetorical practice that allows them to express their skepticism toward "politics as usual," to break out of the exclusionary language through which many discussions of public policy are conducted, to find a shared language of borrowed images that mobilize what they know as consumers to reflect on the political process. Such practices blur the lines between producer and consumer, between consumers and citizens, between the commercial and the amateur and between education, activism, and entertainment, as groups with competing and contradictory motives deploy parody to serve their own ends. These tactics are drawing many into the debates who would once have paid little or no attention to the campaign process. As they have done so, they have brought to the surface both inequalities in participation and deep-rooted hostilities between groups within American society. Democracy has always been a messy business: the politics of parody offer us no easy way out, yet parody does offer us a chance to rewrite the rules and transform the language through which our civic life is conducted.

## NOTES

I am indebted to Colleen Kaman and Steve Schultz for their assistance in tracking down references and materials for this study.

1. For a video archive of the debates, see http://www.youtube.com/democraticdebate and http://www.youtube.com/republicandebate.

2. "Digital Democracy: YouTube's Presidential Debates," *Talk of the Nation*, 18 July 2007, at http://www.npr.org/templates/story/story.php?storyId=12062554.

3. Jose Antonio Vargas, "The Trail: The GOP YouTube Debate Is Back On," *Washington Post*, 12 August 2007, at http://blog.washingtonpost.com/the-trail/2007/08/12/the_gop_youtube_debate_is_back_1.html.

4. Jason Rosenbaum, "It's a Trap!" *Chicago Seminal*, 29 November 2007, at http://www.theseminal.com/2007/11/28/its-a-trap/. See also Micah L. Sifry, "How CNN Demeans the Internet," *TechPresident*, 29 November 2007, at http://www.techpresident.com/blog/entry/14238/how_cnn_demeans_the_internet.

5. Henry Jenkins, *Convergence Culture: Where Old and New Media Collide* (New York: New York University Press, 2006).

6. Sarah Lee Stirland, "CNN-YouTube Debate Producer Doubts the Wisdom of the Crowd," *Wired*, 27 November 2007, at http://www.wired.com/politics/onlinerights/news/2007/11/cnn_debate#.

7. Heather Levi, "The Mask of the Luchador: Wrestling, Politics, and Identity in Mexico," in *Steel Chair to the Head: The Pleasures and Pain of Professional Wrestling*, ed. Nicholas Sammond (Durham, N.C.: Duke University Press, 2005), 96–131.

8. Yochai Benkler, *The Wealth of Networks: How Social Production Transforms Markets and Freedom* (New Haven, Conn.: Yale University Press, 2006), 274–75.

9. Ibid., 275.

10. "Snowman vs. Romney–CNN Reports," at http://www.youtube.com/watch?v=NmVIm_JRHH4.

11. "Walter Williams," at http://www.mrbill.com/wwbio.html.

12. Cain Burdeau, "Mr, Bill Tapped to Help Save La. Swamps," *Associated Press,* at http://www.mrbill.com/LASinks.html.

13. "Mitt Catches S**t over Hillary-Bashing Sign," at http://www.tmz.com/2007/07/21/mitt-catches-s-t-over-hillary-bashing-sign/.

14. "Romney on Osama Sign: 'Lighten Up,'" at http://www.tmz.com/2007/07/23/romney-on-osama-sign-lighten-up/; http://www.dailykos.com/story/2007/7/23/31656/4987.

15. For more discussion, see Henry Jenkins, "Childhood Innocence and Other Modern Myths," in *The Children's Culture Reader,* ed. Henry Jenkins (New York: New York University Press, 1998), 1–40.

16. Benkler, *Wealth of Networks,* 200.

17. Denise Mann, "The Spectacularization of Everyday Life: Recycling Hollywood Stars and Fans in Early Television Variety Shows," in *Private Screenings: Television and the Female Consumer,* ed. Lynn Spigel and Denise Mann (Minneapolis: University of Minnesota Press, 1992), 41–70.

18. Henry Jenkins, "Quentin Tarantino's Star Wars? Digital Cinema, Media Convergence, and Participatory Culture," in *Rethinking Media Change: The Aesthetics of Transition,* ed. David Thorburn and Henry Jenkins (Cambridge: MIT Press, 2003), 281–314.

19. Stephen Duncombe, *Dream: Re-Imagining Progressive Politics in an Age of Fantasy* (New York: New Press, 2007), 16.

20. Ibid., 17.

21. For more on TrueMajority, see Jenkins, *Convergence Culture,* 206–7.

22. Jim Ridley, "Country Boys Can Survive," *Nashville Scene,* 20 September 2007, at http://www.nashvillescene.com/Stories/Cover_Story/2007/09/20/Country_Boys_Can_Survive/index.shtml.

23. *Wired* represented YouTube as central to a new culture of media snacks in "Snack Attack!" *Wired,* March 2007, at http://www.wired.com/wired/archive/15.03/snack.html.

24. Antonio Regalado and Dionne Searchy, "Where Did That Video Spoofing Gore's Film Come From?" *Wall Street Journal,* 3 August 2006, at http://online.wsj.com/public/article/SB115457177198425388–0TpYE6bU6EGvfSqtP8_hHjJJ77I_20060810.html?mod=blogs.

25. Phil De Vellis, aka Parkridge47, "I Made the 'Vote Different' Ad," *Huffington Post,* 21 March 2007, at http://www.huffingtonpost.com/phil-de-vellis-aka-parkridge/i-made-the-vote-differen_b_43989.html.

26. W. Lance Bennett, "Changing Citizenship in a Digital Age," in *Civic Life Online: Learning How Digital Media Can Engage Youth*, ed. W. Lance Bennett (Cambridge: MIT Press, 2008), 2–3.

27. Henry Jenkins, "Manufacturing Dissent: An Interview with Stephen Duncombe," *Confessions of an Aca-Fan*, 23 July 2007, at http://henryjenkins.org/2007/07/manufacturing_dissent_an_inter.html.

28. John McMurria, "The YouTube Community," *FlowTV*, 20 October 2006, at http://flowtv.org/?p=48.

29. Chuck Tyron, "Is Internet Politics Better Off Than It Was Four Years Ago?," *FlowTV*, 29 September 2007, at http://flowtv.org/?p=797.

30. "Transcript: CNN/Youtube Democratic Debate," *Defective Yeti*, at http://www.defectiveyeti.com/archives/002172.html.

31. Each of these examples is taken from images submitted to http://political-humor.about.com.

32. Duncombe, *Dream*, 126.

33. "Interview with Lawrence Lessig, Stanford Law Professor, Creative Commons Chair," *Mother Jones*, 29 June 2007, at http://www.motherjones.com/interview/2007/07/lawrence_lessig.html.

REFERENCES: YOUTUBEOLOGY

anonymousAmerican, "Fuck You, CNN," http://www.youtube.com/watch?v=xJRGb2zlBTo

Ask a Ninja, "Special Delivery 4, Net Neutrality," http://www.youtube.com/watch?v=H69eCYcDcuQ

Bill Holt, "Mitt Romney Meets Jaguar," http://www.youtube.com/watch?v=Swr4JruUTpU

Billiam the Snowman, "CNN/YouTube Debate: Global Warming," http://www.youtube.com/watch?v=-oBPnnvI47Q

Billiam the Snowman, "The Original," http://www.youtube.com/watch?v=BJpZD_pGCgk

Billiam the Snowman, "Billiam the Snowman Responds to Mitt Romney," http://www.youtube.com/watch?v=CtU9ReDhFiE

CNN, "Snowman Vs. Romney," http://www.youtube.com/watch?v=NmVIm_JRHH4

"Donald Trump Fires Bush," http://www.youtube.com/watch?v=RrYXY_JYzX8

"Keep America Beautiful," http://www.youtube.com/watch?v=87SojmdYCWI

Hillary Clinton, "Sopranos Spoof," http://www.youtube.com/watch?v=shKJk3RphoE

Jackie and Dunlap on the CNN YouTube Democratic Debate, http://www.youtube.com/watch?v=ZrPnWoZTjlQ

John Edwards, "Hair," http://www.youtube.com/watch?v=Y1qG6m9SnWI

Lyndon Johnson, "Daisy," http://www.youtube.com/watch?v=63h_v6ufoAo

MadTV, "Hillary vs. Obama," http://www.youtube.com/watch?v=YqOHquOkpaU

Mckathomas, "Bomb Bomb Bomb, Bomb Bomb Iran," http://www.youtube.com/
watch?v=0-zoPgv_nYg

Mike Huckabee, "Chuck Norris Approved," http://www.youtube.com/
watch?v=MDUQW8LUMs8

Obama Girl, "I Got a Crush . . . On Obama," http://www.youtube.com/
watch?v=wKsoXHYICqU

ParkRidge47, "Vote Different," http://www.youtube.com/watch?v=6h3G-lMZxjo

RCFriedman, "Snowman Challenges Mitt Romney to Debate," http://www.you-
tube.com/watch?v=e9RnExM41u4&feature=related

RogerRmJet, "John Edwards Feeling Pretty," http://www.youtube.com/
watch?v=2AE847UXu3Q

SmallMediaXL, "I'm a Democrat, I'm a Republican," http://www.youtube.com/
watch?v=ApNyDMj7zLI

This Spartan Life, "Net Neutrality," http://www.youtube.com/
watch?v=3S8q4FUY5fc

Toutsmith, "Al Gore's Penquin Army," http://www.youtube.com/
watch?v=IZSqXUSwHRI

TPMtv, "I'm Rudy Guiliani and I Approve This Message," http://www.youtube.
com/watch?v=qQ7-3M-YrdA

"YouTubers & Snowmen Unite AGAINST Romney!" http://www.youtube.com/
watch?v=8xvEH-6R16o&feature=related

# Part IV

# Shock and Guffaw
## *The Limits of Satire*

## 10

IIIIIIIIIIIIIIIIIIIIIIIIIIIIIIIIIIIIIIIIIIIIIIIIIIIIIIIIIIIIIIII

# Good Demo, Bad Taste
## South Park *as Carnivalesque Satire*

### Ethan Thompson

In March 2003, the *Hollywood Reporter* noted what seemed a curious meeting of television minds: Norman Lear, the 80-year-old television writer/producer famous for such socially conscious programs as *All in the Family, Maude,* and *Good Times,* was collaborating with Trey Parker and Matt Stone on the latest season of their notorious cartoon, *South Park.*[1] *USA Today*—preeminent arbiter of what constitutes the American "now"—picked up the story and directed the attention of the general public to this curious pairing: Lear, the icon of relevant, liberal-minded TV joining forces with the duo responsible for "Mr. Hanky the Christmas Poo." Though originally intending to collaborate on a single episode about the Declaration of Independence, Lear reportedly influenced a majority of the upcoming season's programs. "Those guys are equal-opportunity condemners," he said of Parker and Stone. "We covered a lot of important ground together."[2]

The *USA Today* article noted that Parker and Stone had first imagined Eric Cartman, the overweight and obnoxiously bigoted *South Park* youth, as an eight-year-old version of Archie Bunker. But the similarities between *South Park* and Lear's programs don't stop there. *South Park* may be the most confrontational sitcom, the most willing to tackle divisive social issues, since Lear's *All in the Family.* Like that program, *South Park* has also managed to successfully connect with audiences in spite of such potentially alienating content. The manner in which it does this, however, is far different from *All in the Family,* not just because the program is animated but because its mode of representation is characterized by an aggressive "bad taste." By the time of the meeting between Lear, Parker, and Stone,

*South Park* had become the longest running sitcom on cable TV. Today, the influences of its aesthetic-with-an-attitude can be seen from FOX's *The Family Guy* to much of the Adult Swim programming block, not to mention the seemingly endless homemade parodies and mash-ups available on YouTube. Critics from across the political spectrum may see this as the "culture" bar having been drastically lowered. *South Park*'s style and content can be dismissed by conservative watchdogs as moral depravity and by academic critics as postmodern nihilism that lacks depth. However, *South Park* uses a symbolically meaningful mode of representation with a long tradition in literary and folk culture—what Mikhail Bakhtin described as the carnivalesque—and stands as an example of how cultural texts created in today's media treat social and political issues in a way that appeals across ideological sensibilities too often simplified as conservative or liberal. When *South Park* subjects explicitly political issues (even candidates) to carnivalesque treatment, this is too easily dismissed as promoting a cynical (and ultimately apathetic) political attitude. Instead, we should recognize how *South Park*'s satire may encourage people to care about important issues not in a "Which team are you on?" but a "What do I think about this?" kind of way.

*South Park* has consistently been the highest-rated program on the Comedy Central cable channel since its debut in 1997 and is credited with raising the profile of that channel, thereby paving the way for later successes such as *The Daily Show with Jon Stewart* and *Chappelle's Show*.[3] Most important, *South Park* quickly proved capable of reaching many advertisers' most desired (and difficult to reach) demographic, males 18–34, routinely outdrawing the broadcast networks during its Wednesday night timeslot.[4] Though *South Park*'s ratings have fallen off from when the show was at the height of its popularity in the late 1990s, the show remains a model of today's narrowcasted television universe: a low-budget production that succeeds in delivering a quality demographic to advertisers. In 2007, Parker and Stone signed a $75 million deal with Comedy Central that extended *South Park*'s run at least through 2011.[5]

The members of that desirable "demo" differ in political sensibilities; it is a cultural sensibility that they share. Nailing down the politics of *South Park* is a tricky—perhaps ultimately futile—exercise. The show has provoked the wrath of Christians for its flippant attitude toward Jesus, while also being embraced for what *South Park Conservatives* author Brian C. Anderson describes as antiliberalism, such as its lampooning of Hollywood politicos like Barbra Streisand and Rob Reiner.[6] But any suggestion that *South Park* is essentially conservative must downplay the program's profound antiestablishment attitude and mocking of self-righteousness throughout the political and cultural spectrum. The carnivalesque mode of representation enables the program to treat controversial content and bridge political differences, creating points of identification that may make the program meaningful in different ways for *South Park* conservatives *and* liberals. Still, this is not to deny that *South Park* can play an important role as a site of articulation of political discourses and a source of the articulation of political identity on the part of its viewers. What *South Park* may most convincingly teach is that politics is too often reduced by the news media to the simplistic binaries that have alienated much of the public—Republican versus Democrat, liberal versus conservative, pro-life versus pro-choice, and so on.

## Cartman's Conceptual Grandfather: From All in the Family to South Park

Though *All in the Family* came from a vastly different television universe (the pre-cable 1970s), that show also owed its existence to an appeal to a smaller, more specific audience. The program was based on the cultural, political, and generational conflicts generated between the racist, sexist, and all-around bigot Archie Bunker and his daughter Gloria and son-in-law Meathead (played, not so ironically, by Rob Reiner). The program's debut followed the gutting of the CBS lineup in 1970, when the network cancelled a number of long-running, highly ranked programs in order to reach the more "quality" audience desired by advertisers. In the 1970s, that meant urban, college-educated adults. Surprisingly, though, by the summer of 1971, *All in the Family* had achieved mass success on a pre-cable, broadcasting scale and remained the top-ranked program for five years.[7]

David Barker has described how the multicamera mode of production of *All in the Family* encoded the social meaning of the program. Because the cameras never cross the proscenium and enter the performers' space, there are no reverse angles. The viewer never shares Archie's perspective; instead, the cameras typically cut to Archie's face for his "mugging" reaction. Thus, the audience is encouraged to laugh at Archie's dinosaur-like attitudes, not with him.[8] Still, Archie's outrageous comments can be very funny, and the show's long-standing success at the top of the ratings suggests that it appealed not just to those urban, liberal, "quality" demographics but to their more conservative parents and neighbors as well. Despite its production techniques or the intent of Lear, its chief writer/producer, some people were laughing with Archie, not at him.[9]

By looking at the style and content of one episode, it is possible to see how the program's mode of representation built in enough ambiguity or polysemy to accomplish this. In the episode "Equal Time," Archie and Meathead get into an argument about gun control after seeing the owner of a local television station advocating more gun regulation. Meathead challenges Archie to demand equal time to respond to the editorial. Archie records a typically obnoxious response (including the suggestion to stop hijackings by giving all airplane passengers guns), which the family watches together, then goes to the neighborhood bar to celebrate. As they sit, a man comes in and recognizes Archie from his TV editorial, shakes his hand, and praises Archie's ability to speak the truth. Though Archie initially revels in this vindication that the "common man" sides with him, the table is turned when the man pulls a gun and robs the bar and the Bunkers, ending the episode. The preferred reading, given the series' history and Lear's liberal sensibilities, would be that Archie becomes a victim of his naive (conservative) ways of thinking about guns and crime. Archie's beliefs are lampooned, and he gets his comeuppance. However, as Archie would undoubtedly point out—were he afforded the narrative codas now common in the continuity segments between programs—if he had had a "rod" himself, he could have stopped the guy from robbing the joint.

While *All in the Family* brought social relevance to the sitcom, the realistic treatment of that content did not undergo an aesthetic transformation of the magnitude that takes place in a typical episode of *South Park*. Though *All in the Family,* like most sitcoms, had a pronounced sense of theatricality since it was taped before a live audience and maintained a proscenium style of shooting, its mode of representation was fundamentally realistic. The show's visual palette, for instance, was dominated by beige and brown, resulting in a relatively "gritty" look for a sitcom. The debates within the Bunker household likely took place at higher volumes and with greater frequency than in typical American homes, but the ways in which the characters engaged cultural issues and the conversations that ensued played out realistically—albeit with the expected sitcom ending to tie up the conversations for the week.

*South Park*'s radical deviation from the typical sitcom aesthetic is not one of narrative structure. Horace Newcomb, writing at height of *All in the Family's* popularity in the early 1970s, described the narrative structure of the typical sitcom: some "situation" upsets the narrative equilibrium, complications ensue, then a resolution returns the program to narrative equilibrium.[10] In *South Park,* the situation usually has to deal with the outside world coming to *South Park,* and the boys (Stan, Kyle, Cartman, and Kenny) somehow complicate matters, involving more citizens of the town, until some bizarre or extreme turn brings the episode to an end. Stan signals each episode's narrative resolution by recounting the lesson the boys have learned from the events. This lesson is always sorely inadequate to account for the excesses of the episodes, which often include substantial cases of both physical and ideological destruction. *South Park* thus mocks the notion that a "lesson learned" can tie up all the possibilities and problems raised by the sitcom. In its relentless treatment of controversial issues, the realization of the inadequacy of narrative closure to contain the excesses of style and content is an important starting point. No half-hour television show (let alone a cable cartoon) can adequately find or offer the best answers to the most difficult questions. *South Park* acknowledges that the raising of issues, the way they are raised (the televisual mode of representation), and how they are put in dialogue with one another (the dialogic nature of the mode of representation) are more important than how a single episode ends. *South Park* thus offers another example of why scholars, including Newcomb, have suggested that television be understood as a cultural practice that raises questions and opens discussion, not a product that answers and ends conversations.[11]

The cultural transformations that take place on *South Park* have two fundamental components necessary to understand the treatment of controversial content, and thus *South Park* as satire. First, the paper cutout style of the program further exaggerates the ironic gap between the childish appearance of the program and its grown-up content. That *South Park* is animated removes it a degree from *All in the Family's* style; that it makes no pretense to realistic rendering removes it further. Though done with computers, the show looks low-tech, even sloppy. This low-tech approach has benefited the show in a number of ways. Though it reads as an ironic clash between childish form and mature content, the "crude" style fits the "crude" content. The animation style has also helped the show maintain an incredibly quick turnaround time. Episodes are sometimes made in a matter of days and turned in to Comedy Central shortly before airtime. This undoubtedly stresses out the network, but it protects the show from significant wrangling over content as there is seldom time to make substantial changes to the end product. Parker and Stone can respond quickly to satirize current situations, and by waiting to the last minute to finish the episodes, they inoculate themselves against having changes imposed on them to lessen controversy. South Park, thus, may very well be the most current non-news (or non-news satire) program on television.

The clash between childish style and grown-up content has undoubtedly provoked some of the backlash against the program. But the animated transformation ultimately pales in significance to the second key component of aesthetic transformation, the all-permeating bad taste and offensiveness with which *South Park* transforms historical reality into animated TV. In 2002, the Parents Television Council, a conservative media activist group, issued a report singling out *South Park* as the worst source of objectionable TV content on basic cable. The group reported that the show averaged 126 instances of sex, violence, or foul language per half-hour episode. While *All in the Family* had sparked a national debate over whether comedy could be an effective tool in combating racism and prejudice, *South Park's* aesthetic was criticized as being offensive for offense's sake, for pushing boundaries for no reason other than simply exercising bad taste. For example, the Parents Television Council had noted 166 counts of "shit" in one evening's basic cable programming. Of these, 162 came in a *South Park* episode specifically parodying Americans' obsession with "bad words." "To take that episode out of context," responded Comedy Central executive vice president and general manager Bill Hilary, "shows that they don't get the idea of irony."[12]

The key to evaluating how *South Park's* "offensiveness" works is not to focus on how particular groups are offended, or to count obscenities, as if these are there just to titillate the 18–34-year-old males expected to be watching. Rather, the key is considering how the offensiveness is a component of a consistent aesthetic that constructs an alternative language for interrogating contemporary cultural discourses. *South Park's* offensive style and content do not simply "get in the way" of cultural criticism or ameliorate controversial content; they are essential to the structure of the show and its critical and comedic aesthetic. *South Park* has mocked or attacked Scientologists, animal rights activists, homosexuals, environmentalists, the handicapped, and everyone in between. But those specific attacks are built on a foundation of unrelenting indecency that mocks the very notion of good taste.

## Understanding the Carnivalesque:
### Why Farting, Vomiting, and Cursing Matter

*South Park*'s mode of representation, the combination of its televisual style and content—the way it tells these stories—conforms to Bakhtin's characteristics of the carnivalesque. In his analysis of the eighteenth-century French novelist Rabelais, Bakhtin identified elements of a textual mode that bore characteristics of the social practice of carnival and the "low" language of the marketplace. The carnival was a special time and place where normal rules of social decorum didn't apply. People were expected to release themselves from social inhibitions and drink, dance, curse, and just be rowdy in general. Bakhtin suggests that, although lasting only a short time of the year, carnival was symbolically central to medieval folk culture. Its systems of signification were complex and, though often indecent, were fundamentally tied to power relationships that governed medieval life. During carnival, those relations were inverted through rites and traditions of a truly participatory popular culture. Bakhtin described the dramatic shift in the social order that takes place during carnival as a "temporary suspension of all hierarchic distinctions and barriers among men and of certain norms and prohibitions of usual life." Meanwhile, "an ideal and at the same time real type of communication, impossible in ordinary life, is established."[13] Bakhtin emphasizes how carnivalesque laughter isn't a negative laughter that places itself above the object of ridicule; the carnival is about rebirth: "This carnival spirit offers the chance to have a new outlook on the world, to realize the relative nature of all that exists, and to enter a completely new order of things."[14]

Robert Stam, John Fiske, and others have persuasively argued that Bakhtin's literary concepts, even those derived from medieval folk culture, can be applied to the study of today's mass media.[15] Television today is the preeminent sphere of what Bakhtin calls "heteroglossia," the collision between competing discourses that defines human communication and the experience of culture, rather than any singular system of meaning. Increasingly, we respond to those experiences through new media where we may find more competing discourses in dialogue, but it is still television that remains the common culture to which we react. According to Fiske, "Television, in this sense, constitutes an electronic microcosm . . . which reflects and relays, distorts and amplifies, the ambient heteroglossia."[16]

Within TV's heteroglossia, *South Park's* carnivalesque mode of representation parodies official language and maps the relations between competing discourses, tracing out the power relations that define and make sense of the world. We can look to Bakhtin's formulation of the carnivalesque not because we think *South Park* is essentially subversive, progressive, or even neoconservative but because doing so allows us to recognize how seemingly diverse aspects of the *South Park* narrative are consistent with an overall aesthetic approach to making sense (and fun) of culture.

In his examination of genre hybridity and *The Simpsons,* Jason Mittell questions the productivity of labeling the show a "postmodern" text. "How does this further our understanding of the text or its cultural life?" he asks.[17] Though seemingly objecting to the need to engage the question, Mittell effectively argues for the centrality of the tensions between the genres of the sitcom and the cartoon in *The Simpsons,* thus debunking its supposed postmodernism, which downplays the significance of genre conventions in encoding and decoding texts. Similarly, one might question the usefulness of laboring to establish the carnivalesque status of *South Park.* How is applying a label created for literary and folk culture to contemporary, industrialized culture a useful form of criticism? The answer is that it helps us understand not just our own cultural moment but how popular culture changes. It also shows how the liminal space of the carnival, whether existing in actual physical space or as a literary or televisual mode, remains a space for meaningful play. In the case of *South Park,* the carnivalesque is a signifying system that successfully (and efficiently) incorporates contemporary elements outside of its own narrative universe, both from television culture and historical reality, in order to connect with audiences.

Jeffrey Sconce has written that the central challenge facing producers of contemporary television programs, dealing with both the limited material economy of television and plentiful narrative economy, is the need to generate repetition with difference.[18] How can TV writers and producers repeat a compelling premise while still keeping things fresh? A rash of programs have succeeded in recent years by combining tried and true television formats with a self-conscious, parodic approach to television and political culture that both is funny and produces a sense of social relevance. Much as *All in the Family* took the formula of the domestic sitcom and used current events and social conflict as the "situation" for the weekly episode, *South Park, The Daily Show, The Colbert Report, Family Guy, Chappelle's Show,* and *Mind of Mencia,* not to mention *Saturday Night Live* and *MADtv,* take preexisting television forms and hybridize them through parody and satire steeped in ironic cultural references. And like *All in the Family*, which had a specific liberal agenda (if not effect), this hybridization is not simply about parodying television form. Rather, parody is the language through which a liminal space is created for considering contemporary political and social discourses.

While pointing out the elements of *South Park* that could be considered in bad taste may seem unnecessary to even the occasional viewer, a close look at the first episode of the program, "Cartman Gets an Anal Probe," shows the consistency of the carnivalesque aesthetic that is deployed in most all the shows, even though the first episode does not explicitly deal with any particular political issue. From Bakhtin's descriptions of the cultural forms of folk carnival, we can identify these key characteristics of carnivalesque culture, both as lived human experience, and as a mode of representation:

1. Laughter. The preeminent response produced by carnival rituals and carnivalesque texts. The carnivalesque is not a somber—or even rational—form of cultural engagement or critique.
2. Bodily excess/scatological humor. By featuring the grotesque or drawing attention to the "lower bodily stratum," the carnivalesque celebrates the antithesis of what human bodies are supposed to look like and how they are supposed to behave: as restrained and subordinate to the mind.
3. Billingsgate. Language "games" such as insults and cursing that constitute an alternative response to official, legitimate language.
4. Inversions or reversals. The inversions of the usual social roles and power relations, frequently including the mocking of authority.

The episode begins with Cartman recounting a vivid dream of being kidnapped by aliens and given an anal probe. Though Cartman refuses to acknowledge this was anything but a dream, Kyle and Stan immediately believe it actually did happen, and these suspicions are confirmed when a telescoping eye emerges from his pants. Across town, Officer Barbrady assures a rancher that there is nothing unusual about a recent rash of cow mutilations. He and the other adults (with the notable exception of Chef, the cafeteria cook and boys' confidant) dismiss the suggestion that there are aliens invading South Park, even after Kyle's little brother is abducted. Stan courts Wendy Testaburger but vomits every time she talks to him. Kenny is hit by a car, stampeded by cattle, and eaten by rats. The boys refer to one another as "fat ass," "Jew," and "dildo," even as they work to-gether to save Kyle's little brother. The aliens ultimately apologize to the cows and leave, certain that cows are the most intelligent creatures on the planet. Cartman is taken by the aliens but is spat out the next morning with a bad case of pinkeye, reportedly given to him onboard the space-craft by minor 1980s heartthrob Scott Baio.

The carnivalesque elements, even in this brief plot summary, are clear. Cartman's body is grotesque and unruly: it is excessive not just in size but exceeds his ability to control its bodily functions. The alien probe causes flaming gas that disrupts the elementary school classroom and sets Brit-ish exchange student Pip on fire. Other episodes have featured Cartman "bulking up" on steroids or eating a treasure chest full of fake gold, which swells him to immense proportions. Stan's nervous vomiting is another out-of-control bodily function. The birds that alight, bathe, and feed on his vomit, as well as the rats that eat Kenny's dead body, are carnivalesque degradations like those Bakhtin describes that also connote some sense of regeneration or rebirth. At both these moments (the rats and the birds), the narrative pauses for what seem to be self-indulgent flourishes of bad taste—moments when the program purposefully goes another step be-yond what is already in bad taste. These moments, which feed into the criticism that *South Park*'s creators are indecent just for indecency's sake, are examples of the narrative reveling in the grotesque.

The folk culture of carnival that Bakhtin discusses featured rituals of inversion and reversal, where religious or feudal authorities were mocked and derided. The social order of *South Park* is inverted in that the kids are the only ones who actually recognize the presence of aliens. Throughout the series, the adults and the authorities (exemplified not just by the par-ents but by Officer Barbrady and the school counselor, Mr. Mackey) muck things up, and the kids—though indignant at adult incompetence—try to patch things together. To make matters worse, the cows are recognized by the aliens as superior in intelligence to humans. Of course, through it all the boys cuss like sailors and insult each other at every opportunity.

Identifying the elements of the carnivalesque in the first episode of *South Park* allows us to recognize how *South Park*'s "offensiveness" works in episodes that deal more explicitly with controversial social issues. *South Park* articulates an alternative, unofficial, offensive language—a carnivalesque response to the official discourses that are brought under scrutiny as the sitcom's necessary disrupting "situation." While the poli-tics of *All in the Family* might be described as liberal in intention, if not necessarily in effect, *South Park*'s are more slippery due not just to Parker's or Stone's intents but to the carnivalesque mode of representation, as well as characteristics that have been described as common in postmodern culture, such as nihilism, irony, and pastiche. To "subvert" through the carnivalesque is to call into question, to undermine, official, legitimate discourse. This creates opportunities for the articulation of political identity from a number of perspectives, even if it doesn't ultimately endorse a specific alternative path. In *The Politics and Poetics of Transgression,* Peter Stallybrass and Allon White suggest that the notion of a rational public sphere contributed to the marginalization of other modes of discourse by other people. "The emergence of the public sphere required that its space of discourse be *de-libidinized* in the interests of serious, productive and *rational* discourse."[19] South Park also uses the carnivalesque to recapture the public sphere, reopening the discussion of "serious" affairs to a crude language that signals that anyone can participate in it.

## Politics and the Carnivalesque: "Vote or Die, Mother(bleep)er!"

As a more explicitly political example, we can look to "Douche and Turd," an episode that first ran the week before the 2004 presidential election. The episode follows the typical treatment of social issues by translating the "issue" into a situational disturbance of the *South Park* narrative equilibrium that will be excessively complicated then inadequately resolved by Stan's token "lesson learned." These narrative complications tie in various other contemporary discourses, bringing them into dialogue with the central social issue of the episode. In "Douche and Turd," the 2004 presidential election finds carnivalesque representation as a hard-fought campaign over a new South Park Elementary School mascot. This campaign is initiated after the animal rights group PETA (People for the Ethical Treatment of Animals) interrupts a pep rally in protest of the school's current mascot, the cow. Disgusted by being forced to give up their cow mascot because of PETA, Kyle nominates a giant douche, while Cartman's candidate is a turd sandwich. Stan is uninterested in voting, finding the choices equally unattractive. His apathy sets off a hostile reaction from his friends, family, and the town of South Park at large, which literally banishes him until he has changed his mind and recognized the importance of voting.

Giant Douche and Turd Sandwich are not specifically characterized in ways that make them readable as real-life 2004 presidential candidates John

Cartman and Butters hit the campaign trail for Turd Sandwich,
greasing palms with butterscotch candies.

Kerry or George W. Bush. Instead, they are interchangeable as grotesque
mockeries of the undesirable choices available to voters. The mascot candidates are derived from what Bakhtin referred to as "those parts of the body
that are open to the outside world . . . the open mouth, the genital organs,
the breasts, the phallus, the potbelly, the nose."[20] The candidates don't just
bear symbolic characteristics of the bodily lower stratum; they are literally
products of and for that stratum. But *South Park*'s critique doesn't stop as a
complaint about the desirability of our political candidates, which is fairly
commonly heard in popular culture. This is really just the starting point
for calling into question other characteristics of the political environment,
particularly, the dominance of political discourse by those on the fringe and
self-serving celebrity and corporate get-out-the-vote campaigns. "Haven't
you seen the 'Rock the Vote' stuff?" Kyle asks Stan. "Or Puff Daddy's 'Vote
or Die'?" Kyle references campaigns that are ostensibly nonpartisan, public service messages but suggests they are based on whom those voters are
likely to vote for. "We've got to make Stan understand the importance of
voting," he says, "because he'll definitely vote for our guy."

Puff Daddy's "Vote or Die" campaign is made literal, as he visits Stan's
house with posse in tow, pulling a gun and telling Stan to vote or he will

indeed shoot, stab, or by other means kill him. Puff does so in song, and this portion of the cartoon simulates a rap video, complete with the fish-eyed lens techniques familiar in music videos, particularly those directed by Hype Williams. His "Vote or Die" rap also contains segments typical of the sort frequently criticized in hip-hop as misogynist, Puffy relating what he wants "bitches" to shake in the voting booth and what he plans to do with his "jimmy" in there as well. These inclusions not only articulate "Vote or Die" within contemporary hip-hop rhetoric but again are examples of bodily excess and bad taste, not to mention a pastiche of hip-hop video tropes.

Though Parker and Stone treat Puff with the opprobrium they typically set aside for celebrities, the main carnivalesque criticism of the episode seems directed toward the political activist group, PETA. After the town's citizens rip off pieces of Stan's clothing, spit on him, and send him off on a horse, he winds up at PETA's wilderness fortress, where its members live with animals as equals. As a PETA member explains this "natural way" to Stan, he stops, pulls down his pants, and defecates. He then introduces Stan to a number of PETA members who are "married" to animals, one of whom has managed to procreate with an ostrich, producing a hideous creature that repeatedly begs to be killed. When Puffy follows Stan to the compound in order to finally follow through on his "Vote or Die" vow, a PETA member dumps a bucket of blood on him for wearing a fur coat. Puff's posse breaks out the guns and massacres the PETA members, whose bodies are immediately desecrated by the animals they supposedly live in harmony with. A dog urinates on its dead owner's head; a goat eats the face of another. Like the birds and rats in the first episode, these, too, are carnivalesque flourishes.

Before the melee, a PETA member encourages Stan to return to town and explains that almost every election from the beginning of time has been between a turd and a douche—"the only ones who will suck up enough to make it in politics." Again, the episode indicts not specifically Kerry or Bush but more generally the state of American politics. Prompted by this comment, and the Puffy/PETA melee, Stan returns to South Park. He tells everyone why he came back as he recites the episode's lesson: "I learned that I better get used to having to pick between a douche and a turd sandwich, because it's usually the choice I'll have." His vote ultimately doesn't change the outcome, however, as the giant douche wins in a landslide. Upset, he is reminded by his parents that he can't say his vote didn't matter just because his candidate didn't win. When it is announced that all the PETA members have been killed, however, the school decides they don't need a new mascot anymore. "*Now* your vote doesn't matter," Stan's Dad reassures him.

The carnivalesque in the episode works as a response to the "official" discourses on voting and politics familiar to *South Park* viewers in 2004. The primary discourse that seems upended is the purported sanctity of voting—more specifically, the frequent (and frequently patronizing) public service campaigns designed to get young Americans to vote. *South Park* doesn't so much suggest that voting itself doesn't matter but that those who suggest they are impartial and only want people to vote are both self-righteous and disingenuous. It attacks the "official" ways of thinking about voting—that is, the way the establishment (the school principal, MTV, Puff Daddy) suggests it is disinterested in encouraging voting. This is further emphasized when Stan's parents, after being shocked at his apathy, quickly begin fighting over the proper candidate and by Kyle's repeated comments that they must get Stan to vote because he'll vote for his side. *South Park* dramatizes how painfully binaristic politics has become and how alienating this divisiveness is, then suggests that there are other important things going on beyond party politics.

The most grotesque figures in the episode are the PETA members, drawn as unkempt hippies. *South Park* attacks them as examples of how fringe political interests now dominate political discourse. PETA makes an easy target of political correctness run amok. They violently boycott the seemingly innocuous selection of the cow as elementary mascot. They rescue the horse Stan has been banished on, not Stan. They don't just love animals—they *love* animals. Their advocacy of animal rights is hyperbolized as a delusional obsession that undermines common sense and, yes, decency. Yet it is one of the PETA members who ultimately convinces Stan to vote, reminding him that the choices of candidates are always undesirable. PETA's "eco-terrorism" brings about the vote, and their demise renders it unnecessary.

Rather than articulating a consistently conservative or liberal voice, *South Park*'s carnivalesque mode creates a space for viewers to engage multiple social discourses from a variety of political subjectivities, while undermining the supposed legitimacy of those discourses. The episode can be read as conservative because of its portrayal of PETA as a leftist political fringe group whose members are not simply misguided but insane. However, the show certainly doesn't offer a Republican endorsement. Cartman's logo for the turd sandwich mimics the Bush/Cheney 2004 logo, and he bribes voters with butterscotch candies. *South Park*'s carnivalesque treatment of voting creates points of identification for various political identities—left, right, and center. This, no doubt, helps explain its broad appeal across that desirable demographic, males aged 18–34.

If the carnivalesque, as Bakhtin repeatedly notes, is fundamentally ambivalent, degrading in order to suggest rebirth, what optimistic possibilities does this *South Park* episode suggest? Is there a cultural meaning beneath the surface, more to the text than material for ideological identification from already existing political perspectives? If the carnivalesque creates an ideal sort of communication, impossible in everyday life, that communication ought to be saying something, to offer some alternative to the "official" discourses and power structures. The kids nominate Giant Douche and Turd Sandwich not out of a disdain for the democratic process but because they are upset by the extremist political action that brought about the controversy. Stan doesn't want to vote because he resents the self-interested parties encouraging him to do so. This episode of *South Park* articulates a critique of contemporary political discourse as dominated, on the one hand, by extremist organizations removed from the mainstream and, on the other hand, by the condescending public relations campaigns that, through their claim of political disinterest, stand for nothing. *South Park*, through its carnivalesque treatment of these poles, suggests that there ought to be a vast, reasonable, democratic middle. The tone of this social criticism is appropriately irate and rowdy because it is adopted on behalf of the people fed up with official political discourse— the fabricated photo-ops, the scripted debates and talk show appearances, and the legitimate news media that help produce them rather than demand something more.

Though *South Park* is consistently topical and offensive, occasionally, in its "bad" episodes, the program's carnivalesque characteristics can seem uninspired and betray a lack of substantial engagement with any particular social or political discourse. The carnivalesque can also be used as a "paint by numbers" formula with the necessary bodily functions, sexist characters and comments, violence, and cultural references to produce a new episode. At its worst, then, even when engaging the most politically overt of content, *South Park* can become a carnivalesque pastiche—little more than an offensive echoing of contemporary discourse rather than a subversive alternative.

An example of how South Park's carnivalesque may function as a whole lot of offensive noise, signifying nothing—even when it seems it ought to

A bomb-sniffing pig locates the "Snuke"
inside Hillary Clinton.

be at its most meaningful—is the 2007 episode titled, "The Snuke." The episode is structured as a parody of the critical and popular hit, *24*, which at the time was in its sixth season after winning the Emmy for best drama for its fifth season. The program was also the subject of considerable criticism (even from the Pentagon) over its representation of torture as an effective tactic for interrogating suspected terrorists. Cartman takes over the role of superhero and counterterrorist Jack Bauer, tracking down what he believes is a terror plot involving a Muslim family that has just moved to town. Inadvertently, he exposes a plot involving presidential candidate Hillary Clinton's upcoming visit. Besides using *24*'s signature digital clock as an intertitle, the narrative includes such *24* standbys as a diversionary plot for a much larger threat, along with interrogation scenes where Cartman tortures two suspects by repeatedly farting in their faces. Since the bomb plot is only a diversionary tactic, *South Park* must offer a larger threat to American safety and finds an appropriately absurd one in the British. Not contemporary ones, mind you, but eighteenth-century era "red coats." Thus, the boys can again learn a valuable lesson: "We shouldn't profile one race of people, because most of the world hates us."

When Clinton first appears to make her speech in town, it seems that *South Park* might be about to critique the emptiness and predictability of campaign rhetoric. Clinton offers the familiar refrain "I campaign in small towns like these because it is in small towns like South Park where you find the true America," affecting a southern accent (even though

South Park is in Colorado). Unfortunately, besides that, she says little for the rest of the episode. Rather than engage Clinton's vast cultural and political persona, she is rendered nothing more than a handy carnivalesque site for the diversionary plot: a nuclear bomb is inside her. Typical of 24's outlandish plots and carnivalesque bodily preoccupations, "The Snuke," we learn, is the name for "a suitcase nuke that fits in a woman's snizz." An officer warns that no one's been inside there for 30 years, and, ultimately, the man who attempts to disarm the snuke is attacked and eaten. The first female presidential candidate with a legitimate shot at winning thus becomes the *vagina dentata*. Grotesque, perhaps, but it's tough to read this as somehow upending any kind of sexist norms. This is especially true when viewing the episode during its later, post–safe harbor airing, a time when *South Park* is often framed by commercials for the infamous softcore pornography video series, *Girls Gone Wild*. Indeed, one should understand that *South Park's* carnivalesque culture is not always political; its critique is often muddled and may as reliably violate as articulate progressive politics.

## Conclusion

"The Snuke" appeared during the earliest stages of the 2008 presidential campaign, and *South Park* again made news. CNN reported on the episode and again betrayed the inability of "real news" coverage to conceptualize the political potential of *South Park's* carnivalesque satire.[21] The piece dutifully pointed out that the episode took swipes at both the left and the right, but in summing up its political significance seemed to be at a loss, ultimately asking, "Will *South Park* influence its young viewers to vote?" Rather than acknowledging that political involvement is about thinking before it's about voting, CNN fell into the myopic trap of seeing television viewing as either a distraction from or a mere prelude to meaningful social activity.[22] More specifically, CNN echoed a common misconception about how televisual satire works or should be evaluated, effectively suggesting that all that matters is voting for the Turd Sandwich or the Giant Douche, ignoring *South Park's* assertion that there are more important issues at stake.

*All in the Family* sought to connect with a "quality" audience demographic in the 1970s through an emphasis on bringing relevant content into the traditional sitcom format. The treatment of that content—the representation of how the characters struggled with social change, and the narrative resolutions to the situations and issues raised—enabled *All in the Family* to connect with a mass audience across ideological boundaries. *South Park*'s carnivalesque mode similarly enables the program to treat controversial content while still appealing to a demographic defined by age and gender, not politics. That *South Park*'s mode of representation is fundamentally one that calls into question official, legitimate forms of producing ideology suggests that its audience has a (bad) taste for challenging authority and the status quo. The computer-animated, cutout style of *South Park* has proven to be an effective mode of production, suitable to the material economy of a basic cable program and appropriate to the creative and intellectual economy of its writer/producers who wish to routinely incorporate timely, controversial content into the show. The *South Park* aesthetic is more than a visual style—it's a distinctive mode of making sense of controversy and the "real world" social context.

The cultural status of *South Park* got a shot in the arm in 2006, when the program was given the Peabody Award—regarded as the Pulitzer Prize of television. While 31 other programs received Peabody awards that year, including historic news coverage of Hurricane Katrina, a prestigious Martin Scorsese–directed documentary about Bob Dylan, and the cult Sci-Fi series *Battlestar Galactica,* the *South Park* award garnered all the attention in the press. "The judges felt that it was a bold program that probably offends just about everybody at some point and in doing so reminds us that we need to be tolerant," awards director Horace Newcomb was quoted as saying.[23] Though the height of *South Park*'s popularity may have been behind it, the award seemed to signal the end of a cycle of cultural taste. *South Park,* possibly the most intentionally offensive program in the history of television, had been awarded the most prestigious award in television—for being offensive.

Long before becoming Peabody director, Newcomb was one of the first academics to take the time to look at the sitcom and think about how it works: both as narrative entertainment and as a cultural form that shapes the ways in which people make sense of their world. Likewise, the award suggests that *South Park* has not only influenced the aesthetic landscape of television but also has altered the accepted ways of rendering the social landscape. Such was the effect of *South Park* on Norman Lear, anyway. What were the manifestations of the elder-statesman's influence on Comedy Central's enfants terribles? An exploration of why Kenny's family can't escape persistent poverty? Cartman transformed after a visit to the

Museum of Tolerance? Not quite. In the season premiere, Earth was revealed to be a reality show staged by aliens. Lear's touch: the show's host was a giant taco that pooped ice cream. Perhaps Lear was inspired by *South Park*'s demonstration that pooping on politics does not equate with having no politics or even having cynical politics. Instead, *South Park* uses the carnivalesque to recapture politics for a pissed-off public, refusing to endorse the official ways of speaking that limit political debate and participation to either/or, left or right, "vote or die" binaries. A rude, crude mode of representation can be a powerful—and economic—way to make television that makes people think.

NOTES

1. Andrew Wallenstein, "Lear Joins 'South Park' Family," *Hollywood Reporter*, 14 March 2003.

2. Bill Keveney, "TV Icon Norman Lear Is Goin' Down to 'South Park,'" *USA Today*, 17 March 2003.

3. Ray Richmond, "'South Park' Will Subvert through '05," *Hollywood Reporter*, 31 March 2003.

4. Scott Hettrick, "Hanky Panky," *Hollywood Reporter*, 6 April 1998.

5. Andrew Wallenstein, "Ads Add Up for 'South Park,'" *Hollywood Reporter*, 28 August 2007.

6. Brian C. Anderson, *South Park Conservatives: The Revolt against Liberal Media Bias* (Washington, D.C.: Regnery, 2005), 82.

7. Tim Brooks and Earle Marsh, *The Complete Directory to Prime Time Network TV Shows, 1946–Present* (New York: Ballantine, 2003), 34.

8. David Barker, "Television Production Techniques as Communication," in *Television: The Critical View*, ed. Horace Newcomb, 6th ed. (New York: Oxford University Press, 2000), 173.

9. For a compelling discussion about the politics of *All in the Family* in an interview with Lear, see *Color Adjustment*, dir. Marlon Riggs (California Newsreel, 1991).

10. Horace Newcomb, *TV: The Most Popular Art* (New York: Doubleday, 1974).

11. Horace Newcomb and Paul Hirsch, "Television as Cultural Forum," in *Television: The Critical View*, ed. Horace Newcomb, 6th ed. (New York: Oxford University Press, 2000).

12. John M. Higgins, "Loose Standards Shock," *Broadcasting and Cable*, 28 January 2002, 16.

13. Mikhail Bakhtin, *Rabelais and His World*, trans. Helene Iswolsky (Bloomington: Indiana University Press, 1984), 15–16.

14. Ibid., 34.

15. Robert Stam, *Subversive Pleasures: Bakhtin, Cultural Criticism, and Film* (Baltimore: Johns Hopkins University Press, 1989); John Fiske, *Television Culture* (London: Metheun, 1987).

16. Fiske, *Television Culture,* 220.

17. Jason Mittell, "Cartoon Realism," in *Television: The Critical View,* ed. Horace Newcomb, 7th ed. (New York: Oxford University Press, 2006).

18. Jeffrey Sconce, "What If? Charting Television's New Textual Boundaries," in *Television after TV: Essays on a Medium in Transition,* ed. Lynn Spigel and Jan Olsson (Durham, N.C.: Duke University Press, 2004).

19. Peter Stallybrass and Allon White, *The Politics and Poetics of Transgression* (Ithaca, N.Y.: Cornell University Press, 1986), 97.

20. Bakhtin, *Rabelais and His World,* 26.

21. CNN, 30 March 2007.

22. My thanks to Jonathan Gray, Avi Santo, and Yael Sherman for their comments on this episode and news clip.

23. Paul J. Gough, "Peabodys Go Down to 'South Park,'" *Hollywood Reporter,* 6 April 2006.

# 11

# In the Wake of "The Nigger Pixie"
## Dave Chappelle and the Politics of Crossover Comedy

### Bambi Haggins

When Dave Chappelle left behind his incredibly successful Comedy Central series (and a $50 million paycheck) for his South African walkabout, it was in the wake of the "Nigger Pixie," a character created and played by Chappelle. The aforementioned pixie, clad in the costuming of minstrelsy (blackface, white lips and gloves, red vest and a Pullman Porter's cap), was the centerpiece of a controversial sketch screened as part of the "Lost Episodes" of *Chappelle's Show* in which culturally and racially specific devils exhorted individuals to react "naturally" and perform the stereotypical tropes of racialized masculinity.[1] When Chappelle greeted journalists between takes, he apologized for his appearance, slyly adding, "Bet you never met a real live coon."[2] During the initial part of the taping, the comic explained, "The premise of the sketch was that every race had this . . . pixie, this racial complex . . . The reason I chose blackface . . . was [because] this was going to be the visual personification of the 'N' word."[3] Chappelle later described the experience of doing the sketch in terms that differed substantially from his pre-taping impressions. Loud and long laughter from one of the white members of the crew gave the comic a moment of pause. Chappelle later stated that this reception of the Nigger Pixie was the beginning of the end: "I felt like it had gotten me in touch with my inner 'coon.' . . . When that guy laughed, I felt like, man, they got me."[4] On one hand, one might argue that the Nigger Pixie sketch is no more transgressive than other provocative comedic fare dealing with stereotypical tropes from the first two seasons. On the other, regardless of whether there was a sliding scale of outrageousness and offensiveness that afforded greater or lesser sociocultural resonance to the historical (or ahistorical) construction of the pixies, it was Chappelle who questioned whether this use of internalized racism as a part of broad satire was crossing an ideological line. In the wake of the Nigger Pixie, Chappelle acknowledged the possible dangers inherent in comedy that challenges cultural, social, and political sensibilities and questioned whether his comedic discourse—as exemplified in his creation of little specters of racial self-hatred—was becoming progressively more open to [mis]interpretation.

The comedy of Dave Chappelle has always existed at the intersections of multiple comic trajectories in black comedy: the embodiment of de facto crossover. Chappelle's comic voice—in his standup and his series—reflects the dynamic, complex, and conflicted nature of sociopolitical comedic discourse in the post–civil rights moment. *Chappelle's Show's* consistent engagement with the politics of racial representation was the element that cast the series as both anomaly and model within the niched and narrowcasted televisual milieu of the post-network era. The series, like the comic, enjoys dual credibility through ties to the Afrocentricism of the black hip-hop intelligentsia, as well as the skater/slacker/stoner ethos of suburban life. This cred allows Chappelle to speak for and to Gen X and Gen Y subcultures in both the black and white communities.

As civil-rights-era comic pioneer Dick Gregory stated simply, "When you mention his name among young folks, it's like mentioning Jesus in a Christian church."[5] In industrial, sociocultural, and aesthetic terms, attaining de facto crossover affords the performer a lofty and lucrative space in American entertainment and popular culture—and, as Chappelle discovered, this is a precarious space to occupy. The comic's awareness of both the industrial and cultural cachet that *Chappelle's Show* had amassed was compounded by the pressure and responsibility that came with that coveted position: it would also eventually make Chappelle question whether his series was exploding stereotypes or merely reinforcing them. In this essay, I explore disquieting questions about the price of de facto crossover for the comic, the industry, and American popular culture at large when those of us in the audience may—or may not—be discerning the politics of racial representation embedded in the satire.

Over the life of the series, the sociopolitical significance of *Chappelle's Show* becomes clearer as the fragile mixture of biting satire and gratuitous outrageousness becomes muddied.[6] The problematic aspects of this discursive muddiness are exacerbated by the multiple reading positions of the decidedly diverse audience.[7] As a sketch comedy program on a basic cable network (Comedy Central), *Chappelle's Show's* ability to inspire admiration and imitation from frat boys and backpackers (as well as the occasional scholar) raises questions about the nature, the source, and the subject of their laughter. Through the analysis of deliberately sociopolitically provocative sketches in the series, "The Racial Draft," "Reparations," and "Black Bush," as well as the most controversial sample from the Lost Episodes, "The Nigger Pixie," one can trace the escalation of the comedic stakes: how the power of being a cultural phenomenon complicated and confused the comic's intentions for the satire and ultimately made even his basic cable refuge untenable. Before examining the products of the honeymoon period at Comedy Central—and subsequent estrangement— a greater understanding of Chappelle's failure to connect in network (and netlet) programming is required.

### *The Middle Passage: Chappelle's Road to De Facto Crossover*

Although as early as 1996, when Black Block counterprogramming strategies had taken hold on the netlets (and some enthusiasm still existed for singular black comics on network television), Chappelle had signed a series of development deals with Disney to make sitcoms for Touchstone Television. Only one of the 11 pilots proved to be palatable to either the comic or the networks. The singular "success," *Buddies,* was an interracial buddy comedy that had a 13-episode run on ABC.[8] The show treated the professional partnership between the two leads (Chappelle as Dave Carlisle, black buddy; and Christopher Garlin as John Butler, white buddy) as a monumental feat—a victory of the civil rights era. "It was a bad show," said Chappelle on a *60 Minutes* interview.[9] The central problem with this series (and the other 11 pilot attempts) was an inability to find an appropriate vehicle within the 22-minute programming framework to allow the friendly subversiveness of Chappelle's comic sensibility to make more than a cameo appearance. The comic's inability to find a "niche" in the age of "niche-marketing" signaled that his comic persona was not ready for sitcom prime time.

By the late 1990s, the changing network/netlet climate made it even more difficult to find an appropriate vehicle for Chappelle's comic persona. When Chappelle developed a series for FOX television based on *his* life as an up and coming comic in New York City with Peter Tolan (*The Larry Sanders Show* and *The Job*), television success seemed imminent. After all, they were dealing with FOX, not only the home of *Married . . .*

*With Children, Martin,* and *The Simpsons,* but the originator of Black Block programming, dysfunctional domcoms, and boundary (and taste)–challenging television fare. Unfortunately for Chappelle, by 1998 FOX had virtually gained network status and was, for the most part, out of the Black Block business. The WB and UPN were still looking toward black comedy programming to open up the "urban" (read: nonwhite) audience. Both broadcasting entities catered to black viewers—seeking to fill a niche not adequately served by the major networks—at least in terms of the sitcom.

With six episodes ordered and the show slated as a midseason replacement in January 1998, negotiations between Chappelle and the network fell apart when FOX executives, seeing the Touchstone-produced sitcom as "too black," suggested that the lead female character be changed from black to white, in order to "broaden" audience appeal. Chappelle and Tolan walked away; in the case of the comic, he did not do so quietly. Chappelle spent the better part of the next year (and multiple appearances on *Late Night with Conan O'Brien*) venting about FOX's network practices: "This network built itself on Black viewers . . . [but] tells every Black artist no matter what you do, you need whites to succeed."[10] The FOX debacle, like Margaret Cho's experience with the network dictating what her Asian American experience should look like, soured Chappelle on both the genre and the networks.[11] In many ways, given the restrictiveness of the genre and the openness and fluidity of Chappelle's comic persona, the lack of "fit" between the two is not surprising. As Chappelle himself noted, "I tried sitcoms before, and it's something about the way I'm funny that is not for that venue. People never know the extent of how funny I was. I'd be Urkel. I'd be rich, but I'd be Urkel."[12]

When *Chappelle's Show* found a home on the network that championed a cartoon featuring a misanthropic and pathologically self-centered "big-boned" little boy with a foul mouth (Cartman of *South Park*) and a fake news program whose anchor lampoons the absurdities of domestic and foreign policy with the same ease he interviews movie stars and former and current heads of state (*The Daily Show with Jon Stewart*), it seemed Chappelle had found in a little corner of basic cable the niche that eluded him on network television. As *Chappelle's Show* cocreator Neal Brennan, stated: "We're trying to push the genre and make stuff that's more interesting and personal. . . . We went to a place, Comedy Central, that sort of needs us and gave us a lot of freedom. . . . We didn't get much money, but that was the trade-off—you get control."[13]

The series' contentiousness, as well as its conflicting ideological and comedic impulses, positioned *Chappelle's Show* as the product of *our* sociohistorical moment. The program, which the comic described as "hip-hop Masterpiece Theater," spoke directly to the first decade of the new millennium—an era when duality seems the norm. From its midseason premiere in 2003, *Chappelle's Show* engaged issues of race, class, ethnicity, and popular culture with irreverence, candor, and a decidedly black sensibility rarely seen in prime-time television comedy.

The duo that brought us *Half Baked* rejuvenated sketch comedy that they described as "cultural rather than political," infused it with a hip-hop sensibility, and the espoused creative ethos of "dancing like nobody's watching."[14] However, given that the show averaged a viewership of 3.1 million per episode *on basic cable,* people were watching in droves. While the situation comedy is almost always about containment—within the 22-minute format, within cultural norms, within certainties of narrative closure—sketch comedy always has great potential for transgression and, in this particular post-network era, "edgy" is considered good for business.[15] That is, as long as it's not "too edgy"—a judgment call that, ironically, in the end, would be more problematic for Chappelle than for Comedy Central. Nevertheless, in its consistent engagement with performances of Blackness and Whiteness, *Chappelle's Show* walked the razor's edge of provocative comedic sociopolitical discourse.

Just as significantly, I would argue that *Chappelle's Show's* de facto crossover appeal facilitated and problematized its unique status as an industrial and cultural phenomenon. The intertextual pleasures of the series (especially those rooted in popular cultural referencing) provide viewers with a degree of cultural cachet as a reward for being "down"—meaning hip to the sociocultural positioning of black language, style, music, and humor embedded in the texts. As with any form of cultural acuity, there are multiple levels of "down-ness." Insider/outsider, black/white, Boomer/Gen X and Y sensibilities—from these different reading positions, segments of the audience discern cultural traces and treatises produced in these comedies, which, in turn, inform notions of race in contemporary American society. *Chappelle's Show* told stories inflected by multiple identities designed for multiple forms of identification.

In the process of partaking in all of these moveable cultural feasts, however, the spectatorial palates of all the consumers were not always sensitive enough to discern all the ideological ingredients in the series. But, arguably, such is the nature of the subgenre of sketch comedy, where catchphrases are often appropriated while context is lost. The libratory potential of the subgenre of sketch comedy, in general, and *Chappelle's Show*, in particular, must be seen within the context and constraints of American television. Even on basic cable, the potential to transgress, the pushing of aesthetic and generic boundaries, and the incredibly difficult task of being funny and original take place within and not outside of the industrial constraints of American commercial television. Nevertheless, with the interracial writing team of Chappelle and Brennan at the helm, in its freshman and sophomore seasons, the series thrived on speaking the unspoken and, in so doing, laying bare the absurdities and hypocrisies that often inform "polite" conversations about race relations.

In each season of *Chappelle's Show*, one can see moments where the mobilization of stereotypes arguably confront *and* conform to popularly, if silently, held racial stereotypes. Historian and cultural theorist George Lipsitz makes an unequivocal statement about the power and function of race in American society: "Race is a cultural construct, but one with sinister structural causes and consequences. Conscious and deliberate actions have institutionalized group identity in the United States . . . [including] the dissemination of cultural stories."[16] No doubt the way in which specific cultural stories are read can either contribute to or undermine hegemonic notions of race. Few moments of comedy have been positioned more tenuously on that particular ideological razor's edge than a sketch titled "The Racial Draft" from the premiere episode of the second season.[17]

The sketch begins with a fairly innocuous lead-in: Chappelle talking about how Americans are "all mixed up . . . genetically" and recounting how he and his wife (who is Asian) argue about "which half of Tiger Woods is hitting the ball so good." What follows is an astute and absurd "solution" for the ambiguity of racial classifications for multiracial America: a racial draft. With the *Monday Night Football* theme blasting as the draft's anthem, the sketch replicates the theatricality, media blitz, and fan frenzy of ESPN's coverage of the NFL or NBA draft: team representatives onstage; integrated anchor/expert team of Chappelle, Bill Burr, and Robert Petkoff in the booth; and crowds of partisans in the balcony, separated by racial and ethnic rather than team affiliation. Because the draft was designed to decide once and for all the racial affiliation of the best and brightest of the biracial in sports and entertainment, the (literal) representatives of their races and their choices speak to preconceptions about how race is performed and who is (and is not) considered "down" with their race or ethnicity. When Rondell (Mos Def), the black delegation rep, takes Tiger Woods as the first pick, the balcony rocks with the cheers of a jubilant black delegation (as the disappointed Asian delegation glares silently at the victors). As Chappelle as Woods approaches the stage (clad in his signature golf gear with putter in hand), the commentators' assessments praise the logic of the black delegation's pick: "The richest and most dominant athlete in the world. His father, Black, and his mother, Thai, but that doesn't matter anymore because now he is officially Black." Chappelle's Woods possesses a goofy intensity that, in the end, is almost childlike as he speaks of being relieved to know *what* he really is. A banner on the bottom of the screen displays "Tiger Woods: 100% Black," as Woods exclaims (through a prosthetic-enhanced toothy grin), "Goodbye fried rice. Hello fried chicken. I love you, Dad." Constructed as awkward and decidedly *un-down*, the No. 1 pick performs a notion of blackness informed by style rather than culture exemplified by Woods's gleeful (and almost childlike) parting remark: "I've always wanted to say this: *fer shizzle.*"

Each of the ethnic delegations' representatives and their picks play with stereotypes and current issues associated with their group: the Orthodox Jewish rep chooses singer Lenny Kravitz, whose mother, Roxy Roker (Helen Willis, *The Jeffersons*) was black, and whose father was her white, Jewish lawyer ("a Jew was her lawyer . . . I couldn't make that up"); the Latina delegation's female rep picks Cuban Elián González to prevent the white people from trying to "adopt him—*again.*" However, the final picks from the white and Asian delegations raise questions about race by affiliation rather than lineage. Chappelle revisits the role of anchorman Chuck Taylor, costumed in bad wig, whiteface, and country club slacks and blazer. Jeers from the minority delegations are replaced with incredulous gasps and stunned silence when he picks Colin Powell. Confused banter ensues in the booth as commentator Burr blusters, "What? Colin Powell's not white; he's not even an eighth white. He's 100 percent Black." Following a stock photo of Colin Powell on screen, with the banner "Whiteness under Review," Rondell (Mos Def) responds to the whites' seeming breach of protocol: "We of the Black delegation accept the white delegation's offer to draft Colin Powell on the condition that they also accept Condolezza Rice as part of the deal." A shot of Rice and banner declaring that she was "Given away by Blacks" follows, and Taylor, "on behalf of white people everywhere," accepts the deal.[18]

Finally, just in case the absurdity of the sketch's premise did not seem clear to all, the Asian delegation makes their pick—perhaps, at least partially, in response to the loss of Woods: "The Asian delegation chooses the RZA, The GZA, Raekwon, Ghostface Killah, ODB—The Wu-Tang Clan." The RZA and the GZA take the stage and embrace their new racial identity—as does the entire Asian delegation, which chants "Wu-Tang" while throwing the "W" hand sign. The GZA's final line provides the last dollop of outlandishness and cultural misappropriation: "Konnichiwa, bitches." While some insider humor might be lost on the viewer, if they were unfamiliar with the philosophical ties between Wu-Tang Clan and Eastern thought, the division of loyalties with Latino communities over where and with whom Elián should grow up, or the oft-raised questions about how Rice feels about black people (and how black people feel about her), the satirical bite of the sketch remains fundamentally intact.

In this sketch, stereotypes are mobilized in a comic campaign of shock and awe that requires the viewer to recognize the play between the politics and performance of race and racial representation without offering a pedantic or oversimplified moral, which, one might contend, is both a good and a bad thing. On one hand, one might argue that Brennan and Chappelle's steadfast adherence to the notion that theirs was a "personalized" form of comedy takes the ideological edge off of the racially charged nature of the humor in sketches like the "Racial Draft" and, thus, affords a greater degree of discursive freedom. On the other hand, the ideologically idiosyncratic ethos might also serve to facilitate the view that the series neither endeavors nor aspires to engage in more complex (or confrontational) forms of sociocultural critique.

In her analysis of *In Living Color*, Norma Miriam Schulman reminds us that "appropriating a language of stereotypes in order to undermine the dominant order is an age old device employed by persecuted groups to subvert the status quo."[19] The "Reparations" sketch from the first season of *Chappelle's Show* presents a litany of stereotypical constructions of blackness, mostly annunciated by the "white" media. Correspondents from Action News present stories of what happens when black people "get paid."[20] On some level, the pleasures of this particular text are based in (minimally) dual recognition—the laughter impulse rooted in the "that's just wrong" response to constructions of African American taste culture and another more self-reflexive commentary that speaks to playing with "their" (read: outsider) understanding of our (read: insider) cultural foibles.[21] The line is hundreds of people long at the check-cashing liquor store, because as the perky blonde correspondent chirps, "there are no banks in the ghetto because banks hate black people." This is the first of many reparations-induced news stories explained by a white-faced Chappelle (as anchorman Chuck Taylor), who "makes sense" of the phenomenon for the virtual and literal audience. The finance reporter's announcement of 8,000 new record labels being formed in the last hour, the market implications of Cadillac Escalades and gold going through the roof while stock in watermelon stayed "surprisingly low," and the newly merged world's largest company, FuBu/KFC, leave few stereotypes unstated. The litany of racialized tropes includes the transformation of Al Roker–esque weatherman, Big Al, from one who jovially performs amenability to his "true" self, a "straight up gangsta."

Perhaps the most interesting character is the individual who is said to usurp Bill Gates as the world's richest man, "a Harlem native known simply as 'Tron.'" In matching grey PNB Nation oversized basketball jersey and shorts, Chappelle plays Tron as a stylish street hustler with gold ropes hanging on his arms. Tron explains to the white female reporter that his new status was acquired by virtue of "a hot hand at a dice game, baby girl." Tron also taunts Taylor—"I got your girl, Chuck"—just before asking the white female correspondent to give "a lap dance for the world's richest man."²² Offering a cringe-worthy embodiment of stereotypes, the sketch (somewhat) congenially calls the audience out while also acting as a reminder of the *issue* of reparations for the legacy of slavery that still informs aspects of the African American experience. Amid the deliberately absurd performances of race, assertions are made about being black in urban America (before the national amends are made) that tie black life to that of the underclass, such as banking at check cashing places, "making money work for you" means a dice game, and having to perform whiteness to "make it" in the American mainstream. Along with the blatant lampooning of intolerance and a sort of "I know you've thought this stuff, too" sensibility, the sketch seems to simultaneously espouse the impossibility of "compensating" for centuries of oppression and its legacy, while still not rejecting the idea that amends need to be made.

While there is clearly a sociopolitical resonance to both "The Racial Draft" and "Reparations," "Black Bush" is the most overtly political sketch in the entire series.²³ Chappelle introduces the sketch by immediately placing it in a "them versus us" context regarding both perception and policy: "If our president were black, we would not be at war right now—not because a black person wouldn't have done something like that, [but] because America wouldn't let a black person do something like that without asking them a million questions."

Black Bush (Dave Chappelle) grabs the microphone like an angry M.C.

Thus, the premise of the sketch becomes facetiously educational: making it clear to nonwhites why they wouldn't trust the government either if it was being run by "Black Bush." The broadness of the sketch (including Mos Def as a gangsta George Tenet, who assures the press that his napkin full of actual "yellow cake" proved that Saddam Hussein did, indeed, have weapons of mass destruction) did not undermine the fact that Bush's actions (if not his rhetoric) had more than a touch of "street" sensibility. In a segment of a faux documentary entitled "Path to War," Black Bush performs "presidentially" by discussing the times as being "ripe for regime change." This performance of decorum fades quickly as Black Bush gets "real," with White House counsel Donnell Rawlings at his side providing back up:

> BLACK BUSH: But, if I can be real.
> RAWLINGS: Be real, son.
> BLACK BUSH: Can I be real?
> RAWLINGS: Be "real" real, son.
> BLACK BUSH: He tried to kill my father, man. I can't play that shit.
> RAWLINGS: Say Word. He tried to kill your father.

Jumping up from his seat, Black Bush grabs the boom mike like an angry M.C., and says (in melodramatic outrage), directly to the camera, "The nigger tried to kill my father." To this Rawlings as his "back up" replies, "Word to everything we love. We're coming to see y'alls."

The image of Black Bush, in all its "thugly" nuance, and his Pentagon posse getting ready to roll, replicates any number of moments in black gangsta-inflected films—from *Menace II Society* to *Baby Boy*—particularly if one substitutes "boy" for "father." The pleasure added here for the insider is rooted in knowledge of other black cultural productions—like Black Bush naming Afrika Bambaataa and his Universal Zulu Nation as part of the coalition of the willing. However, the central premise that if one examines the actions of the administration, the emotional illogic of the foreign policy that seems more about turf, pride, and "cream" than exporting freedom can be understood without being able to decipher the hip-hop currency in the text. In these sketches, the conflation of race and culture provide *at least* two viewing positions from which to understand the comedy—but that does not prevent the viewer or this scholar from discerning the direction of the comedic discourse.

## When De Facto Crossover Goes Terribly Wrong

When Chappelle provided an assessment of the body of his television work, he seemed acutely aware of the problematic aspects of his show: "I was doing sketches that were funny but socially irresponsible. I felt like I was deliberately being encouraged and I was overwhelmed. It's like you are cluttered with things and you don't pay attention to things like your ethics."[24] His ethical conundrum was resolved when Comedy Central chose to cobble together the sketches taped before Chappelle's self-imposed exile (including "The Nigger Pixie") and air them expressly against the wishes of the comic. Thus, the much anticipated and thrice-delayed third season consisted of an abbreviated three-episode run, entitled *Chappelle's Show: The Lost Episodes*. And so, we return to the Nigger Pixie. In truth, the day the sketch was completed, the death knell began to sound for *Chappelle's Show* and the "Lost Episodes" were simply the wake that not everyone in the family attended. Like a perfect storm, all of the elements—media frenzy (including a "Where's Dave?" campaign on Comedy Central), the conflicts between Chappelle and Brennan (over the content, as well as the directives, of the comedy) and industrial imperatives (the $50 million incentive to keep one of the cable network's cash cows on the air) served to feed the groundswell of controversy around the Lost Episodes, in general, and "The Nigger Pixie" sketch, in particular, while diluting the artistic and ideological strife that drove Chappelle away from the series.

In general, the Lost Episodes are unremarkable—along with the narrative bookends for sketches that were sprinkled with jokes riffing on the "Where's Dave?" premise. There was, however, both anticipation and curiosity of the sketch that sent Chappelle on his initial walkabout. When "The Nigger Pixie" sketch was finally introduced, Charlie Murphy's lines (although not his delivery) mimicked the typical Chappelle setup: "Have you ever been in a situation where you may have felt racially insecure? . . . I'm talking about a situation where you actually alter your behavior because you are afraid how someone of a different color might react—that they might possibly think you're living up to a stereotype. Check this out."[25]

Chappelle is seated in the first-class section of a plane, and a cheerful blonde flight attendant asks him whether he would prefer the fish or chicken. Enter the Nigger Pixie; like a minstrel version of Tinkerbell, the pint-sized sambo howls: "OOOOOOOweeeee! I just heard the magic word—chicken. Go on ahead and order you a big bucket, nigger, and take a bite . . . Black motherfucker." The pixie follows his tirade with an all-too-jaunty little tap dance. When Chappelle requests the fish, the pixie admonishes him ("You son of a bitch, you don't want no fish.") and mocks him when his choice of entrée is unavailable ("Back in the game, baby . . . you can't beat fate, nigger, eat the chicken."). With a hand crooked to his ear, the pixie waits for a reply to Chappelle's inquiry regarding the preparation of the chicken. When she replies that "it's fried," the pixie's jubilance cannot be contained as his cries of "Hallelujah" are accompanied by a sort of "busting his buttons" dance, intercut with reaction shots of an increasingly uncomfortable-looking Chappelle, whom the pixie calls a "big-lipped bitch." Once the chicken is ordered, the pixie calls for music, and a pickaninny-like accompanist (Mos Def) emerges, dressed in shabby newsboy garb, blackface, black fright wig strumming the banjo and shufflin' around.[26] Together the pixie and the pickaninny sing a little "make way for the bird" ditty, which ends with the exclamation, "Chicken's on the deck," the sound of a ship's whistle, and overly ceremonious salutes. There is, then, a sort of unintended poetic justice to the fact that in the sketch, Chappelle walks away from the taunts of the Nigger Pixie.

Chappelle as "Nigger Pixie" from the *Lost Episodes* DVD.

Other stereotypical specters appear throughout the sketch, such as Chappelle's Latino Pixie, dressed as a matador with oversized castanets and a voice like an East Los Angeles cholo's, and his Asian Pixie, clad in quasi-samurai robes, with topknot and facial hair reminiscent of Ming the Merciless performing "yellowface." One could argue that the virulence of the racist tropes is diluted by the absurd constructions of the particular self-hating specters as they tempt and implore their charges to do the wrong thing. With Donnell Rawlings's introductory cry, "This is for all the crackers in here," the White Pixie is introduced. The White Pixie, whose appearance fits Chappelle's usual version of whiteface, invokes a fear of and disdain for all that is associated with the ethnic and racial other. As he offers faulty advice to his white guy (an ironically uncredited player) about using "their vernacular," and then reprimands him for dancing with a voluptuous Latina ("For God's sake, don't freak her . . . Damn BET"), the White Pixie speaks with a stern and serious voice reminiscent of Ward Cleaver ordering the Beaver to tell the truth or Chappelle's own Chuck Taylor doing the evening newscast. While this pixie's construction of whiteness can be located through intertextual referencing, the cultural assumptions about whiteness refract stereotypes about other minority groups (i.e., the "scary" black men and the hypersexualized Latina). As was true with the Latino and Asian Pixies, the Nigger and White Pixies fail to convince their color-coded wards to perform the stereotypical behaviors. However, only the Nigger Pixie manages to use both the historically rooted and minstrel show–branded assertions and epithets to berate his charge (Chappelle): in other words, the Nigger Pixie is an angry, self-hating pixie.

Playing on the popular and critical buzz associated with the pixie sketch, Comedy Central offered what I would argue was a cynical gesture of "programming responsibility" and PR repair in its "very special" interactive audience moment at the episode's end. Charlie Murphy and Donnell Rawlings, in direct address to the camera (with a television monitor showing a freeze frame of Chappelle at the beginning of the Nigger Pixie sketch in the background), introduce the audience feedback segment. Both speak with an air of seriousness. Murphy states, "As some of you may know, Dave had some problems with the pixie sketch." The sequence that follows begins with a close-up of the May 23, 2005, cover of *Time* with Bill Gates and the X-Box and the headline "Exclusive: Dave Chappelle Speaks." As the pages of the magazine flip to near its end, quotations are highlighted, enlarged, and superimposed over the entire text of the article focusing on the passage where Chappelle "wonders whether the new season of the show had gone from sending up stereotypes to merely reinforcing them." In the next frame, Rawlings confesses, "We didn't know whether we should air the sketch or not, so we asked the audience what they thought about it."

Accordingly, the responses were generally supportive of the sketch and the decision of Comedy Central (through their agents, Murphy and Rawlings) to play it. The closest thing to criticism that the session yielded was one black male's assertion that it didn't really show the white race in the same terms it did the others—that, in the end, whiteness was the "generic race" and was not subject to the powerful fallout that stereotyping can bring. Murphy restated the assertion by saying that the critique "wasn't hard enough [that it was] the softest one." The final audience comment, given by a thirty-something black woman, was the one that justified both the existence of the series and the impossibility of controlling (or, even guiding) the reading of the sketch by a diverse audience: "Even if it is being a responsible comedy show, no matter how responsible you are, you are not going to be able to educate everybody in the world so you have to stick to what your true goal is—making people laugh." (Cheers in the audience abound.) Clearly, this "the people have spoken" moment was designed to support the cable outlet's position, and the cachet of the audience's comments are lessened by the probability that anyone who felt strongly about the concerns expressed by Chappelle regarding the pixie sketch and the third season, would not have been in the audience for the Lost Episodes.[27]

## Politics of Race and Satire in the "Post-Pixie" Era

In *Laughing Mad: The Black Comic Persona in Post-Soul America*, I describe Chappelle as the "Provocateur in the Promised Land": one whose comedic discursive imperative is to challenge generic, industrial, and social boundaries (as well as his audience), and I would argue that the comic succeeded—but not without paying an economic, ideological, and psychological price. I often tell my students, many of whom want to be media makers, that once you put your work out there, it ceases to be yours, and the meaning made from your ideas, images, and words is out of your hands.

In Chappelle's case, his acknowledgment of his powerlessness and his complicity in producing comic discourse that could be—and was— mobilized in myriad unintended ways, eventually made it impossible for him to continue his relationship with Comedy Central. In the wake of the Nigger Pixie, Chappelle's desire to return to a space where reading the audience, correcting interpretation, clarifying politics, and disavowing misappropriated bits of comedic social discourse led him back to the direct autonomy and intimacy of stand-up. While one might assume a $50 million paycheck could go a long way in terms of assuaging the comic's anxiety about the broader impact of superficial [mis]readings of his subversive comic texts and how his racial satire was (or was not) being read, this wasn't enough. Being onstage with the microphone and the audience in the palm of his hand, Chappelle is, once again, "dancing like no one is watching." The unfortunate thing is that, in comparison with the salad days of 3 million viewers per episode on Comedy Central, for all intents and purposes, no one *is* watching—and that's not a good thing.

In the post-network era, everyone in network, netlet, and cable programming is looking for "the next big thing." Even in the era of the niche and the narrowcast, being labeled "edgy with broad appeal" in the 18–34 demographic is the signifier of a programming Holy Grail. *Chappelle's Show* filled that bill—a sort of de facto crossover Camelot of sketch comedy. The series didn't last because it couldn't. The transgressive aspects of the comedic discourse were key to the series' success—the fire in the belly of the show, if you will, depended on a sort of comic alchemy in order to produce a sketch series that was smart and funny, as well as culturally and intellectually *honest*. For two brief seasons, Chappelle played with comic discursive fire . . . brilliantly so. But the directives of a *commercial* medium (and Comedy Central, a minion of Viacom, would most certainly be bound by those directives) differed from those of Chappelle.

While Comedy Central encourages creative teams to "push any boundaries" as long as it generates revenue, reflection on the impact of the comedic discourse is simply not a priority, and *Chappelle's Show* was a cash cow for the basic cable network. The fact that the series existed in a television landscape where expansive representations of genuine racial diversity is still an anomaly was not Comedy Central's concern, although it clearly became a source of consternation for Chappelle. By the arrival of the much-delayed third season, the comic got burned by his own actions, as well as Comedy Central's: the cable network may have aired "The Nigger Pixie" against the comic's wishes, but it was Chappelle who, both literally and figuratively, brought him to life. Nevertheless, there is plenty of culpability to be spread around in regard to the fundamental quandary faced by *Chappelle's Show:* viewers and actors, creators and network executives, producers and critics unequally share in the credit and the blame for the rise and fall of the most successful racial satire in television history. Satire reflects, refracts, and reconstitutes the fundamental beliefs and mores of a segment of the world in order to critique its practices—giving a through-the-looking-glass image of a particular swath of society with all defects in full and enlarged view. As long as the assumptions implied by the race-baiting little demons (the Nigger Pixie and his brethren) resonate in the hidden recesses of popular consciousness—not as critique but as confirmation—the road for racial satire, regardless of media outlet—will be arduous. In other words, as long as there is racism, doing racial satire will be problematic.

NOTES

1. Devin Gordon, "Fears of a Clown," *Newsweek*, 16 May 2005, 60. Gordon describes how Chappelle, in his Nigger Pixie regalia, greeted journalists between takes: he apologized for his appearance, slyly adding, "Bet you never met a real live coon."

2. Ibid.

3. Ibid.

4. Christopher John Farley, "Dave Speaks," *Time*, 23 May 2005, 68.

5. Gordon, "Fears of a Clown," 60.

6. *Chappelle's Show* has the ability to mix sly sophistication and popular cultural savvy to interrogate issues of race. However, when mining other categories of marginalization for comic fodder, ethnicity, gender, and sexuality are either elided or exploited. Moreover, some of the most popular characters in the series' comic stable can be seen as fundamentally apolitical and even bordering on minstrelsy.

7. Those familiar with *Chappelle's Show* are undoubtedly aware that the two most popularly cited characters in the series—and their patented catchphrases—occupy the fringe of Chappelle's comedy. Like parsley on the *Chappelle's Show* discursive plate, the comic's portrayal of a cocaine-frenzied Rick James in "Charlie Murphy's Hollywood Moment," as well as the nonsensical mimicry of the King of Crunk, Lil Jon, using his callbacks as his primary mode of expression, while undoubtedly funny, add color but little substance to the televisual meal. Regardless of their most-quoted status, these sketches provide little to no sociocultural context, yet award the trappings of cultural cachet.

8. The series was a spin-off of *Home Improvement*.

9. Dave Chappelle, interviewed by Bob Simon, *60 Minutes*, CBS, 20 October 2004.

10. "Comedian Chappelle Accuses *FOX* of Racism for Show Fumble," *Jacksonville Free Press*, 15 July 1998, 13.

11. Cho details this experience in her first concert film, *I'm the One That I Want*, dir. Lionel Coleman (Winstar, 2000).

12. "Dave Chappelle: The Reason Grandmas Know Who Lil Jon Is," *MTV News*, 6 June 2004, at http://www.mtv.com/news/articles/1488068/20040601/lil_jon_1.jhtml (accessed 8 November 2004).

13. Hillary Atkins, "Chappelle's Show," *Television Week*, 31 May 2004, 36.

14. Neal Brennan and Dave Chappelle, *The Charlie Rose Show*, PBS, 28 April 2004.

15. The qualifying "almost" in this statement is required by animated "radical" sitcoms, including *The Simpsons, Family Guy,* and, of course, *South Park*. See Thompson on *South Park*, chapter 10 in this volume.

16. George Lipsitz, *The Possessive Investment in Whiteness: How White People Profit from Identity Politics* (Philadelphia: Temple University Press, 1998), 2.

17. 21 January 2004.

18. In an attempt to "hustle" another pick, Rondell requests Eminem; he is denied. Taylor offers another deal: whites keep Eminem, and blacks take O. J. back. Rondell agrees, to Burr and Petkoff's subtle glee and Chappelle's chagrin.

19. Norma Miriam Schulman, "Laughing across the Color Barrier: In Living Color," in *Gender, Race and Class in Media: A Text Reader*, ed. Gail Dines and Jean M. Humez (Thousand Oaks, Calif.: Sage, 1995), 439.

20. 12 February 2003.

21. When discussing the insider humor and "that's just wrong" impulses of the comic ethos of *Chappelle's Show*, inevitable comparisons between the Comedy Central series and FOX's *In Living Color* arise. For detailed examination of the two series, along with the short-lived *The Richard Pryor Show*, see Bambi Haggins, *Laughing Mad: The Black Comic Persona in Post Soul America* (New Brunswick, N.J.: Rutgers University Press, 2007), 207–27.

22. When, later in the season, Tron reappears in *Mad Real World*, a racial reversal of the MTV reality series, he again acts the antagonist to whiteness—this time to the lone white "innocent," Chad, who is placed in the house with a cornucopia of characters who occupy "ghetto" constructions of urban blacks by constantly partying, never working, and, "without provocation," hating the white man. In this sketch, Tron acts as a facilitator for the token's downfall when he beds Chad's not so virginal girlfriend (on film)—as does Charlie Murphy as Tyree, the prison-hardened thug, who, over a "look," "shanks" the white guy's father—and makes the final house meeting pronouncement that Chad has to go (because, as one of the black female housemates says, they "don't feel safe" with him). The absurdity of this statement is a direct response to the premature exit of David Edwards on *The Real World LA*. Edwards, with whom Chappelle grew up, was the first cast member to be kicked out of the house. On the season's DVD commentary, Chappelle remembers (with what seems like a trace of anger) his response when the same phrase was used when David was asked to leave: "Don't feel safe . . . the guy weighs maybe a buck-twenty. It was ridiculous."

23. 14 April 2005.

24. Dave Chappelle, interviewed by James Lipton, *Inside the Actors Studio*, BRAVO, 12 February 2006.

25. 16 July 2006.

26. It is interesting to note that on the DVD version of the sketch, Mos Def as the blackfaced buddy does not appear. One might hypothesize that, while Comedy Central owned the footage of Chappelle's pixie outright, perhaps, after the initial broadcasts, Mos Def's pixie sidekick became a free agent, and Chappelle's friend opted out.

27. Since Chappelle began instructing his fans not to watch whatever fragments of the abortive season 3 that Comedy Central might choose to broadcast (and to boycott any DVDs of said material), both the advertising for and the buzz about season 3 of *Chappelle's Show* faded from popular media memory, until advertising for the Lost Episodes went into rotation in the early summer of 2006.

# Of Niggas and Citizens
## The Boondocks *Fans and Differentiated*
## *Black American Politics*

*Avi Santo*

Aaron McGruder's *The Boondocks* is a successful transmediated brand with a loyal community emotionally invested in its controversial and satirical take on black cultural politics and political culture from a black American perspective. Loyalty is expressed both through the community's purchasing power and through their ongoing conversations about *The Boondocks,* generating buzz and effectively advocating for the brand. While many brands cultivate and exploit positive emotional associations from their communities, *The Boondocks* largely trades on the power of controversy. *The Boondocks* has faced repeated accusations of political propagandizing for its explicit anti-Bush, anti–Homeland Security, and anti–Iraq war commentaries (to name just a few).[1] It has also been repeatedly labeled racist by many of its detractors for its provocative depiction of black popular and political culture and has been cancelled or temporarily pulled from newspapers across the country on numerous occasions.[2] Each time, these uproars have generated added publicity.

Though largely driven by the economic logics of contemporary media industries, *The Boondocks* also serves important cultural and political roles in providing outlets for social criticism and community engagement. In this chapter, I analyze how the community that has formed around *The Boondocks* TV series uses it to engage in political conversations and articulate a differentiated black cultural citizenship. I argue that the community invests in politics differently than traditionally imagined informed citizens, privileging identity over partisanship and emphasizing the importance of value-laden, commonsense political actions and language that speaks directly to black American concerns. I also argue that the *Boondocks* community tries to resolve particular tensions activated by the series over the current state of black American cultural citizenship. In so doing, the community often resorts to populist and exclusionary tactics that overemphasize personal responsibility in the face of continued structural inequality in the post–civil rights era. The community also readily points an accusatory finger at particular classed and generational subgroups of black Americans who they hold responsible for perpetuating black stereotypes and failing to help the black community as a whole move forward.

Ultimately, I argue, the community stresses the importance of economic success for black cultural survival but is ambivalent toward the ways material wealth destroys community solidarity. As such, the community often uses nostalgic strategies to resolve these tensions, imagining the decades leading up to the civil rights moment as a period of community solidarity and economic prosperity. In other words, even as they use *The Boondocks* to articulate a differentiated black American citizenship, they still attempt to reign in differences within the black community. In the end, I argue that scholars must pay attention to the potential—especially for marginalized groups—for popular entertainment to serve as an alternate space for political engagement, as well as populist impulses to resolve community tensions that shape and limit the dialogic potential of these political communities.

*The Boondocks* features the Freeman family—Huey, the ten-year-old Black Nationalist; Riley, his eight-year-old wannabe Gangsta brother; and Grandad, their guardian, who moves the family from Chicago to the affluent and predominantly white suburb of Woodcrest, Maryland, for a taste of the good life. It was first published as a comic strip in January 1998 in the University of Maryland's *Diamondback* newspaper and made the leap to national syndication in 1999 after being picked up by the Universal Press Syndicate and sold to over 160 newspapers across the United States.[3] *The Boondocks* launch was one of the largest in comic strip history and, in part, spoke to a dearth of minority representations in the funnies up to that point.[4] By 2006, *The Boondocks* appeared in over 350 newspapers across the country.[5]

The 2005 *Boondocks* animated series distributed by Sony Pictures and appearing as part of Cartoon Network's Adult Swim line-up extended the brand's reach and audience, attracting a younger demographic than the comic strip's readership.[6] Adult Swim, which shares channel space with its parent company Cartoon Network but effectively operates as its own separate cable channel, is currently the number one rated network among men 18–34.[7] The Boondocks premiered on November 6, 2005, drawing 2.3 million viewers, 1.1 million of whom fit Adult Swim's desired demographic, placing the show twelfth among ad-supported cable's list of top 50 shows.[8] By the time the series' tenth episode had aired, it had already been renewed for a second season.[9] In addition to the comic strip and animated television series, The Boondocks has been packaged as a series of best-selling collected anthologies in a DVD set, as well as a range of products ranging from t-shirts to posters to signature ringtones. A major motion picture is allegedly also in the works.[10] The Boondocks website receives significant traffic, and its message boards—along with McGruder's MySpace page—are well attended by an active and loyal fan community.[11]

Many of these conversations have addressed The Boondocks' penchant for attracting controversy. One such example is "The Return of the King" episode that aired in conjunction with Martin Luther King Day on January 15, 2006. The episode imagined King surviving his 1968 assassination—lapsing into a coma instead—and waking just in time for the 2000 election. Immediately, the civil rights leader is thrust into contemporary race politics when he is turned away from the ballot station due to voting irregularities. Branded a traitor in the wake of 9/11 for advocating a nonviolent strategic response, King is despondent until he runs into Huey Freeman at a book signing. Huey convinces King that he needs to organize a black political party and rally the black American voters for change. Quickly, however, this new "Black Party" descends into a "block party." Seeing the political apathy and ignorance of young black voters, King rails against the community, retooling his famous "I Have a Dream" speech in order to indict the crowd as a "bunch a ignorant Niggas," and promptly announces that he is moving to Canada. Huey tells the TV audience that King's speech finally got people angry enough to take action. The episode ends with a montage that includes BET founder Robert Johnson apologizing for the channel's degrading programming, all black NBA players refusing to step onto the court until there is a full troop withdrawal from Iraq, and angry black protesters in front of the White House. In this alternate reality, King dies in 2020, the same year Oprah Winfrey is elected president. As the credits roll, Huey admits that, "sometimes, it's nice to dream."

Perhaps not surprisingly, the episode came under some fire. Civil rights leader Al Sharpton came out strongly against the show for having King say the word "nigga" and threatened to organize a boycott of Cartoon Network.[12] McGruder appeared on *Nightline* defending his creative decisions and fired back against Sharpton in his daily comic strip as being out of touch and misdirected in his priorities. For *The Boondocks* community, the episode provides a space where black American political and cultural concerns can be addressed. Community members come together to exchange and construct knowledge about myriad topics activated by the episode, ranging from the current state of black leadership to the Bush administration's response after Hurricane Katrina. In so doing, they articulate a differentiated citizenship that addresses political and cultural concerns as they relate to the black community.

For this discussion, I analyze threads that directly respond either to the "Return of the King" episode or to the controversy that surrounded it found on two popular *Boondocks* message boards: the first located on the official *Boondocks* website hosted by Sony Entertainment (www.theboondockstv.com), and the second called *Talkin' Videos: The Latest HATE on Hip-Hop TV, Movies and Music Videos* (http://blogs.sohh.com/videos/rapontv/the-boondocks/), a blog that regularly reviews black popular culture. These two websites were chosen based on the amount of traffic and the high number of comments that readers left. From *The Boondocks* website, I look at seven threads with 222 total posts, and from *Talkin' Videos,* I look at one thread with 62 total posts (eight threads and 284 posts in all). Of these, I identified 105 posts by 77 different posters (37 percent), which spoke to the political and cultural tensions described above.[13]

## *Articulating Differentiated Citizenship through Popular Entertainment*

Cultural citizenship is an expanded notion of citizenship rights that extends past civil rights to encompass the protection, preservation, and depiction of identity-based cultural differences. The term is often used to articulate the increasing significance of identity politics to political and civic engagement, wherein the importance of respecting difference—cultural and experiential—to the attainment of equality is foregrounded. Whereas earlier notions of citizenship are based on civil rights—equal access and opportunity to resources under the law—cultural citizenship advocates the right to different treatment with equal opportunity. John Hartley maintains that television not only has become central to struggles over cultural citizenship but also has emerged as the predominant post-print space for reformulating a republic of letters. Building on Thomas Paine's conjoining of textuality, nation, and citizenship as mutually necessary for the formation of a republican society, Hartley argues that "no citizenship evolved anywhere without citizen readers" and that, as "citizenship evolved increasingly from the political toward the cultural domain, and from obligations to a state toward self-determination by individuals . . . [television's] textuality may also have been a site for new forms of cultural engagement and even civic participation through which emergent forms of citizenship could be discerned."[14] Hartley also suggests that the advent of "do-it-yourself" social networking and digital authoring tools allow readers to talk back to the text and among each other in new ways that potentially complete the process of citizen participation through textual engagement.[15]

In effect, Hartley argues that popular entertainment and media culture are increasingly (and, perhaps, always have been) sites for political mobilization, especially as the lines between readers and writers blur; and these domains provide new opportunities for marginalized groups to articulate and share a differentiated citizenship, both among themselves and with the general public that is otherwise unavailable to them through traditional political outlets.

*The Boondocks* community uses the episode in question to articulate a differentiated black cultural citizenship. The community not only discusses political events, but they do so in ways that reimagine how citizens engage with politics. Rather than discussing national politics along traditional partisan party lines, the community foreground identity as the single most important factor in articulations of citizenship and primarily engage in political conversations that have perceived consequences for the black American community. Moreover, *The Boondocks* community frequently translate elitist political speak into everyday language that better reflects their concerns over black cultural citizenship.

Many *Boondocks* community members use the episode in question to call for greater mobilization among all black Americans. For instance, poster 3A angrily states, "all I know is mothafuckas need to wake the fuck up and help each other, the government isn't going to do and they haven't for the past 400+ years so wake the fuck up," while poster 10A similarly suggests, "This Show is what we need. It's not for kids and shouldn't be.

It's for adults who need that wake up call." Other members see the series as providing an alternate site for political mobilization through the combination of McGruder's provocations and the community's ability to dialog about them: "Enjoyed the show. I am enjoying the dialog it has created even more though. Speakup, no need to be profound, just be heard. 'In the end, we will remember not the words of our enemies, but the silence of our friends.'"[16]

Beyond providing new spaces for political mobilization built around community interests, *Boondocks* community members also speak about politics in ways that diverge from traditional notions of informed citizenry as "rational-critical actors."[17] Hartley contends that we currently live in a redactional society, where the instant availability of information has become overwhelming and citizens necessarily engage in careful editorial practices to make sense of the world.[18] These editorial practices can connect a broad set of events separated by time and space as they also filter out all unnecessary clutter by stitching together only bits of information relevant to a particular individual or community.

The various political topics that emerge within the *Boondocks* community are all in service of a fairly focused conversation about contemporary race politics in the United States.[19] Politics matter only to the extent that particular issues are seen as directly affecting the black community. For example, conversations about the war in Iraq range from confusion over Condoleeza Rice's claim that the current military initiative is comparable with the civil rights movement because they are both fights for freedom to debates over whether black parents should support sending their children into battle. This fits well with Jeffrey Jones's assertion that "[contemporary] political culture is increasingly marked by a lack of commitment to traditional institutions, yet composed of temporary alliances around issues and values linked to everyday life. These alliances can be associated with new social movements or 'identity politics' but are generally ones that offer more individualistic forms of expression."[20]

Within the filter of black cultural politics, community members often have little problem jumping from one topic to the next, making connections that are loosely based on identity rather than more tangible policy or legal frameworks. For instance, in debating the current state of black American citizenship, members easily contrast the war in Iraq to the fallout from Hurricane Katrina in New Orleans. Poster 23A asks, "Why is dying for one person or one group's point of view patriotic, but allowing entire races of American citizens to die senseless deaths and live like 3rd world citizens [not]. PETA can locate and prosecute any animal offender within this country but we didn't have the resources to get black folks out of New Orleans." When poster 20A rebuts that being black is not a separate form of citizenship and that the federal government is not responsible for administering disaster relief to victims of Katrina, poster 23A questions what would have happened if the events of 9/11 would have been approached with the same bureaucratic attitude toward federal intervention. These conceptual links point not only to a perception of government hypocrisy (even as it blurs legal differences in government jurisdiction over disaster relief and acts of war) but also to the ways contemporary citizenship practices tend to survey a wide spectrum of topics in order to form political opinions about particular issues even as they demonstrate undetailed knowledge about any one topic.

Finally, members often use the language of identity politics to assess political events. In analyzing discourse about the "Return of the King" episode, it is essential to recognize the centrality of language to contemporary political participation. As John Gibbons and Bo Reimer assert, "Politics in postmodernity . . . is 'recognized to be constructed in language; politics *is* language.'"[21] For instance, poster 14's response to a prowar sentiment is, "Should I hit you because you have the *potential* to hit me? . . . That's some gangster isht." The reframing of U.S. foreign policy by comparing it with a widely circulated stereotypical image of black criminality not only personalizes the political, supporting Jones's assertion that viewers want "conversations on TV to resemble those that occur at home in language [and] conversational style," but also potentially disrupts official discourses by demonstrating their absurdity when rewritten along racial lines.[22]

Even when directly addressing the content of the episode, *The Boondocks* community repeatedly discusses black political engagement and social status through the filter of identity politics in an effort to articulate a differentiated set of American citizenship concerns, rights, and experiences. Community members repeatedly distinguish between blacks or African Americans and "niggas," usually identifying themselves as belonging to the former camp. "I love The Boondocks for separating black people from 'niggas.' Fuck 'niggas'! Death to you all!"[23] Whereas "blacks" or "African Americans" are described as active and engaged in minority politics, "niggas" are described as lazy, uneducated, and unteachable: "Why when a black man/woman wants to start some movement, niggas always wanna drag their fucking feet. Oh well, as the saying goes 'niggas never learn.'"[24] Poster 22A goes as far as to describe "niggas" as "the strongest inhibitors in the African american's progress," while poster 4A positions "niggas" as essentially choosing to exist outside of American society. "Niggas (including latinos) could have still been in them third world countries . . . super strugglin,' without even a means of getting money. We are in the land of opportunity, so niggas need to take advantage." As discussed in the next section, black "citizens" are described as taking personal responsibility for their economic situation while remaining community conscious (a combination that many posters have difficulty navigating).

In this section, I demonstrate how political conversations taking place among *Boondocks* community members support Hartley's and Jones's claims that television and popular entertainment are sites of public engagement with the political process. I also argue for the ways in which marginalized groups can use popular entertainment to articulate differentiated citizenship experiences that also necessarily require new modes of political engagement that are loosely knit and rooted in everyday language. I now turn to analyzing the discursive strategies that *The Boondocks* community employs (consciously or not) in addressing tensions raised by the "Return of the King" episode over the continued struggles of the black American community in the post–civil rights era. These strategies, though intended to mobilize the black American community to action and address internal concerns over the effects of materialism and popular culture on community standards, solidarity, and leadership, inevitably rely on both populist and exclusionary rhetoric that overemphasize black personal failures in the face of continued institutional inequalities while also attempting to cast blame along classed and generational lines.

## The Cult of Personal Responsibility and the Politics of Exclusion

In slaughtering a sacred cow, McGruder told *Nightline:*

> It comes with the territory of being a satirist. . . . It's our job to be out there on the edge . . . but the points are there and to me at least they justify the language. . . . In the episode King is critical of our apathy and our inactivity. . . . We carry the blame of our own apathy and our own inactivity. . . . We deserve to take a look at that and be honest about it.[25]

Many community members also identify Martin Luther King's speech—and the Boondocks in general—as expressing a painful, but much needed

truth about the black community: "The speech Dr. King gives at the political party information meeting-turned-house party was both painfully truthful and eye-opening. Through Dr. King, McGruder has again
touched on the harsh truths that so many African-Americans are afraid to
acknowledge."[26] Satire can serve an important social function in revealing
underlying truths through humor by rendering complex ideas and processes as commonsense statements that supposedly wipe away all ambiguity. Jones suggests that there is a populist impulse in our society to tell
jokes that subvert existing power hierarchies and that the joker's disrup-
tive ability to render elite sense nonsensical by adopting the "tonalities of
common sense" expose underlying—if alternate—truths about the social
fabric of reality that are shared by the audience being addressed.[27] Bambi
Haggins asserts that, "historically, the black comic has retained the ability
to get the audience laughing while slipping in sociocultural truths."[28]

Even as multiple posters assert that the episode in general—and King's
speech in particular—reveals some sort of underlying truth about the
black community, there is no consensus within the community over what
that truth is. Rather, several overlapping and contradictory interpretations
emerge. Many rely heavily on populist strategies that either overemphasize the role of personal responsibility (i.e., black problems are solvable if
the community simply behaves better or makes smarter choices) or blame
ongoing community problems on particular subgroups of black Americans. These subgroups intersect along classed and generational lines, with
young and old, rich and poor all at varying points facing accusations of
holding blacks back. While economic prosperity is singled out as the
benchmark for community success (and failure), there is a tremendous
ambivalence expressed toward the effects of materialism on the community, as well as toward wealthy blacks who are believed to have struck it
rich by exploiting stereotypical black cultural representations of gangsta
and ghetto lifestyles—that is, by selling aesthetics and values associated
with poverty. Many (but not all) community members express nostalgia
for the civil rights era (or earlier), selectively remembering this period as
one of both economic opportunity and community solidarity. Others feel
that the civil rights generation have simply cowed to white society and
have abandoned the current generation as it struggles to articulate a differentiated citizenship identity, one that guarantees blacks equal opportunities while respecting their different cultural and political experiences.

A common refrain among *Boondocks* posters is that the current
black community has not lived up to the expectations of the civil rights

generation or the freedoms they fought and died to earn for the current generation. Many posters agree that King would be disappointed in the current generation's failures, comparing this generation's actions unfavorably with those of civil rights activists. For example, poster 36 asserts, "I am haunted by the notion of Martin Luther King seeing humanity today. We have not lived up to our responsibilities. People struggled and gave their lives to get our country somewhere and so much of that progress has been reversed." Then poster 17 further extends King's disgust to include contemporary black leadership: "MLK would be shocked and appalled and probably, well no probably about it, he would read the whole AA community the riot act as well as the 'leaders' that he left behind to continue the fight. The problem is once we got the freedoms that they fought for we took those freedoms and abused them."

Community failures are often articulated as digressions in terms of educational, familial, and personal behavioral standards. For example, poster 21A addresses the perceived devaluation of education within the black community as the source of contemporary black problems: "We've got to the point where parents and teachers push kids through school not learning a damn thing. Its very sad to see 7th graders that can't multiply or read at a 2nd grade level, but can recite every word of Busta's new song 'Grillz.'" The same poster also points a finger at poor parenting: "But the real issue is a lot (not) parents not being responsible today. Don't want to watch the kids? Let the babysitter, TV, PSP, DVD, watch them. Is your kid hungry? Feed them some cheap crap from KFC, Taco Bell, Burger King, Whitecastle, and so on." Finally, poster 25A singles out black criminality as the reason for continued black American struggles: "I am seriously sickened to my stomach everytime I see another black person arrested for something stupid. Survival is one thing, but people are getting arrested for stuff that doesn't even make sense."

Joe Feagin argues that of the three ways of explaining the causes of poverty—individualistic, structural, and fatalistic—Americans generally favor the first, which supports the myths of romantic individualism and meritocracy while blaming the poor for their continued problems.[29] What many of these declarations have in common (beyond a nostalgic gesture backward to the civil rights era—discussed further below) is an emphasis on bad behavior and a lack of personal responsibility as the causes of black failures. As 33 succinctly states, "if blacks actually got up and done [*sic*] something already, we would be less likely to be stereotyped and stepped on." The community repeatedly overlooks institutional barriers for many blacks and highlights individual actions and behaviors as keys to overcoming continued economic, political, and social marginalization.

While this emphasis on personal responsibility fits well within McGruder's stated objective for the episode to mobilize the black community to action and combat political apathy and stagnation, it also runs the risk of blaming members of the black community who are unable to rise above structural conditions and fails to see their "bad" behaviors as the effects of continued economic, institutional, and political inequalities rather than the causes for them. Critiquing Bill Cosby's widely circulated May 17, 2004, attack on poor blacks during a speech given at a gala commemorating the fiftieth anniversary of the decision in *Brown v. the Board of Education*, Eric Michael Dyson suggests that "we must never lose sight of the big social forces that make it difficult for poor parents to do their best jobs and for poor children to prosper. . . . Cosby's overemphasis on personal responsibility, not structural features, wrongly locates the source of poor black suffering—and by implications its remedy—in the lives of the poor."[30] Perhaps unsurprisingly, several members of *The Boondocks* community reference Cosby as a role model. The few that openly oppose Cosby do so on generational grounds, not because of his bias toward the poor.

While it might be asking too much of the average American to recognize the roles that structural inequalities play in perpetuating poverty cycles, several posters went as far as to suggest that poor blacks are simply not taking advantage of the structural conditions available to them:

> People (black people) need to understand that the legislation of civil rights is already here. We still got problems, but its on us, cause them white folks ain't givin too many more hand outs. racism still exists, and the only way we can prevent it from affecting us is to be in a position where it doesn't matter what they do. Its fuckin America and we have to understand that we are lucky and gifted.[31]

Others invert the logic, insinuating that poor blacks are taking advantage of those opportunities to their own detriment: "Too many of us wait for handout, wait for apologies, while holding back those of our own just because we don't know."[32]

Many of *The Boondocks* community's comments hint at class biases that repeatedly look down at practices like eating fast food or the lack of full parental supervision, without ever considering how poor economic conditions might require parents to work night shifts or make chain restaurants like McDonalds both necessarily affordable and time-efficient options. Dyson argues that class politics among black Americans has never simply been about economic status but "embraces style and behavior as well."[33] Thus, comments like those made about children knowing all the lyrics to rap songs but being unable to otherwise read are necessarily tinged with classed assumptions, even if these are not always explicitly stated. This blurring of economic and behavioral class affiliations is perhaps best captured by poster 31A's assertion that "Yes we can get jobs but half of us would rather be on welfare. . . . Yes we can eat in the same restaurant but we always go through the drive thru. . . . Wake up black people . . . we were civilized but we made ourselves 'ghetto' . . . we are digressing." Finally, poster 1A selectively identifies the keys to overcoming black problems as entirely rooted in class behavior: "Sure I'm not leaving my cushy suburban crib to live amongst my peoples. Nor am I forsaking my white friends, they pay for drinks at the bar . . . and tip. . . . What I will do is continue to be the opposite of the stereotype. . . . I will be the best man I can be. . . . That's my version of the dream."

Though it is impossible to know for certain whether *The Boondocks* community consists primarily of middle-to-upper-class blacks (most posters do self identify as black),[34] their attitudes toward the poor are consistent with philosophies of racial uplift and moral enforcement that date back over a century to the emerging black aristocracy, who sought to both police and teach poor blacks to behave in ways that would grant them recognition as "human" within white society.[35] As poster 3A suggests, "We all know the niggas that we talking about are the poor niggas so why can't we uplift them. Teach them to do better." Others question whether it is the responsibility of successful black Americans to help out poor blacks, especially when the latter are seen as responsible for their own impoverished condition:

> So are you saying that it is the duty of every black person to drop whatever they are doing or quit any job they have when someone with the same skin color is having trouble? . . . Are you saying that successful and ambitious blacks are evil and selfish? . . . If two rival gangs are fighting over territory, what would you have a black lawyer or banker do about it?[36]

Posters generally look down on what they perceive as the attitudes, behaviors, and values of the poor, and they make clear distinctions between themselves and that community:

Remember [McGruder] is trying to get his point across to a portion of black Americans out there he feels are a bunch of Rileys. [McGruder] was trying to speak on a level he believes to be the only level on which his target demographic communicates. . . . Us brainy guys—those of us on the message board, we didn't need to hear the N word. We KNEW what MLK was getting at.[37]

At least one member categorically contrasts economic value with moral values in order to legitimate the superiority of wealthy blacks over their poor counterparts: "When have you ever seen Oprah do some dumb nigga sh*t . . . who better to lead us than the richest black person in America."[38] Once again, the significance of language, of which demographic gets labeled as "niggas" and which does not, is front and center. While the community exhibits mixed feelings about the possible damage to King's image by having him say the word "nigga," they demonstrate no such concerns over using that label to describe poor blacks.

Nonetheless, there is often a tension expressed by posters between economic prosperity equaling success and the ethical choices and social responsibilities made by those blacks who do succeed:

The problem isn't the blacks who are struggling to get a good job, education, and hustling to put food into their stomachs. It's those who actually made it into white America and forgot where they came from. . . . The people who can afford to put a diamond encrusted logo on the back of their car, but at the same time people in Katrina are still homeless.[39]

The diamond-encrusted logo is clearly marked as excessive and in poor taste in light of the struggles of the black community at large. Poor taste crosses economic lines and demonstrates the malleability of classed values. As Dyson explains, classed-values are not tied to the size of one's bank account in the black community.[40]

*The Boondocks* community also frames black failures along generational lines. While several posters use the episode in question and the controversy surrounding it to point out broad differences between the civil rights generation and the current black community in terms of attitude and style, without ascribing value judgments, most community members clearly prefer one generation over another. For example, poster 35 simply delineates the characters of Grandpa and Huey on the series:

With grandpa, the issues of his day were black folks being brutalized and deprived of basic human rights. Having won the battle of not getting beaten over the head and called ni99er, he's through. . . . Huey, being generations removed from the tangible manifestations of racism (by tangible I mean dogs and fire hoses and overt codified segregation) is stuck in a kind of honorary anger. Almost all of his anger comes from things he personally hasn't experienced.

Similarly, poster 22 makes a nonpartisan assessment of Sharpton's criticism of the episode: "Like him or not Al is old school and hearing ni**er/nigga/nukka whatever on TV is gonna be offensive to him. . . . He's just not gonna have a sense of humor about MLK. My parents are from the same era and they just don't get the show. It's blasphemy to them."

Concerns over the episode's public use of the word "nigga" are often couched in generational terms, transferring community anxieties onto an older black population. Other community members, however, are not as willing to accept different behavioral practices as a reason for the older generation condemning the episode. Poster 20.2 responds by suggesting that the older generation is hypocritical: "Watever about being old. Once again we got the word usage from them. There parents said it, they said it, we say it." Poster 15A articulates this generational divide as a matter of betrayal, essentially accusing the older generation of being complicit with white norms, as having sold out or fallen in love with white values at the expense of fighting for black causes or investing in black cultural practices:

Our older generation definitely believes in white is right. They have been increasingly submissive and afraid to disrupt things because they don't want to lost that "good job" or make boss man mad. They are willing to accept their brothers and sisters dying all around them as long as they can move themselves away from the struggle and closer to the white folks who run from us whenever we move to their town and then idolize and imitate us behind closed doors.

Poster 25 extends the older generation's ineptitude to include financial and moral failures, which the poster argues have had a devastating economic outcome for the younger generation:

It is your economic failure resulting in our lack of inheritance why we cannot afford higher education and have no foundation upon which to build our house both figuratively and literally. . . . Instead of spreading wealth as a weapon of self defense you spread the ideology of handouts leaving us defenseless. . . . Many of you have been compromised by allowing our enemies to finance you instead of creating your own wealth.

The majority of posters, however, actually take the opposing view when it came to generational divisions, even as they agree in theory with poster 25's focus on the significance of economic prosperity to black cultural and political survival. Many posters do see the older generation as providing a better model for integrating financial success and community standards. Much of the discourse on *The Boondocks* message boards is nostalgic toward the civil rights generation and disparaging of the current generation's failures to live up to those standards. For example, poster 5A states: "Back then they marched and protested and make things happen. Now on MLK Day is nothing but a goddamn nigga party." Similarly, poster 32 argues: "It seems that our race has went down ward from marches to ignorant word calling!!!" Poster 31A flips an iconic civil rights moment on its head in proclaiming, "Sure we can sit in the front of the bus but we choose to sit in the back."

Nostalgic discourse about the civil rights era and earlier tends to selectively remember a generation of communal harmony and positive role models who grew stronger because of their struggles against racism.[41] For example, poster 28A suggests that black Americans were morally better off before the civil rights movement than they are currently:

I hate to say it but we as a black community were better off in the 1900s-1960s when we were segregated and devoted all of our time to keeping our families strong and our communities safe and close nit. It seemed all of America was against us then, and it made us better as a people. We had focus, and positive ambition. We worked hard for what we had and taught our kids to do the same in everything they did. . . . Well that's all for me, just a brotha tired of niggas missing the point and tryin to sound like they got it.

This discourse also often suggests that blacks were better off financially before the passing of civil rights legislation. Whereas certain community members blame the older generation for current black economic struggles, others locate economic prosperity as a thing of the past that blacks need to reclaim. Poster 13.1 states, "Look at what's going on in our finances. We don't own banks anymore, now we're overjoyed because Chase and Citibank finally decided that our money was just as good." Poster 38 adds, "Before the 1960's there were successful Black towns and cities where little Black children had professional Black role models . . . doctors, lawyers, teachers, etc."

Clearly, a recurring theme among *Boondocks* community members is to stress the importance of economic prosperity in overcoming current black struggles. For the most part, the community advances a populist position that stresses personal responsibility as the key to overcoming black financial failures through simply adopting the correct values. The community also posits blame on particular classed and generational groups who, in their estimation, espouse the wrong values, placing greater burden on the community as a whole. However, in failing to resolve tensions that emerge between advocating for material success and promoting communal integrity in the face of the perceived threat of materialism, *The Boondocks* community repeatedly looks to an imaginary past where prosperity and cohesiveness supposedly coexisted in spite of (or because of) racial inequalities and segregated citizenships. In my conclusion, I offer some tentative reasons why these tensions exist and why they are resolved in these manners.

## Conclusion

First, it must be restated that *The Boondocks* community under investigation, while providing certain opportunities for black Americans to engage in more-focused political conversations relevant to that particular community, in no way represents a microcosm of the entire black American population. The digital divide spans class and age and necessarily limits the breadth and narrows the scope of community dialogue there is to be had. This, in turn, qualifies scholarly assertions that television and do-it-yourself digital technologies produce greater opportunities for a refurbished republic of letters. Even Hartley notes this tendency to substitute the part for the whole when he states, "the readership for a given platform was most likely to be taken as 'the' public during its initial ascendancy and popularity."[42]

Second, part of what might account for *The Boondocks* community lashing out against poor blacks and emphasizing personal responsibility over continued structural inequalities has to do with ongoing tensions over how to articulate a differentiated yet equal cultural citizenship based on identity politics. As Hartley suggests, the politics of difference stretch traditional notions of citizenship based on equality to their limits.[43] As such, there is a risk that difference becomes the very ground on which failures to achieve equality are justified, even as there is agreement that authentic differences based on ethnicity, gender, or sex need to be equally recognized. While *The Boondocks* community largely supports the notion that black cultural experiences must be recognized as different from those of other Americans (and are quick to attack posters that suggested otherwise), there is no consensus within the group about what those authentic black cultural differences are and how they can best translate into greater economic mobility for the black community as a whole.

Thus *The Boondocks* community walks a fine line between promoting a differentiated cultural citizenship for black Americans and policing cultural differences between black Americans of different socioeconomic and generational categories. In the process, certain articulations of difference are demonized or excluded in favor of those that promote particular classed black identities. As poster 20A summarizes:

> We have to be careful how we choose an identity for a black person because as long as being successful or living in a nice house is considered a "white thing" or the "submissive thing" instead of a "good thing," then we really have blown it, and being broke and living in the projects will always be the "black thing" since we have made the alternative so unpopular.

Where Hartley and Jones refer to popular television's liberal democratic possibilities for promoting discourse, even as *The Boondocks* offers its community a "working through space" to address black cultural and political concerns, it does so by encouraging them to focus on personal—as opposed to institutional—factors that constrain black success, which is inevitably a much easier means of explaining continued marginalization.[44] Though the community often debates complex black cultural, economic, and political concerns without consensus, the overwhelming vilification of certain classed and generational subgroups held accountable for continued black struggles provides an easy means of resolving these issues and delineating the community's shared cultural politics by splitting itself off from an "other" perceived to be holding them back. This has the unfortunate effect of shutting down potentially fruitful conversations about shared political concerns that might unite the black community or encourage dialogue across its various socioeconomic and generational factions.

On rare occasions, some community members have attempted to resolve classed and generational tensions differently, by not only recognizing the positives and the negatives of *all* subgroups within the black community but also pointing out that in *The Boondocks* world, these subgroups are represented as kin. According to poster 36, Huey and Riley might "stand in opposition to one another, but they are still brothers." Similarly, poster 28 provided an astute breakdown that recognizes how each of the show's main characters embody positives and negatives attributes associated with these various subgroups:

Huey
Represents the most progressive and best educated elements of Black society.
Examples: Cornell West, Henry Louis Gates
Pro: Intelligent, educated, thoughtful, knows history
Con: Constantly aggrieved, will probably never be satisfied, has great ideas that don't necessarily connect to reality

Riley
Represents the poor and disenfranchised portion of Black society as well as the media's representation of Blacks. Examples: 50 Cent, NWA, Allan Iverson
Pro: Proud of their Blackness, strong-willed, unafraid, scares the $hit out of white people
Con: Ignorant, uneducated, nihilistic, scares the $hit out of white people

Granddad
Represents the Black political establishment. Examples: Jesse Jackson, Charles Rangle
Pro: Have significant past accomplishments, established within the system
Con: Complacent, happy just not getting called ni99er, unwilling to accept that things have changed and need to be approached in a different way.

In these examples, the institution of the family becomes the space for exploring potential solidarity across classed and generational lines, while pointing both to their shared commonalities and the contributions and limitations offered by all sides. As a family, the Freemans may not always like one another, but they are also beholden to one another in ways that exceed mere personal responsibility. The exceptionality of these statements, however, underscores the greater mobilization of differentiated politics around clearly demarcated lines and the general absence of dialogue recognizing the shared political concerns of black Americans that traverse class and generational divides.

What does all of this suggest about the roles satirical series like *The Boondocks* play in activating politically engaged differentiated citizenries? Clearly, *The Boondocks* community makes active use of the episode in question to debate and discuss black political concerns and cultural politics, but those conversations alone are not cause for celebration. The tendency within *The Boondocks* community to interpret and engage with the episode in ways that divide blacks from "niggas" along classed and generational lines inevitably forestalls larger group solidarity even as it demonstrates the heterogeneity of black perspectives. Without lessening the significance of popular entertainment as a politicized space, scholars must also examine how particular communities use these spaces both productively and reductively (often at the same time). In the case of *The Boondocks* community, populist impulses (to overstate personal responsibility; to blame poor "niggas") repeatedly get in the way of politicized discussions of class and ideology in U.S. society that might productively challenge questions of "difference" and power along racialized lines.

## NOTES

1. One week after 9/11, McGruder had Huey call the FBI, offering information on who might have helped fund Al-Quaida: R-E-A-G-A-N. Later, pointedly satirizing the unabashed racial profiling policies proposed by the Office of Homeland Security, McGruder had John Ashcroft introduce the "Turban Surveillance Act" on national television. Responding to accusations that he was being unpatriotic, McGruder replaced *The Boondocks* with the mock über-nationalistic "Adventures of Flagee and Ribbon," in which an anthropomorphized U.S. flag and commemorative ribbon exchanged xenophobic faux-jingoistic rhetoric about America's greatness before announcing that the best way to show one's patriotic spirit would be to purchase Flagee and Ribbon action figures.

2. The strip was perhaps most famously cut by the *Washington Post* during a week-long segment where Huey and his coconspirator, Caeser, devise a plan

to end U.S. overseas warmongering by finding Bush's top international advisor, Condoleeza Rice, a boyfriend. The incident sparked a series of angry letters accusing the newspaper of censorship. Black conservative radio talk show host, Larry Elder, a subject of much derision in both *The Boondocks* comic strip and TV series, has suggested that an award for the "Dumbest, Most Vulgar, Most Offensive Things Uttered by Black Public Figures" be called the "McGruder," while Bob Johnson has proclaimed that BET employees do more for black Americans in a single day than McGruder has accomplished in his entire life. See Ben McGrath, "The Radical: Why Do Editors Keep Throwing 'The Boondocks' Off the Funnies Page?" *New Yorker,* 19 April 2004.

3. Steve Jones, "'Boondocks' Dives into Adult Swim," *USA Today,* 4 November 2005, 11E.

4. While peoples of color were regularly and derogatorily caricatured in the funnies from the late 1800s onward, it was not until 1965 and the debut of Morrie Turner's *Wee Pals* that a syndicated cartoon strip by a black man regularly appeared in newspapers. At the time of *The Boondocks'* national debut, there were only two other comic strips created by black Americans in circulation: Ray Billingsley's *Curtis* and Robb Armstrong's *Jump Start.* Neither was particularly politicized in its content.

5. Neely Tucker, "Like It or Not, 'Boondocks' Will Finally Hit the Airwaves," *Washington Post,* 26 October 2005, C1.

6. McGrath, "Radical."

7. Kimberly Nordyke, "Adult Swim Makes Splash," *Hollywood Reporter,* 28 February 2007.

8. Anthony Crupi, "Boondocks Ratings Up 24%," *Mediaweek,* 15 November 2005.

9. Lola Ogunnaike, "'Boondocks' Renewed," *New York Times,* 26 January 2006, E2.

10. McGrath, "Radical."

11. As of 13 September 2007, *The Boondocks* MySpace page had 122,525 friends.

12. "Sharpton Criticizes 'Boondocks' for Showing King Saying the N-Word," *USA Today,* 25 January 2006.

13. Of course, there were also myriad posts within these threads about topics ranging from whether or not other community members had recorded the episode to who sang the song featured in the episode. In the discussion in this chapter, posters are identified by an assigned number and are differentiated according to website by the letter "A." If a number is followed by the letter "A," it is from the *Talkin' Videos* site; without an "A" from *The Boondocks* site. If a number has a decimal point after it (i.e., 23.1), this is to indicate the particular numbered comment by a repeat poster (some posters were more vocal and posted more frequently than others).

14. John Hartley, "From Republic of Letters to Television Republic? Citizen Readers in the Era of Broadcast Television," in *Television after TV: Essays on a Medium in Transition,* ed. Lynn Spigel and Jan Olsson (Durham, N.C.: Duke University Press, 2004), 406–7.

15. Ibid., 408.

16. Poster 18A.

17. Jeffrey P. Jones, *Entertaining Politics: New Political Television and Civic Culture* (Lanham, Md.: Rowman and Littlefield, 2005), 18.

18. Hartley, "From Republic of Letters to Television Republic?" 402.

19. In the message board threads looked at for this essay alone, overt political discussions included conversations about Hurricane Katrina, the war in Iraq, 9/11, the Terry Schiavo case, Barack Obama's bid for the presidency, Condoleeza Rice, and Al Sharpton.

20. Jones, *Entertaining Politics,* 20.

21. John Gibbons and Bo Reimer, *The Politics of Postmodernity* (London: Sage, 1999), quoted in Jones, *Entertaining Politics,* 20.

22. Jones, *Entertaining Politics,* 24.

23. Poster 8A.

24. Poster 3A.

25. *Nightline,* ABC, 17 January 2006.

26. Poster 1A.

27. Jones, *Entertaining Politics,* 138–39.

28. Bambi Haggins, *Laughing Mad: The Black Comic Person in Post-Soul America* (New Brunswick, N.J.: Rutgers University Press, 2007), 6.

29. Joe R. Feagin, *Subordinating the Poor: Welfare and American Beliefs* (Englewood Cliffs, N.J.: Prentice Hall, 1975), 95.

30. Michael Eric Dyson, *Is Bill Cosby Right? Or Has the Black Middle Class Lost Its Mind?* (New York: Basic Books, 2005), 2–5.

31. Poster 4A.

32. Poster 22B.

33. Dyson, *Is Bill Cosby Right?,* xvi.

34. Though no statistics are available detailing the average income and age of posters on the sites, it may be inferred—based on the statements made by members and broad statistical data about the makeup of the online black American population in general—that it skews toward younger and middle-class blacks. According to the 2005 Pew Online Life Report on African Americans and the Internet, only 36 percent of black Americans are currently online.

35. Dyson, *Is Bill Cosby Right?,* 197.

36. Poster 20A.

37. Poster 37.2.

38. Poster 39.

39. Poster 34.2.

40. Dyson, *Is Bill Cosby Right?*, xiv.

41. Many histories of African American life in the first half of the twentieth century argue that there was great heterogeneity of economic and communal experiences along class lines during this period. For example, Rod Bush, *We Are Not What We Seem: Black Nationalism and Class Struggle in the American Century* (New York: New York University Press, 1999).

42. Hartley, "From Republic of Letters to Television Republic?," 391.

43. Ibid, 408.

44. John Ellis, *Visible Fictions: Cinema, Television, Video* (New York: Routledge, 1992), 55.

||||||||||||||||||||||||||||||||||||||||||||||||||||

# About the Contributors

GEOFFREY BAYM is Associate Professor of Media Studies at the University of North Carolina–Greensboro. He is the author of *From Cronkite to Colbert: The Evolution of Broadcast News* and numerous articles and book chapters on the changing nature of news media and political discourse.

AMBER DAY is Assistant Professor in the English and Cultural Studies Department at Bryant University. She received her Ph.D. in Performance Studies from Northwestern University. Her current research is on performative satire and political agitation.

JONATHAN GRAY is Assistant Professor of Communication and Media Studies at Fordham University. He is author of *Watching with The Simpsons: Television, Parody, and Intertextuality* and *Television Entertainment* and coeditor of *Fandom: Identities and Communities in a Mediated World* and *Battleground: The Media*.

BAMBI HAGGINS is Associate Professor of Screen Arts and Cultures at the University of Michigan in Ann Arbor. Her book, *Laughing Mad: The Black Comic Persona in Post-Soul America*, examines the place of black comedy as comedic social discourse in U.S. popular consciousness.

HENRY JENKINS is Professor and Director of the Comparative Media Studies Program at the Massachusetts Institute of Technology. He is author or editor of 12 books, including *Democracy and New Media*, edited with David Thorburn, and *Convergence Culture: When Old and New Media Collide*.

JEFFREY P. JONES is Associate Professor of Communication and Theatre Arts at Old Dominion University. He is the author of *Entertaining Politics: New Political Television and Civic Culture* and coeditor of *The Essential HBO Reader*.

DAVID MARC is the author of six books and more than 300 articles for publications ranging from peer-reviewed journals to in-flight magazines. His most recent book is *Our Movie Houses: A History of Cinematic Innovation in Central New York* (2008); his most modern, *Comic Visions* (1989); most postmodern, *Bonfire of the Humanities* (1995); and most ancient, *Demographic Vistas* (1983). He has taught American civilization at Brown University, communication at Syracuse University, film studies at the University of California, Los Angeles, English at California Institute of Technology, and plenty of other subjects at plenty of other places.

JOANNE MORREALE is Associate Professor of Communication Studies at Northeastern University. She is the author of *A New Beginning: A Textual Frame Analysis on the Political Campaign Film* and *The Presidential Campaign Film: A Critical History* and editor of *Critiquing the Sitcom: A Reader.*

HEATHER OSBORNE-THOMPSON is Assistant Professor of Radio, Television and Film at California State University–Fullerton. She received her Ph.D. in Cinema-Television Critical Studies from the University of Southern California. Her current work focuses on the relationship between popular television remakes, feminism, and postfeminism.

AVI SANTO is Assistant Professor in the Department of Communications and Theater Arts at Old Dominion University. His work has been published in *Framework: The Journal of Cinema and Media, Continuum: The Journal of Media and Cultural Studies,* and the *International Journal of Cultural Studies.*

ETHAN THOMPSON is Assistant Professor of Communication at Texas A&M University–Corpus Christi. His essays have been published in *Television and New Media* and *The Velvet Light Trap,* and he is currently working on a book, *What, Me Subversive? Parody and Sick Comedy in Postwar Television Culture.*

SERRA TINIC is Associate Professor of Media Studies in the Department of Sociology at the University of Alberta, Canada. Her research focuses on critical television studies and media globalization. She is the author of *On Location: Canada's Television Industry in a Global Market.* She has published in a number of scholarly anthologies and journals, including *Television and New Media, Journal of Communication, Social Epistemology,* and *The Velvet Light Trap.* She is currently working on a book project, *Trading in Culture: The Global Cultural Economy of Television Drama.*

# Index